The Pittsburgh School of

Routledge Studies in Contemporary Philosophy

For a full list of titles in this series, please visit www.routledge.com

The Pittsburgh School of Philosophy

Sellars, McDowell, Brandom

Chauncey Maher

Routledge
Taylor & Francis Group

NEW YORK   LONDON

First published 2012
by Routledge
711 Third Avenue, New York, NY 10017

Simultaneously published in the UK
by Routledge
2 Park Square, Milton Park, Abingdon, Oxfordshire OX14 4RN

First issued in paperback 2014

*Routledge is an imprint of the Taylor & Francis Group,
an informa business*

Library of Congress Cataloging-in-Publication Data
A catalog record has been requested for this book.

ISBN 978-0-415-80442-4 (hbk)
ISBN 978-1-138-81355-7 (pbk)
ISBN 978-0-203-09750-2 (ebk)

Typeset in Sabon
by IBT Global.

**Dedicated to my parents,
Kathleen and Chauncey Maher III**

Contents

Abbreviations

SELLARS

BLM	"Behaviorism, Language and Meaning" (1980)
CDCM	"Counterfactuals, Dispositions, and the Causal Modalities" (1958)
EAE	"Empiricism and Abstract Entities" (1963)
ENWW	"Epistemology and the New Way of Words" (1947/2005)
EPM	"Empiricism and the Philosophy of Mind" (1956/1963)
FD	"Fatalism and Determinism" (1963)
FMPP	"Foundations for a Metaphysics of Pure Process" (1981)
IM	"Inference and Meaning" (1953/2005)
LRB	"Language, Rules and Behavior" (1949/2005)
LTC	"Language as Thought and Communication" (1969)
ME	*Metaphysics of Epistemology* (1989)
MFC	"Meaning as Functional Classification" (1974)
MGEC	"More on the Given and Explanatory Coherence" (1979)
NO	*Naturalism and Ontology* (1980)
P	"Phenomenalism" (1963)
PPPW	*Pure Pragmatics and Possible Worlds* (1980/2005)
PSIM	"Philosophy and the Scientific Image of Man" (1963)
SM	*Science and Metaphysics* (1967)
SRLG	"Some Reflections on Language Games" (1954/1963)
TA	"Thought and Action" (1963)
TC	"Truth and 'Correspondence'" (1963)
TTP	"Towards a Theory of Predication" (1983)

BRANDOM

A	"Asserting" (1983)
AR	*Articulating Reasons* (2000)
BSD	*Between Saying and Doing* (2008)
HAPHFCS	"How Analytic Philosophy Has Failed Cognitive Science" (2009)

KSASR	"Knowledge and the Social Articulation of the Space of Reasons" (1995)
MIE	*Making It Explicit* (1994)
PPT	"Pragmatism, Phenomenalism and Truth-Talk" (1987)
REA	"Reference Explained Away" (1984)
RP	*Reason in Philosophy* (2009)
SG	"Study Guide" (1997)
TMD	*Tales of the Mighty Dead* (2002)
TP	"The Centrality of Sellars's Two-Ply Account of Observation" (2002)

MCDOWELL

APM	"Another Plea for Modesty" (1997/1998)
BIR	"Brandom on Inference and Representation" (1997)
BO	"Brandom on Observation" (2010)
CDK	"Criteria, Defeasibility and Knowledge" (1982/1998)
EI	*The Engaged Intellect* (2009)
HWV	*Having the World in View* (2009)
IDM	"In Defense of Modesty" (1987/1998)
KI	"Knowledge and the Internal" (1995)
KIR	"Knowledge and the Internal Revisited" (2002)
MI	"Motivating Inferentialism" (2005/2008)
MIWLP	"Meaning and Intentionality in Wittgenstein's Later Philosophy" (1993/1998)
MW	*Mind and World* (1994)
OSPLA	"One Strand in the Private Language Argument" (1989/1998)
PI	"Pragmatism and Intention-in-Action" (2011)
SRIA	"Some Remarks on Intention in Action" (2011)
WCIA	"What is the Content of an Intention in Action" (2010)
WFR	"Wittgenstein on Following a Rule" (1984/1998)
WQ	"Wittgensteinian 'Quietism'" (2009)

Acknowledgements

Many people helped me write this book. Mark Lance, James Mattingly and Terry Pinkard advised and encouraged me when I first came up with the idea. Matt Burstein, Nathaniel Goldberg, Michael Wolf, and Susan Feldman offered improvements on the first chapters. Nat Hansen and Zed Adams helped me improve several chapters, but also brainstormed with me about the big picture and the point of this book. Mark Pitlyk commented carefully on nearly the whole manuscript, helping me find the right voice for my audience. Willem deVries and Jeremy Wanderer had never met me but graciously agreed to read the penultimate draft of the manuscript. As I had hoped, they spotted ideas and inaccuracies that I had overlooked. Their encouragement also gave me the confidence to push through the final stages of writing. I am grateful to all of them. And Erin: thank you for indulging my endless worries and for showing me the value of being forthright.

Introduction

> The aim of philosophy, abstractly formulated, is to understand how things in the broadest possible sense of the term hang together in the broadest possible sense of the term.
>
> Sellars, Philosophy and the Scientific Image of Man, p. 3

Galaxies attract one another; waves erode shores; leaves rest on grass; bees pollinate flowers; dogs chase squirrels; humans dance to music. Things affect each other.

But we humans aren't simply affected by things. We have beliefs about things. The book in front of you, for instance, isn't merely affecting you, as a leaf affects the grass on which it rests. You can think about the book. Moreover, you can have better or worse support for what you think. What you think about the book is *answerable* to facts about the book. For instance, if you thought that the book was made of cheese, your thought would be false, since the book is (I presume) not made of cheese. Likewise, we don't simply affect things around us. We often do so deliberately or intentionally. When you turn this page, for instance, you don't merely affect the page, as an ocean wave affects the shore. You intend to turn the page, and know what you are doing as you do it. Moreover, you can have better or worse support for what you do. What you do is *answerable* to what you intend. For instance, if the page doesn't actually get turned—perhaps because a breeze blows—then your intention has been thwarted, unfulfilled.

Those issues about thought and action are the focus of the Pittsburgh School, a group of philosophers consisting centrally of Wilfrid Sellars, Robert Brandom, and John McDowell. This book is an introduction to the School's views on those issues.

Although Sellars, Brandom, and McDowell do not agree on everything, they share some distinctive ideas. In brief, they reject the idea that thinking about things can be assimilated to being merely affected by things; thinking requires a capacity to reason, to know what does and does not follow from a thought; likewise, they reject the idea that acting intentionally can be assimilated to an ability to affect things; acting intentionally also requires a capacity to reason; that capacity, in turn, requires sensitivity to *norms* or *evaluative standards* of proper reasoning; reasoning is fundamentally language-like; moreover, initiation into "the space of reasons" comes with initiation into natural languages like German, Japanese, and English; thus, thinking and acting intentionally are skills we acquire as we become so initiated.

Sellars, Brandom, and McDowell are the *Pittsburgh* School because Sellars taught in the Department of Philosophy at the University of Pittsburgh for more than twenty-five years until his death in 1989, and Brandom and McDowell continue to teach there, now for more than two decades. They are the Pittsburgh *School*—and not just a mere group—because they share concerns and views. That's the main point in calling them a "school." Other philosophers also share those concerns and views, and thus plausibly count as part of the School, but I won't try to say who else is or is not part of the School. Although I will not explicitly defend the claim that they are a school in some interesting sense of that word, I think that idea will be plausible by the end of this book.

Although the views of the Pittsburgh School are influential, their writings can also be very hard to read.[1] And they have written a lot. This book aims to make their ideas more accessible. It is mainly for people who have not read much of their work. I wrote it thinking of undergraduates who have had several classes in philosophy. I hope that it will help such readers as they begin to read their work. Perhaps this book will also be useful to people who are already familiar with their work.

This book focuses on one set of ideas that Sellars, Brandom, and McDowell share, highlighting some of their disagreements. It doesn't cover everything that they have written, nor even everything that is most important to each of them. For that, there are overviews, edited volumes, and monographs on them as individual philosophers.[2] While many of those works consider connections between Sellars, Brandom, and McDowell, and while many contemporary philosophers certainly do think of them as a school, this book is distinctive in part because it explicitly treats them together, as a school.[3]

You can think of this book as a sketch of the Pittsburgh School's views of human rational engagement with the world, focusing on our abilities to know about, think about, and act intentionally in the world. Thus, in Chapter 1, I present their critique of some views of justification and knowledge; in Chapter 2, I present their views of belief; in Chapter 3, I present their views on following rules—which is, for them, essential to having beliefs at all; in Chapter 4, I present Sellars's and Brandom's views on meaning, on what it is for a claim to be linguistically meaningful; in Chapter 5, I present their positive views of knowledge, filling out the sketch begun in Chapter 1; and in Chapter 6, I present their views of intentional action.

I start in Chapter 1 with their rejection of "the Given." Many philosophical views about justification and knowledge begin from the worry that justification and knowledge suffer from a vicious regress. That regress emerges as we start to reflect on the structure of justification and knowledge. Suppose B is my reason for thinking A. It would seem that I am justified in thinking A only so far as I have reasons for thinking B. Suppose C is my reason for thinking B. Here again it appears that I am justified in thinking B only so far as I have reasons for thinking C. It looks like this could iterate indefinitely; it looks like we have a regress. If that regress does not stop somewhere, I would seem to know nothing. It looks like we need a *foundation* of justification or knowledge, something that will halt the regress, something that one can justifiably believe or know without any further reasons or knowledge. In the simplest case, one might think that simply being "face to face" with an object would suffice for knowing something about that object. For instance, simply touching a rock might by itself enable me to know that it is hard. That sort of picture of knowledge—as a process of simply being "given" something by the world—has recurred throughout the ages, lending some intuitive support to the idea of a foundation. For the Pittsburgh School, the idea of such a foundation is the idea of "the Given," which can take various forms. Despite its apparent appeal, they hold that there is no such thing. They think it is a mere "myth."[4] Roughly, the problem with the Given is that there is nothing one can know prior to and independently of knowing anything else, which in turn enables one to know further things. Having any knowledge at all requires taking a position in the "logical space of reasons," which requires one to know many things. Simply touching a rock does not suffice for that. To hold otherwise would be to accept a form of the Given. But that is just one form that it can take. For the Pittsburgh School, it is essential to understand the different ways of appealing to the Given and what's wrong with them. That's the main aim of Chapter 1.

Chapter 2 focuses on some of the ideas underlying the rejection of the Given, ideas about what it is to think *about* something—what philosophers call *intentionality*. Belief, one important kind of thought, is the specific focus of the chapter. Philosophers and cognitive scientists generally hold that all thinking requires concepts; a capacity to *conceive of* things. For instance, to think about red things, one must be able to conceive of red things; one must have the concept of red. Thus, to understand thinking, hence believing, one must understand concepts. What does it take to have a concept of something? How does one "get" a concept? According to one intuitive picture—a picture ultimately rejected by the Pittsburgh School— we abstract concepts from experience. For instance, by encountering a red object or several red objects, one gets the concept of red. That concept then allows one to "sort" or "classify" further objects that one encounters as red. In this picture, believing consists mainly in being able to classify things that one encounters, as when you believe that a particular apple is red. That ability can be had before one learns to use a language. Indeed, in this picture, one's ability to speak is explained by appeal to one's prior possession of concepts. Words are simply tools for the conveyance of thoughts that one can have prior to and independently of putting them into words.

The Pittsburgh School rejects that picture of beliefs and concepts. While they agree that beliefs and concepts do have an essential connection to experience, they also hold that beliefs and concepts have an essential connection with *reasoning*. For them, to believe that things are thus-and-so, one must have some idea of what does and does not follow from that belief; otherwise, one has no grasp of what one putatively believes. And one does not genuinely have a concept until one can think in terms of it, by forming relevant beliefs. They hold further that thoughts can be helpfully modeled on overt speech. Roughly, a concept is like a word; a judgment—a manifestation of what one believes—is like an "inner assertion;" and the reasoning that we do "in our heads" is like what we do when we engage in rational discourse, what Brandom calls "the game of giving and asking for reasons." Both talking and thinking require responsiveness to norms of proper reasoning. One cannot talk or think unless one sufficiently complies with "the rules." Indeed, for the Pittsburgh School, the very meaning of our words and the content of our thoughts is constituted by norms of reasoning. Much more contentiously, the School holds that having beliefs and concepts—in the way that normal adult humans do—depends on our ability to use a language. That is, one learns to think in the course of learning to speak a language. Full-fledged thinking is not possible prior to and independently of the ability to use words properly; words are not mere tools for the conveyance of thoughts. Sellars, McDowell, and Brandom each have their own reasons for thinking that, which we will consider in due course.

Chapter 3 focuses on the Pittsburgh School's views of rules and rule-following. Like their views about beliefs, their views about rule-following grow out of a rejection of a faulty picture of the phenomenon. In that faulty picture, following any rule requires following another rule for the first rule's proper application. For instance, to follow the rule 'Stop for red lights,' I must know how to interpret those words. Do they mean 'Stop for the red lights in that store window'? Or do they mean 'Stop for red *traffic* lights'? Those are two incompatible ways of understanding the initial rule. Thus, for me to follow that rule properly, the rule itself would seem to require another rule. And that would seem to launch another regress, this time a regress of rules. As with the regress of justifications in Chapter 1, this regress seems to demand something to stop it, a rule that can be followed without need of any other rule, a rule that one cannot fail to follow. The Pittsburgh School thinks such a thing is ultimately unintelligible— indeed, McDowell thinks it's just another form of the Given. Instead, they think we should resist the need for a regress-stopping rule by resisting the assumption that starts the regress in the first place, the idea that following any rule requires following another rule for the first rule's proper application. They recognize a challenge here: we must avoid turning genuine rule-following into merely *regular* or *habitual* behavior. Genuinely following a rule seems to involve awareness of the rule, as when a person observes and drives within the posted speed limit on a street. By contrast, merely regular behavior need not involve such awareness, as when a dog happens to have a habit of running slower than the posted speed limit on a street. So, the real trick is to avoid the regress, without turning rule-following into merely habitual behavior. Sellars, Brandom, and McDowell have different views about how to do that.

Chapter 4 focuses on linguistic meaning. We learn, in Chapter 2, that for the Pittsburgh School, norms or rules of reasoning are important not simply because one must be responsive to them in order to think or speak at all, but also because they constitute the very meaning or content of our thoughts and claims. Put roughly, the big idea is that the meaning of a term or a whole sentence is its norm-governed role in rational conduct, broadly construed to include perception, thinking, speech, and deliberate action. Sellars's and Brandom's attempts to develop that idea are the focus of Chapter 4.

Chapter 5 begins where Chapter 1 ends, with the rejection of the Given. The Given is supposed to stop an apparent regress of justification or knowledge that would lead to skepticism. So, rejecting the Given seems to leave one with that regress and that threat of skepticism. Sellars, Brandom, and McDowell, however, are not skeptics; they think skepticism can and should be rejected. Their task is to develop a view of knowledge that avoids both the Given and the regress into skepticism. Those views are the topic of Chapter 5. I delay presenting them until then because they are easier to understand, I think, when one has some grasp of the ideas in Chapters 2, 3, and 4. Sellars, Brandom, and McDowell all think that we should reject an assumption underlying the regress, but they disagree about which assumption. Sellars and Brandom think we should deny the assumption that knowledge is "static" and can be justified "all at once." McDowell holds that the key is to deny the assumption that we could think or have experiences at all without yet having any knowledge. They all think that the right view requires getting clearer about the relation of experience to knowledge and intentionality.

Chapter 6 focuses on intentional action, but it's important to notice that behavior is a running theme of the book. In Chapters 1 through 5, it will emerge that the Pittsburgh School is partly reacting against pictures of one's mind that make it seem like a mysterious "inner" realm, tenuously in touch with the world and inaccessible to others. One of its basic aims is to develop an alternative picture of one's mind that shows it to be rationally engaged with the world and accessible to others in the various things one *does*, one's *behavior*. Chapter 6 focuses on a specific sort of behavior, intentional action, those things we do intentionally, or deliberately, with understanding of what we are doing. Such behavior differs from events that merely befall us, as when a book falls on your toe, but also from the voluntary motion of non-human organisms. The philosophical task is to understand those differences. Traditionally, philosophers have done so by appeal to "the will," which is really just a name for our ability to act intentionally. Sellars, Brandom, and McDowell can be thought of as part of that tradition. For them, the trick is to think about the will in a way that avoids treating the mind as a mysterious inner realm. In particular, they want to explain how certain things that happen with our bodies can be seen not as mere effects of something that precedes it, but as *rational* responses to what we think or intend. In developing their views, they are all guided by the idea that intentional action is structurally similar to experience. Just as experiences of the world are capable of *rationally supporting* further thoughts, claims, and action, so intentional actions are capable of being *rationally supported by* thoughts and claims.

In each of the chapters, I track some of the important agreements and disagreements between Sellars, Brandom, and McDowell. One philosophical goal they share is to keep an eye on "the whole." For instance, they hold that what one thinks about knowledge bears rationally on what one thinks about mind, language, and action. In developing a view on any one of those topics, one should consider what effect it will have for one's views on the others. In holding that commitment, one thing that distinguishes the Pittsburgh School from others is their idea that so-called practical philosophy—the study of how to live and act—and theoretical philosophy—the study of what there is and how we know it—are not as easily separated as some have thought, for both are concerned with *norms*.

In this book, my aim is to introduce the views of the Pittsburgh School. I hope it will help you understand them by letting you glimpse them as a whole.

1 The Given

[T]he framework of Givenness . . . has . . . been so pervasive that few,
if any, philosophers have been altogether free of it.

-Sellars, Empiricism and the Philosophy of Mind, §1

INTRODUCTION

In trying to understand how we know things, it is tempting to appeal to
the idea that something is simply "given." What any particular philosopher means by that often depends on other ideas she holds. In this chapter,
I want to show you one of the main reasons for appealing to something
"given," and why philosophers in the Pittsburgh School think that such
appeals are always problematic.

1. A REGRESS

Suppose that Mark and Sarah enter their house and walk into the kitchen
to put away some groceries. Remembering that the air conditioning is on,
Sarah asks Mark, 'Is the door shut?' Mark peeks into the hall, sees that the
door is shut and says so. Here Mark voices what he sees, passing his knowledge on to Sarah, who now knows that the door is shut.

When we say that some person S knows that P, we credit her with a
certain status. Not only does S believe that P, but P must also be *true*. We
would not say, for instance, that Sarah knows that the door is shut, even if
it isn't. 'Knows' is a verb of success. Moreover, in crediting S with knowledge, we generally take it that her belief does not merely happen to be true,
as though she had no idea that what she believed was really true, as though
she had no defense at all for holding that belief. Rather, we think that S is
also *justified* in having that belief; for instance, she could say why she has
it; she could provide justification for believing what she believes. So, on the
standard view of knowledge, tracing back to Plato, knowledge is justified,
true belief.[1]

The fact that knowledge requires having reasons seems to spark trouble,
for one's knowledge would seem to be only as good as one's justification.
Surely one cannot count as having knowledge if one's reasons for what one
believes are lousy. For instance, Sarah's knowledge is based on what Mark
said. If Mark's claim is false, then it's questionable that Sarah knows that

the door is shut. A true belief that's based on a false or unsupported premise doesn't seem like knowledge.[2] One's justification itself must be good for one to count as having knowledge. And it seems as though it must be good in just the same way as the original putative piece of knowledge; it too must be known. For Sarah to count as knowing that the door is shut, she must also count as knowing, for instance, that Mark is reporting things accurately. But that fact sparks an infinite regress. On what grounds does Sarah believe that Mark is reporting things accurately? Perhaps because she recalls Mark accurately reporting such things in the past, and that this situation is no different. And on what grounds does she believe these further things? One piece of knowledge seems to rest on further knowledge.

Now notice that the case of knowledge that we have been considering is not special or unusual; indeed, it seems to be a representative case of knowledge. One person comes to know something on the basis of the reliable testimony of another person. There are, of course, many other things I might claim to know. For instance:

> The moon is mountainous.
> Atoms have electrons.
> Some people like ice cream.
> There are seven days in a week.
> Einstein was a scientist.
> Gold is a metal.
> 2+2=4
> Torture is wrong.
> I am thinking.

If our representative case faces a regress, then it's likely that these other cases do too.

If the regress does not stop somewhere, there would seem to be no knowledge at all, for we cannot know infinitely many things.[3] That is, skepticism would reign.

2. FOUNDATIONALISM AND THE GIVEN[4]

The most natural response to the regress is to identify something that stops it, a grounding or foundation of knowledge.[5] The idea that there is or must be a foundation of knowledge is typically called 'Foundationalism.' However, as Michael Williams has emphasized, the regress is really part of a larger problematic, the "Agrippan Trilemma."[6] He writes,

> According to the Agrippan skeptic, any attempt to justify a claim either opens a vicious regress or terminates in one of two unsatisfactory ways:

we run out of things to say, thus making an ungrounded assumption; or we find ourselves repeating some claim or claims already entered, thus reasoning in a circle. . . . The Agrippan problem is to avoid the regress without lapsing into circularity or brute assumption. (Williams, 1977/1999, pp. 183–4)

For the Agrippan skeptic, an ungrounded assumption, reasoning in a circle, and a regress are all equally unacceptable. The Agrippan Trilemma constrains Foundationalism: a foundation cannot be a mere assumption or one of the very pieces of knowledge which we are seeking to ground.

Can Foundationalism be made to work? What else would a foundation need to be?

It would have to be capable of supporting the rest of one's knowledge, while relying on no further knowledge.

Let me say a bit more about the nature of this reliance. Consider again the case of Sarah and Mark. Sarah gets her knowledge from Mark. Not only is he a *causal or physical link* between Sarah and the door, but what Mark said also serves as a *premise* for Sarah's knowledge that the door is shut. From his claim she is able to *infer* that the door is shut. In this regard, Sarah's knowledge seems to be based on inferring or reasoning.[7] In contrast, Mark's own knowledge that the door is shut is not similarly based on reasoning. He just sees that the door is shut. It's true that there are probably many causal or physical intermediaries of Mark's knowledge, such as the glasses resting on his nose, but those intermediaries do not serve as premises to any inferences that he draws. Because Mark's knowledge is not based on reasoning or inference, it is *non-inferential*.

At a minimum, a foundation of knowledge would need to be non-inferential. For if it were a piece of inferential knowledge (as Sarah's seems to be), it would clearly rest on the knowledge from which it was inferred, and therefore would not halt the regress.

While Mark's knowledge that the door is shut is non-inferential, it nevertheless *depends* on other knowledge that he has. Specifically, it seems doubtful that Mark would know that the door is shut if he did not also know what a door is, under what conditions such a thing counts as being shut, and that the specific door in question was in such a condition.[8] So, although Mark's knowledge is non-inferential, it is not *independent* of other knowledge. Since it depends on other knowledge, what Mark knows would not halt the regress.

Thus, in general, it would seem that foundational knowledge needs to be independent knowledge, not simply non-inferential knowledge. In Williams's useful phrase, such knowledge would have to be "intrinsically credible" (Williams, 1977/1999). It is crucial to see that while independent knowledge would have to be non-inferential, the converse is not true, as shown by Mark's case; non-inferential knowledge is not necessarily independent knowledge. A piece of knowledge is independent of other knowledge if and only if it can be had without having any other knowledge at all.

The Given just is the idea that there could be a foundation of knowledge in that sense: there could be something capable of supporting the rest of one's knowledge, while relying on no further knowledge.[9] When we ask about the prospects of Foundationalism, we are asking about the prospects for finding a foundation, which is to ask about the prospects of finding the Given.

In Sellars words, "the point of the epistemological category of the given is . . . to explicate the idea that empirical knowledge rests on a 'foundation' of non-inferential knowledge of matter of fact" (EPM, §3). He elaborates:

> One of the forms taken by the Myth of the Given is that there is, indeed must be, a structure of particular matter of fact such that (a) each fact can not only be noninferentially known to be the case, but presupposes no other knowledge either of particular matter of fact, or of general truths; and (b) such that the non-inferential knowledge of facts belonging to this structure constitutes the ultimate court of appeals for all factual claims—particular and general—about the world. (EPM, §32)

Notice that he says that the point of the Given is to "explicate" the idea that knowledge rests on a non-inferential foundation. Thus, the Given should not be equated with non-inferential knowledge. It is the more specific idea that there is independent ("intrinsically credible") knowledge that can support the rest of our knowledge.

It will be useful for us to have a more exact, general formulation of the Given. In his book on Sellars, Willem deVries provides an especially clear and general formulation of what the Given is supposed to be. I believe it helps unify what Sellars, McDowell, and Brandom say about the Given. DeVries writes:

> (EI) The Given is epistemically independent, that is, whatever positive epistemic status our cognitive encounter with the object has, it does not depend on the epistemic status of any other cognitive state.[10]
>
> (EE) It is epistemically efficacious, that is, it can transmit positive epistemic status to other cognitive states of ours. (2005, pp. 98–9)

In what follows, when I talk about the Given, I will be relying on this formulation, unless I state otherwise.

What might the Given be?

At the beginning of "Empiricism and the Philosophy of Mind," Sellars observes, "Many things have been said to be 'Given': sense contents, material objects, universals, propositions, real connections, first principles, even Givenness itself" (§1). Intuitively, it would be something that is *self-evident* or *certain* or *indubitable*. Descartes, for instance, claims that one cannot doubt that one is thinking, for even to doubt is to think. And he goes on to treat that knowledge as a sort of foundation. However, he himself realizes that this particular piece of knowledge is not the best candidate for a foundation, for it is not clear how one could build the rest of one's knowledge upon such a minimal fact. In addition to something that is self-evident or indubitable, we need something that will justify our knowledge of things beyond our own minds, our knowledge of the world and of other minds. To address that challenge, Descartes famously appeals to his knowledge of God.[11] Hume derides that move as a "very unexpected circuit" (Hume, 1748/2011).[12]

The trouble with Descartes's appeal to his knowledge that he is thinking is that it is too narrow. That problem represents a general struggle in searching for a foundation of knowledge: there is a tug of war between the two conditions for a foundation. It needs to be narrow to be properly secure and independent of other knowledge; yet it also needs to be broad to provide adequate support for the rest of our knowledge.

So, it looks like the Given needs to be broader, broad enough especially to support what we know beyond the fact of our own thinking, or the contents of our own minds. Perhaps, then, the foundation should be something perceptual, something rooted in experience of the world.

That idea is partly reinforced by the apparent truism that we validate or invalidate our thoughts and claims about the world by appeal to what we encounter in that world. For instance, we ultimately check the claim that the door is shut by actually looking at the door. Because experience looks like an "ultimate court of appeals," it appears to be a good candidate for the Given. Moreover, experience or knowledge of it seems to be non-inferential. We just have it; we don't reason our way to it. That's a further reason to think it could be the Given.

Is it?

In a rudimentary picture of visual experience, a mere visual encounter with an object gives the perceiver knowledge.[13] For example, a mere visual encounter with a tomato would immediately give you knowledge of certain things about it, such as *that is red*. Simply encountering an object that *is* red (a tomato) is sufficient to make you aware of it *as* red. On that picture, one might not know everything about an object simply by looking at it, such as where it was grown or what variety it is. But there are at least some basic features of objects that one can know that those objects have merely by being presented with those objects, features such as being red. No other knowledge is necessary. That picture reinforces a certain way of thinking of concept acquisition: we acquire our most basic concepts simply by encountering objects that fall under those concepts.

That picture is obviously appealing for a Foundationalist. If some experiences really are like that, some knowledge is available without reliance on other knowledge and the regress could stop.

The immediate problem with that picture is that there is a difference between merely sensing or being aware of an object and knowing something about it. Being aware of something that is red is not the same as being aware of it *as red*, nor is it the same as knowing that it is red.[14] A person could be in the presence of a tomato and not recognize it *as* a tomato, or *as* a fruit, or even *as* red. That sort of recognition requires the relevant concepts, which one might lack. We will look more at concepts shortly, but for now we can say simply that having a concept seems to require knowing something. Thus, if there is a kind of sensing that amounts to a sensing *as*, a kind of minimal knowledge, it seems that it must rest on further knowledge. But if that's so, such sensing does not stop the regress, for the knowledge afforded by such sensing relies on further knowledge.

A slightly more sophisticated conception of experience grows out of the famous "argument from illusion." According to it, we have experiences that present things as being otherwise than how they really are. For instance, there can seem to be a red tomato, when there really isn't. Those experiences are just like experiences in which things really are how they seem to be. The main difference is just that the first sort of experience gets things wrong, while the second sort gets them right. Since the experiences are otherwise indistinguishable from the perceiver's point of view, there must be something that explains their commonality, a representation of the object or scene. According to that picture of experience, in experience what we experience directly are not things or scenes themselves, but representations of them. 'Sense data' is one name that has been given to these things.

According to the classical version of a sense data theory (e.g. (Russell, 1997/1912)), sense data are not merely directly experienced but also directly *known*. When I have an experience of a tomato I have a direct encounter with a sense datum of a tomato. In my encounter with this datum, I know it directly in the sense that I am directly *acquainted* with it. My so knowing it is like my knowing a town or my knowing a person.

For this knowledge by acquaintance to help stop the regress, it must be or result in the kind of thing that can rationally support other knowledge, propositional knowledge, such as knowledge that *the tomato is red*. Yet if my acquaintance with the sense datum is a mere confrontation, then it does not seem to help with that. As we have already seen, merely being in the presence of a red object does not imply that I am aware of it *as* red or know that it is red. The same goes for being in the presence of representations of such things. Acquaintance has to be more robust to support further knowledge.

Now, it is plausible that knowledge by acquaintance can be something more. When I am acquainted with something or someone, I also know facts about that place or person. For instance, if I know Washington, D.C., I probably know that the Washington Monument is on the Mall. But if we conceive of knowledge by acquaintance that way, it would seem to rely on knowledge of other facts, and our acquaintance with sense data would not halt the regress. That problem pushes us back to the idea that our acquaintance with sense data neither is nor affords any propositional knowledge, but is a mere causal confrontation, which seemed equally unacceptable.[15]

A different theory of experience maintains that in experience people have a kind of basic knowledge of how things look or seem or appear to them.[16] Such theories are usually called 'appearance theories.' As with sense data theories, in experience one does not directly or immediately experience things as they are in themselves; one's encounter with the world is mediated in some way, in this case by an appearance. The basic knowledge that one has in an experience is of a fact of the form 'X appears F to me.' For instance, when I have a visual experience of the red tomato, I know it looks red to me. The object might not be red, so what I know is not that it is red, only that it looks red to me. At least to that extent, what I know in experience is rather modest. I do not know how things are, but only how they appear, and only how they appear to me.

As with the other pictures of experience, this one has some initial promise. How things appear to you does seem to be the kind of thing that you know non-inferentially and which requires no further knowledge. Consider the tomato: for me to know *it looks red to me*, I need not do any reasoning, and I don't seem to need any additional knowledge. Moreover, unlike the sense data theory, in experience I am afforded *propositional* knowledge, something in a form that can support further judgments; experience affords knowledge of *facts*, facts about how things appear to me. That conception of experience seems equipped to stop the regress.

But it is beset by two basic problems. First, it is not clear that such modest knowledge about how things merely appear to me can alone support the rest of my empirical knowledge.[17] (Remember the problem with Descartes.) How can knowledge about how things seem or appear to me by itself ground or justify knowledge about facts beyond that, facts about how things *are*, or facts about how things seem to *others*? It doesn't seem as if it could; for it would need ultimately to appeal to knowledge about the connection between how things seem to me and how things really are (or how things seem to others), which is the very knowledge for which we were seeking support.[18] Hume, of course, is famous for drawing attention to that predicament. The second problem that besets this theory is that it is not clear that even this modest knowledge is really available without reliance on other knowledge.[19] When I know that something *looks red* to me, it would seem that I draw on my knowledge of what it is for something to *be red* or, at least, my knowledge of what redness is.

I have sketched three different pictures of experience.[20] Each seems to have some promise for showing how experience could be the Given, but each also has some immediate problems. I haven't made a decisive case against any of them. What I want you to see is that, and how, they run into trouble.[21] They all have trouble making out the idea that experience supports the rest of our knowledge without relying on any further knowledge. That is, they all have trouble showing how experience jointly satisfies EE and EI.

Our next task is to understand why that is.

3. WHAT IS WRONG WITH THE GIVEN?

DeVries presents Sellars's argument against the Given as a dilemma. I think that's a good way to understand the position of philosophers in the Pittsburgh School in general. In brief the argument is this: the Given must be either conceptual or non-conceptual; nothing conceptual can satisfy EI; nothing non-conceptual can satisfy EE; thus, in either case, nothing can fill the role of the Given.[22] That won't mean much to you at this point, since we haven't attempted a distinction between what's conceptual and what's non-conceptual. We will get to that shortly.

3.1. A Conceptual Given?[23]

Consider a typical observation report. I am looking at a red tomato and think: that looks red. Such a report can seem like a good candidate for the Given, for it is epistemically efficacious. For instance, it would support the thought that *something* is red. And it might be epistemically independent. I don't infer my report from something else, some other piece of knowledge. Moreover, merely recognizing that something looks red does not obviously require further knowledge.

Yet that is where trouble starts to arise. What does it take to recognize that a thing is red? What does it take to recognize that any object has a certain property? One must be able to conceive of the object *as* having that property. That is, it requires having the relevant concept, in this case the concept of red. Intuitively, a concept is something like a label or category or "mental box." But what is required for having a concept?

That's a tough question. We will return to it in the following chapters. Here I want mainly to give you a glimpse of the conception of concepts held by the Pittsburgh School. Along with many philosophers and cognitive scientists, they think it requires, at least, an ability to sort or classify. For instance, to have the concept of red is to be able to distinguish red things from non-red things, though one might make mistakes here and there.

Philosophers in the Pittsburgh School think that the capacity to sort things does not suffice for having a concept. Brandom puts that point by saying that having a mere "reliable differential responsive disposition" to sort red things from non-red things does not suffice to have the concept of red. For instance, a sophisticated parrot that produces a noise that sounds like 'red' when and only when in the presence of red things would not thereby *conceive of* those things *as* red.[24] That is, it would not obviously have the concept of red. There are many similar examples. Something, a machine, for instance, can be a good sorter or detector of things that have property X, and yet lack the concept of X.

What more is needed?

For the Pittsburgh School, as for many other philosophers and cognitive scientists, concepts have their home in judgments.[25] A judgment is a thought about how things are. Its generic form is: A is B, as in 'That is red' or 'The tomato is red.' In this picture of things, judgments are made of concepts, as sentences are made of words. Concepts are the constituents of judgments. The claim from the Pittsburgh School is that one does not have a concept unless one can judge in terms of it. For instance, if one has the concept of red, one should be able to form a judgment, such as *that is red*. That's not to say that whenever one judges that something is red, one invariably judges truly. It's just to say that one must be able to make such judgments.

That requires more than a reliable differential responsiveness to things that fall under the concept. The Pittsburgh School maintains that to count as judging one must be capable of reasoning. For instance, to count as judging of some object that it is red, one must be able to reason in connection with that judgment.[26] That is, one must be able to make correct inferences from and to that judgment. Not just any random inferences will do. For instance, to have the concept red, it wouldn't do for one to infer *that is a sailboat* from the judgment *that is red*. That's generally a bad inference. One must in general make *correct* inferences.[27] For instance, a correct inference from the judgment *that is red* would be *that is colored*. Thus, judging is governed by inferential norms. In turn, so too is having a concept: having the concept C requires abiding by the inferential norms governing judgments in which C occurs.[28] That implies that concept-possession is moderately holistic; one cannot have just one concept. For possessing a concept requires the ability to make various related judgments in compliance with the norms of reasoning. In Sellars's words, having one concept requires "having a whole battery of concepts" (EPM, §19).

Why should we think that the ability to judge requires the ability to reason?

For the Pittsburgh School, if one were completely incapable of correctly inferring from or to a judgment, one would not grasp what one had putatively judged in the first place. And one cannot judge what one does not understand. For instance, our sophisticated parrot might be disposed to respond reliably to red things with noises that sound like 'That's red.' On some occasion, when it produces that noise in the presence of a red object, it might appear to be judging that the thing is red. But that appearance is dubious, since the parrot has no idea what it is saying; it does not comprehend what it is doing in producing those noises. More precisely, it does not know what rationally follows from or supports that putative judgment.[29] The parrot would not be moved by someone who retorted reliably, 'No, it's orange' or 'It's not colored at all.' Nor would the parrot respond reliably to someone who retorted, 'How do you know?' or 'Are you sure?' If the parrot has judged that the thing is red, it should be at least minimally responsive to these sorts of response, but it isn't. Moreover, it's questionable that the parrot could be trained to respond reliably to such challenges. So, although it produces the noises 'That's red,' it doesn't understand them, and it does not make sense to count it as judging.[30]

Thus, according to the Pittsburgh School, concepts require the ability to judge, which in turn requires the ability to reason. That conception of concepts implies that having a concept requires knowledge. For it requires the ability to make relevant judgments, in accord with the relevant norms of reasoning, requiring knowledge of those norms.

Now, the Pittsburgh School is not obviously right about concepts. One potential problem is that their view is too restrictive: it seems to imply that small children and non-human animals do not have concepts, since they are not obviously capable of judging or knowing inferential norms. That is a reasonable concern. We will return to it in Chapters 2 and 5.

But if they are right about concepts, then something that is both conceptual and epistemically independent would not be possible. The very fact of its conceptuality precludes its epistemic independence. So, the Given cannot be conceptual.

3.2. A Non-Conceptual Given?

That should prompt us to consider whether the Given could be non-conceptual. If it were non-conceptual, it would be more likely to be epistemically independent.

What would be a good candidate for a non-conceptual form of the Given?

A visual sensation is a good candidate, such as the stimulation of your eye in the presence of something red. Merely being affected by an object does not involve concepts—it does not involve conceiving of it in any way. Moreover, you can have a visual sensation of something red and yet not know anything about red things, or anything else for that matter. So, a sensation could be epistemically independent.

One might also think that a sensation can be epistemically efficacious. A sensation of something red normally results from something that is red. In that way, it can seem to be an indicator or marker of something red, a clue that there is a red thing in the vicinity. When one actually sees something red, a little image of the object is formed on the retina, as an image of a reflected object appears in a mirror. That image represents the red object of which one is having a sensation; it stands for the object. As such, although the image itself is not conceptual, it could be one's evidence for the application of a concept in a judgment, like *that is red*.

From the Pittsburgh point of view, the trouble is that such an image—here serving as a possible case of a sensation—is not really epistemically efficacious. Having a sensation of a red thing need not tell one anything at all; it need not be evidence of anything. Although a sensation might normally result from something that is red, one cannot take it as evidence for the presence of red things unless one knows that fact. The person having the sensation could be ignorant of that fact. Although the sensation is hers—it occurs on *her* retina—she might not be aware of what kind of sensation it is; what it is a sensation of. She might not know how to classify it. Even if we grant that she is conscious of the sensation, it does not follow that she is aware of it as a sensation of redness.[31] Nor does it help to suppose that the sensation is not simply the image on the retina but something "in" one's consciousness. For even then it's possible that she doesn't know what she is sensing; she might simply be conscious of something happening.

According to the Pittsburgh School, the general problem here is that something non-conceptual cannot be one's basis for further reasoning. One can appeal only to something conceptual for that. As McDowell puts the point:

> ... we cannot really understand the relations in virtue of which a judgment is warranted except as relations in the space of concepts: relations such as implication or probabilification, which hold between potential exercises of conceptual capacities. (MW, p. 7)

Citing that remark from McDowell, Brandom writes, "only what is propositionally contentful, and so conceptually articulated, can serve as (or, for that matter, stand in need of) a justification" (SG, p. 122). And later: "only things with sentential structure can be premises of inference" (SG, p. 128).

The idea here is that only something that "says something" or "makes a claim" can serve as a premise for a conclusion. The idea is not that premises must literally speak to us. Rather, it's that they must be capable of being true or false. The paradigm of an inference is from one claim to another, as in 'That is maroon, so it is colored.' Each sentence there can be either true or false. In contrast, something non-conceptual cannot be a premise or a conclusion because it does not "say" anything; it does not "tell" you that things are one way rather than another; it is neither true nor false. Thus, when we conceive of a sensation as something non-conceptual, we keep it from being truth-evaluable. The sensation of a red object is not true or false; it simply occurs.

If that's correct, something non-conceptual would be epistemically independent at the price of being epistemically efficacious.[32] And that would imply that the Given cannot be non-conceptual.

Now, as with the prospects for a conceptual Given, the Pittsburgh School is not obviously right about the prospects for a non-conceptual Given. For instance, one might reject their claim that only something conceptual can provide someone with a reason.[33] We will return to that issue in Chapter 5. If the argument against a non-conceptual Given were to go through, then the argument against the Given would be complete.[34] There can be neither a non-conceptual nor a conceptual Given.

In summary, the Given must be both epistemically independent and efficacious. Yet anything that is suitably independent of other knowledge—such as a non-conceptual Given—will fail to be efficacious; it will fail to be the kind of thing that can support other epistemic states. Anything that is suitably efficacious—such as a non-inferential, conceptual Given—will fail to be independent of other knowledge; it cannot be had all by itself.

3.3. Placing in the Space of Reasons

Philosophers in the Pittsburgh School have a distinctive conception of knowledge, giving them a distinctive angle on the regress, the Given, and the problems with it.

In a widely cited remark, Sellars holds that "in characterizing an episode or a state as that of *knowing*, we are not giving an empirical description of that state or episode; we are placing it in the logical space of reasons, the space of justifying and being able to justify what one says" (EPM, §36). One thing Sellars is saying is that having knowledge involves having reasons, which is familiar, but he is saying more than that. He is proposing a contrast between the force or point of "empirical description" and the force or point of epistemic attributions.[35] When we offer an "empirical description" of something, such as 'The door is shut,' we are saying how things are with the door. By contrast, when we say that someone knows something, such as 'Sarah knows that the door is shut,' although we may be describing Sarah in some way, we are also "endorsing" Sarah as one who is *authorized* to think what she thinks.[36] According to Sellars, the force of that type of remark is akin to the force of an *evaluation* or *prescription*, as when we say that someone is *right* for doing something, or has done something *well*.[37] To say that S knows that P is (roughly) to say that others (including oneself) are or would be right to rely on S in vindicating their own beliefs or claims that P. Thus, epistemic attributions have a crucial *normative* dimension; attribution of epistemic states or episodes are attributions of normative statuses.[38] That is a central commitment of the Pittsburgh School.

What does it mean to say that knowledge is a normative status? The basic idea is that knowing something or being justified in believing something is like having the *standing*, the *permission* or *authority*, to do something. Outside of epistemology, there are many examples of such permission or authority. Baseball umpires are authorized to call a pitch a strike; police officers of a jurisdiction are permitted to issue citations in that jurisdiction; legislators are allowed to propose and enact legislation; and so on.[39] When one says that knowledge is a normative status, one is saying that it concerns the permission or authority to judge how things are.

That conception of knowledge has implications for thinking about the regress and the Given. On that way of thinking, we embark on the regress when we wonder why we are authorized in judging as we judge. For instance, why is Sarah authorized to judge that the door is shut? The authority of that judgment can be put in question. The Given is supposed to halt the ensuing regress by being the ultimate basis or source of epistemic authority, something that authorizes a person to judge and which in turn requires no further authorization. Thus, appeals to the Given commit to a view about epistemic authority.

In turn, the problems with the Given can be seen as problems for a class of views about the nature of epistemic authority. Let's look at the non-conceptual Given in this light.

Sellars's "placing" remark connects with another crucial remark from elsewhere in EPM. He writes:

> [T]he idea that epistemic facts can be analyzed without remainder—even 'in principle'—into non-epistemic facts, whether phenomenal or behavioral, public or private, with no matter how lavish a sprinkling of subjunctives and hypotheticals is, I believe, a radical mistake—a mistake of a piece with the so-called 'naturalistic fallacy' in ethics. (EPM, §5)

The "naturalistic fallacy" was introduced into philosophical discussions of ethics by G. E. Moore in his *Principia Ethica* (§12). It is the idea that moral properties, such as being good or right, can be defined in non-moral terms or can be "analyzed" into non-moral or purely natural properties, such as feeling pleasant. That idea is considered fallacious by Moore and others because what *should* or *should not* be the case cannot be settled simply by what *is* the case, what *has been* the case, what *is typically* the case, or what *would be the case if* certain conditions obtained. That something exists, or occurs or is likely to occur, is one thing; the correctness, appropriateness, or goodness of it is another.

In that passage from EPM, then, Sellars is proposing that there is a similar fallacy in thinking about "epistemic facts," such as the fact that Sarah knows that the door is shut.[40] The fallacy here would be the idea that such facts could be defined in non-epistemic terms or "analyzed" as non-epistemic facts.[41] Sellars insinuates that this idea is fallacious because epistemic facts are normative, in the way that I've just sketched. If that's right, both "fallacies" stand or fall together.

We can now connect with the idea of a non-conceptual Given. From the Pittsburgh point of view, the non-conceptual states of an individual are not "epistemic facts" about that individual: they can be had independently of any knowledge whatsoever, and they cannot support any knowledge. So, the attempt to ground knowledge on them is an attempt to "analyze" epistemic facts into non-epistemic facts. In effect, a non-conceptual Given attempts to explain your authority to judge how things are by appeal to something that gives you no authority to judge at all. The rightness of something—your judgment—would rest upon or "reduce to" something that was neither right nor wrong—a non-conceptual state of yours. That would be "a mistake of a piece with the so-called 'naturalistic fallacy' in ethics."

One final observation. Sellars's "placing" remark has a further, important consequence: there is a tighter connection between theoretical philosophy and practical philosophy than is sometimes recognized.[42] Theoretical philosophy includes epistemology and metaphysics; practical philosophy includes political philosophy and ethics. It might be natural to assume that inquiry into what it is to know and to think is one thing, while inquiry into who should rule and how we should live is another. However, that idea looks too simplistic once we see the normative character of epistemic attributions and states. Once we see that epistemology is concerned with epistemic authority, we can see a fundamental connection with political philosophy. One of its core concerns is political authority: what, if anything, authorizes some people to govern and control others? For instance, what authorizes the police officer to issue citations? The state, one might say. And what authorizes the state? Well, according to defenders of democracy, it is and ought to be the will of the people. But why does the will of the people have that authority? Whatever the answer, if these questions do not come to a legitimate end somewhere, then it would seem the police officer is not authorized to issue citations. An analogue of the Given emerges here: it would be something that could authorize a person or institution or act without itself requiring any other authorization.[43] For instance, one might imagine that it was somehow self-authorizing.[44] About such a conception of political authority there will be worries analogous to the worries we had about the Give. The big point is that for the Pittsburgh School, theoretical and practical philosophy are not fundamentally different inquiries, for they are connected in their concern for authority and norms.

CONCLUSION

We opened this chapter with a regress of knowledge. That led us to the idea of a foundation of knowledge, something capable of supporting the rest of one's knowledge, while relying on no further knowledge, something that is "intrinsically credible." That is the idea of the Given. We considered whether experience—conceived either conceptually or non-conceptually—might be able to play that role. We found that, according to the Pittsburgh School, nothing can really play that role. But rejecting the Given seems to leave us with the regress and skepticism. Is there a way of salvaging the idea of a foundation? Can the regress be resisted in some other way?

To understand the answers given by philosophers in the Pittsburgh School, we need to look more closely at their conception of belief.

2 Belief

> [A]nything which can properly be called conceptual thinking can occur only within a framework of conceptual thinking in terms of which it can be criticized, supported, refuted, in short, evaluated. To be able to think is to be able to measure one's thoughts by standards of correctness, of relevance, of evidence.
>
> -Sellars, Philosophy and the Scientific Image of Man, p. 6

INTRODUCTION

In Chapter 1, we were focused on knowledge, and a cluster of problems that arise from a certain way of thinking about it. As I mentioned there, the standard conception of knowledge holds that it is a belief that is both true and justified. Thus, knowledge can seem to be a particularly successful form of belief. But what is it to have a belief? What is it to believe something?

In this chapter, I want to begin to explain how Sellars, Brandom, and McDowell think about beliefs. In particular, I want to highlight their contention that beliefs are essentially involved in reasoning; their contention that beliefs are language-like; and their contention that having beliefs is importantly connected with the ability to use a natural language.

1. THE LOCKEAN PICTURE OF BELIEF

In this section, I offer a foil to contrast with the views of the Pittsburgh School, which I will present in the next section. I intend this foil to stand for a common way to think about thought. I will call it the Lockean Picture (LP) because you can find a version of it in John Locke's *Essay on Human Understanding*.[1] Other versions have been held by other philosophers and scientists.[2]

1.1. An Initial Glimpse of Thought

LP begins from some widely shared assumptions about thought. I can wonder where my copy of *Making It Explicit* is. Somehow I'm able to think about it even when it's not around. Moreover, I can think about things that don't exist or haven't happened, such as my ideal vacation home or a future trip to New Delhi.[3] This capacity for "thinking in absence" is an essential feature of thought.[4]

The possibility of such "thinking in absence" reveals the fact that thoughts somehow stand for or represent other things; thoughts have meaning or content; they are *about* something.[5] This aboutness is called 'intentionality;' states that have it are called 'intentional states.'[6]

Talk of thoughts can be ambiguous, for the word 'thought' can be used to refer either to an *act* of *thinking*, or to the *content* that is *thought* in such an act. When we say things like, 'I haven't had a thought all day long,' we are talking about *acts* of thinking. By contrast, when we say things like, 'Joan's thought was mistaken,' we are talking about the content of what Joan thought. 'Belief' and 'intention' also exhibit this ambiguity.

There are many different sorts of thought. Speaking broadly, thinking includes imagining, hoping, doubting, wanting, remembering, calculating, intending, loathing, planning, speculating, and judging.[7] We can draw various distinctions between these types of thought. One important distinction concerns their "directions of fit."[8] States or episodes of believing or remembering aim to represent the world. The mind is supposed to fit the world, so we can say they have "mind-to-world" direction of fit. In contrast, states or episodes of desiring or intending are not like that; they aim to change the world, in a broad sense. For those sorts of thought, the world is supposed to fit the mind, so we can say they have "world-to-mind" direction of fit.

States with mind-to-world direction of fit can be *wrong* in a certain way. One's mind can fail to fit the world. In more familiar terms, you can believe that something is thus-and-so when it isn't; you can have false beliefs. For instance, you can believe that a tomato is red when it isn't. A belief purports to be true, but might not be true.[9] In contrast, states with world-to-mind direction of fit are subject to a different sort of evaluation. A desire can go unsatisfied or an intention can fail to be fulfilled.

Historically, philosophers of mind and epistemologists have been more interested in states like believing or remembering, and less interested in states like desiring and intending. The simple reason is that believing and remembering are more obviously relevant to understanding knowledge. Whether that is ultimately a tenable position is an interesting question.[10] In the rest of this chapter we will focus almost exclusively on states of belief and judgment.[11] We will consider another important type of thought in Chapter 6: intentions.

In Chapter 1, we saw that the contents of beliefs or judgments are commonly thought to be composed of concepts, as sentences are composed of words. Just as we speak by using words, so we think by using concepts. For instance, to think that the door is shut, Sarah must have the concept of a door. Intuitively, to have a concept of X is to be able to conceive or think about X-type things. What it is to have a concept will be a topic throughout this chapter.

I have presented a few shared assumptions about thought: they have intentionality; there are different sorts of thoughts, which can be partly distinguished by their directions of fit; beliefs or judgments have mind-to-world direction of fit and can fail to "fit" the world; such states are (and have been) an important concern of epistemology; thoughts, like beliefs and judgment, are composed of concepts. Any picture of thought, such as LP, should account for these features.

1.2. The Lockean Picture

To think, one must have concepts. One might maintain that they are innate; that would mean that you are born with them.[12] LP has instead an empiricist conception of their acquisition: you don't start with them; you get them in experience.[13] You start with the ability to have experiences. Through experiences of a certain sort of thing you acquire the concept of that sort. For instance, you first have several experiences of red things; detecting a similarity in these things, their redness, you acquire the concept of red. If you have no experiences of red things, you do not and cannot have the concept of red. In general, the concept of X is the result of experiences of X-type things. The concepts that one acquires from experience are one's basic concepts which can then be combined or manipulated to form further, non-basic concepts. For instance, one might form the concept of color on the basis of the concepts of red, yellow, and blue; or one might form the concept of a centaur on the basis of the concept of man and the concept of horse. Because basic concepts are supposed to be abstracted from experience, this view has been labeled 'abstractionism.'[14]

LP thus attempts to account for the intentionality of thought by appealing to experience: you can think about red things, you can think with the concept of red, because you have had experiences of red things. Thoughts "containing" or "composed" with the concept of red are about red because that concept gets its content (what it's about) from experiences of red.

That is what it takes to acquire a concept. Once you have it, you can think in terms of it. For instance, once you have acquired the concept of red, you can think about red things. Thinking about red things, according to LP, consists primarily in the ability to apply it to things that one encounters. For instance, having the concept of red means that when you encounter a red object you can think *that's red*. In that way, possessing a concept is fundamentally an ability to reliably discriminate between things.

We saw earlier that it is possible to have false beliefs. For instance, I might think that something is red when it isn't; I might apply the concept to the wrong sort of thing. For LP, such errors are possible because although I acquire a concept in certain good conditions, I might try to apply it in worse conditions, conditions in which I have trouble discerning whether the concept really does apply.

A further, important feature of LP is its conception of the relation between thought and language. The first important point here is that language, like thought, has intentionality; words, expressions, and sentences have meaning. Besides language, many sorts of thing seem to have intentionality. For instance:

A photograph of a Great Sequoia
A painting of dogs playing poker
A map of the mid-west of the U.S.

A blueprint of a yet-to-be-built house
A record of Howlin' Wolf
The thermostat that indicates the temperature
Bits of computer code
The sideline of a soccer field
John's wave goodbye to Sally

"Intentionality, however, is not all created equal," as John Haugeland says in one essay (1998, p. 129). Some things that have intentionality have it only because it is conferred on them by other things that have it. For instance, we might agree that when I wave to you, you should step on the gas. My waving to you has that meaning only because of our agreement, which itself has intentionality (it's about what you should do when I wave). The wave need not have meant that or anything at all. So, some things have intentionality *derivatively*. But not everything can have intentionality derivatively, on pain of an infinite regress. So, some things must have intentionality *originally*. ("Originally" here just means "not derivatively.") As Haugeland and others stress, a central challenge in understanding intentionality is to understand original intentionality, for without it derivative intentionality is unintelligible.

LP maintains that language derives its intentionality from thought.[15] Language is a tool for the expression of thought.[16] In principle, a person can have beliefs without having a language.[17] A thinking thing might acquire a language, or it might not. Someone who has beliefs but no language might still be able to convey a thought non-linguistically with, say, gestures or non-linguistic drawings; that much is not ruled out. The crucial claim is that one can have beliefs or judgments without yet speaking a language.

That is a claim about the order of being. Beliefs or judgments can *exist* or *occur* independently of the existence or occurrence of language. There is a related claim about the order of understanding (or the conceptual order). For instance, Plato suggested that thought is a "dialogue in the soul" (The-aetetus, 189e). That image suggests that thought (or at least some important species of it) should be understood in terms of language; that is, when we study thought, we should think of it as language-like (but of course that's just a contingent fact about how we have to think about thought). That would make language *conceptually* prior to thought. LP is consistent with that proposal. A claim of conceptual priority does not imply a claim of ontological priority, and vice versa. For instance, one could think that we should think of the contents of beliefs as language-like, but at the same time deny that one must have a language in order to think. Indeed, many philosophers and scientists believe just that.

LP's view of the relationship between thought and language implies a view about communication. What you start with and know most immediately are your experiences. That eventually yields concepts and thinking. With further training, you acquire words, sounds, or scratches standing for your thoughts. You can then use those words to convey your thoughts to others, who have that same language. You are likewise able to learn their thoughts. Thus, words are a tool with which you can know the minds of others. Of course, there is a limit to that, for the meaning of your words is rooted in your thoughts, which are rooted in your experiences. You can share your thoughts with others only to the extent that you share experiences.

Summing up, LP has a few distinctive traits: concepts are acquired in experience; thoughts get their meaningfulness from experience, and words in turn get theirs from thoughts; people know their own minds first and best, subsequently acquiring words and using them to share their thoughts with others, whose minds they learn in turn.

2. BELIEF IN PITTSBURGH

The Pittsburgh School rejects LP, questioning all of its main features. In this section, I will sketch an alternative picture of belief, using LP as a foil.

2.1. Abstractionism

Along with many others, philosophers in the Pittsburgh School reject LP's abstractionism.[18]

Abstractionism has trouble with logical and mathematical concepts.[19] Logical concepts include those that we express with English words like 'not,' 'and,' 'if,' and 'some.' Intuitively, abstractionism should treat these concepts like others: they too must be abstracted from experience. But the difficulty here should be obvious: what experiences correspond to those concepts? Indeed, do any experiences correspond to them? For instance, is there an experience characteristic of the concept of not? We say things like, 'Ann's absence was felt.' Perhaps the concept of not is rooted in such experiences of absence. Yet it's hard to make sense of that idea. Do experiences of absence differ from an absence of experiences or non-experiences? Suppose they do. What exactly is an experience of absence? By hypothesis, it is not a non-experience, so it must be an experience of something. But of what? Any answer we provide threatens to turn experiences of absence into experiences of *something*, in which case it's dubious that we have genuine experiences of absence. No comfort is provided by the thought that experiences of absence are experiences of nothing, for then we are back to wondering how—indeed whether—experiences of nothing differ from non-experiences.

One natural response here is to propose a division between different sorts of concepts, e.g., between those that have content and those that are, in some sense, formal or logical. Abstractionism would concern only the acquisition of content concepts; another story would be needed for formal or logical concepts.

We will see that, to some extent, philosophers in the Pittsburgh School agree with the spirit of that move, even though they reject abstractionism. By rejecting abstractionism, one is left in need of a story about the acquisition of concepts. One could hold that they are had innately. Philosophers in the Pittsburgh School don't take that route; they agree with LP that concepts are importantly connected to experience. What they seek is a more sophisticated story about that connection.

Abstractionism has a more serious problem. It holds that without already having a concept, you somehow notice a feature shared by experiences, and abstract that feature out of those experiences, thereby forming a concept of it. When one has experiences of red things, it is as if one issues an order to oneself, saying, 'Red things fall under the concept of red.' Putting it that way should expose the problem. Like comprehending a command about how to classify a feature, "noticing" that experiences share a feature presupposes that one has a way of *recognizing*—if not a way of *knowing*—what feature it is that they share. Thus, abstraction seems to require that one has a concept before one has it. Sellars says that "instead of coming to have a concept of something because we have noticed that sort of thing, to have the ability to notice a sort of thing is already to have the concept of that sort of thing, and cannot account for it" (EPM, §45). Abstractionism holds that simply encountering objects of a similar sort is supposed to suffice to give you knowledge that they are of that sort. Because it holds that one could know something (that experiences share a feature) without knowing anything else, it is committed to a non-conceptual form of the Given.

2.2. Beliefs Are Involved in Reasoning and Language-Like

What, then, is required for having concepts? For having beliefs?

Philosophers in the Pittsburgh School think that we cannot understand concepts or beliefs apart from their role in reasoning. Furthermore, we understand them best if we take more seriously the idea that they are language-like.[20]

Notice first that LP has trouble explaining how it is that a person's beliefs—acts or contents—could be known by someone else. It holds that the contents of a person's beliefs are rooted in her own experiences and that upon acquiring a language those beliefs can be put into words and conveyed to others. The trouble is that for someone else who hears these words to know what they mean—what belief or thought they express—she must ultimately be familiar with the speaker's own experiences. But it's not clear that or how such familiarity is possible. Normally, no two people share the numerically same experience. Mark and I might both look at a tomato. While we both thereby experience the same tomato—and have "the same experience" in that sense—what I experience, the character and content of my experience, can differ from what Mark experiences. He might see it as a tomato; I might not. It might look more orange to him, and more red to me. Furthermore, any person's attempt to explain in words what her words mean or what her experiences are will simply invite the same worries, for the meaning of the words would again be in question. The problem for LP is that a person's beliefs seem to be available only to that person herself and no one else; they are fundamentally *private*. That leaves communication looking mysterious. Moreover, it leaves empirical psychology looking impossible.

Behaviorism was one prominent response to this problem, among others. There were various forms of behaviorism. "Analytical" or "logical" behaviorism claimed that all *talk* of a person's mind could be exchanged for *talk* of that person's behavioral dispositions.[21] According to that view, the claim that Mark believes there is a tomato in front of him can be shown to be equivalent to a set of claims about Mark's behavioral dispositions, such as claims about his use of the word 'tomato' and his responsiveness to uses of the word 'tomato.' Another form of behaviorism—"radical" behaviorism— held that appeals to the mind or mental states were idle in the explanation of behavior, for a person's mind must ultimately be understood in terms of her behavioral dispositions. On that view, for Mark to believe that there is a tomato in front of him is simply for him to be disposed to act as though there is a tomato in front of him—perhaps by pointing and saying 'tomato,' or by seeing a recipe that calls for a tomato and reaching for it.[22] A person's behavior is not to be explained in terms of her "mental" states, but rather in terms of stimuli and her learning or "reinforcement" history. In both cases, the big idea was to keep the mind from being closed off to others by insisting that it was necessarily displayed in behavior.[23]

Alas, behaviorism had serious problems. Mainly, there seems to be more to the mind than just behavioral dispositions and learning history. Even if the mind has an essential connection to behavior, our claims about the mind cannot be reduced to claims about behavior; likewise, the mind itself cannot be reduced to behavior. Some of what we think and feel is not necessarily manifest in behavior, and is therefore not definable in those terms. For instance, the soreness of my knee is not simply a matter of my acting as if it's sore. Someone could act as if her knee were sore when it isn't. The same is true of a belief. Likewise, some of what we do is not explained simply by appeal to what we've learned, but it is rather something we come up with as the result of thinking, maybe unconsciously, such as our many and various utterances.[24] Thus, while behaviorism might be right to resist pictures of the mind like LP, which make belief mysteriously private, it seems ultimately to be an over-reaction.

The Pittsburgh School resists both LP and the over-reaction that is behaviorism. In EPM, Sellars pursues Plato's suggestion that thought is "a dialogue of the soul."[25] He holds that verbal behavior is a model for thought or "inner conceptual episodes." Specifically, thought is analogous to speech by virtue of having the same kinds of contents that speech has. In a rough slogan, thought is inner speech.[26] That idea is characteristic of philosophers in the Pittsburgh School.

In EPM, Sellars crafts a story about a mythical people—"our Rylean Ancestors"—who can speak, but who do not yet talk of thoughts (EPM, §48). Their language includes words for talking of "public properties of public objects located in Space and enduring through Time" (EPM, §49); it includes logical words like 'not,' 'and,' 'all,' and 'some;' it includes words for talking of dispositions, such as 'If you dropped the glass, it would break'—so-called subjunctive conditionals. And it includes words for talking about meaning, such as "'Rot' means red' and 'What you said is true.' Their language is expressively powerful.

A genius named 'Jones' comes along, wanting to explain their intelligence, particularly their verbal behavior. He proposes that it results from things that occur inside them, analogous to that very verbal behavior. He begins from the fact that Ryleans have dispositions to talk. A Rylean can be disposed to say something even though she might not actually say it on some occasion. In fact, before Jones comes on the scene, the Ryleans already can talk that way about each other. Jones innovates on that ability by proposing that a person can be in a state or undergo an episode that is analogous to uttering a sentence in that it has the same meaning, without actually uttering anything.[27] These things are states or episodes, not mere dispositions to speak; they are occurrences, as are utterances.[28] Because speech results from such inner episodes, any particular utterance can be understood as an expression of the inner episode which is its cause. Jones teaches the other Ryleans to talk that way about each other. Initially, they talk that way only about others. Adams might say of Barnes, 'She is having an episode that's like saying 'That dog is dangerous."' But in time, each speaker learns to apply such talk to herself. Barnes, for instance, learns to say, 'I am in a state like that of saying 'That dog is dangerous."' Crucially, with enough practice, this ability to report her own thoughts is something she can learn to do directly, without need of inferring. In that way, these inner episodes are immediately accessible to her, but they are not so accessible for other people. Thus, the Ryleans learn to talk—and think—of themselves as having non-inferentially accessible, inner conceptual episodes, i.e., thoughts.

That picture of thought rejects a few features of LP. It explains the meaningfulness of thought in terms of the meaningfulness of speech, thereby rejecting LP's claim that language derives its intentionality from speech. Furthermore, by starting with the meaning of utterances as something that is interpersonally available, it makes the contents of a person's thoughts accessible to others, in principle, if not always in practice. Although a person's thoughts may be non-inferentially available to her, they are nevertheless available to others: either through inference or by hearing those thoughts expressed in an overt utterance. Thus, communication is more intelligible in Sellars's picture than it is in LP.

With his "myth" of Jones, Sellars's big suggestion is that thought should be modeled on verbal behavior. In this chapter, we are restricting our attention to one type of thought: belief. Assertion is the sort of verbal behavior that corresponds to it. In Brandom's words, "Assertions are essentially performances that can serve as and stand in need of reasons" (AR, p. 188).[29] The arch idea is that assertions should be understood in terms of their *point*, *function*, or *role* in "the game of giving and asking for reasons."[30]

Like talk of thoughts or beliefs, talk of assertions can be ambiguous, for the word 'assertion' can be used to refer either to *acts* of assert*ing*, or to the *contents* assert*ed* in the act. Suppose John asserts, 'The grocery store is closed.' Imagine also that he does it loudly, thereby frightening you as you nap. When we say that John's assertion frightened you, we are referring to his act of asserting, not to the content of what he asserted. In contrast, if you knew already that the store was closed, you might turn to me and say, 'John's assertion is true.' There you would be referring to the content of what John asserted.

For the Pittsburgh School, both *acts* and *contents* of assertion should be understood in terms of their role in the game of giving and asking for reasons.[31] (In Chapter 4, on meaning, we will see that McDowell has deep reservations about how far this idea can be taken.)

Intuitively, the content of an assertion in a game of giving and asking for reasons would be its rational relations to other contents of other assertions. For instance, asserting 'That is red' supports asserting 'That is colored' and would be supported by asserting 'That is crimson.' There are really two ideas here. First, assertions have content, rather than not, because of their role in the game of giving and asking for reasons. Second, a particular assertion has the particular content it has, rather than some other content, because of the particular role it has in that game.

Crucially, however, the Pittsburgh School holds that assertions are connected to more than just other linguistic acts. They are essentially connected to perception (e.g., the seeing of a tomato) and non-verbal action (e.g., eating a tomato). Sellars calls the "move" from one linguistic act to another an "intra-linguistic" move. A "language entry" is a linguistic response to a non-linguistic stimulus; a "language exit" is a non-linguistic response to a linguistic stimulus (SRLG, p. 329). We certainly often do assert that something is thus-and-so (partly) *because* we perceive it to be thus-and-so; and we often act in such-and-such a way (partly) *because* we assert that something is thus-and-so. Philosophers in the Pittsburgh School want to claim that these "entries" and "exits" are not just accidental, but essential to what an assertion is. Assertions—their contents—can be supported and undermined by perception; and non-verbal action can be supported by assertions. The big idea is to expand our conception of the rational or inferential role of assertion beyond its relation to other linguistic acts. Thus, the content of an assertion would be partly constituted by the experiential circumstances in which it would be appropriate to make that assertion, as well as the non-verbal actions that would appropriately result from it. (We will return to this topic in Chapter 4.)

It is not obvious that or how this trick can be pulled off. In the paradigm case of inferring, one contentful thing is offered as support for another. For instance, I might assert 'That is maroon' to support my previous assertion 'That is red.' As we saw in Chapter 1, the content here involved is typically conceived as having sentence-like structure. Perceptions and non-verbal actions, however, do not seem to be like that. Indeed, we saw this same problem in Chapter 1: experience must be "conceptual" if it is going to rationally support anything. The difficulty is that it's not clear how perceptions can be conceptual, and thus enter into relations of rational support. While there seems to be something right about seeing assertion as having essential connections to other important goings-on, the challenge for philosophers in the Pittsburgh School is to say how we must think about both perception and non-verbal action to vindicate that insight.[32]

Crucially, according to philosophers in the Pittsburgh School, the role of assertions that we have been sketching must be understood in *normative* terms.[33] To make an assertion is to adopt a *normative status*, a status defined in terms of what the assertor rationally *may* (or *may* not) and *should* (or *should* not) say or do. That is a manifestation of the normative character of epistemic states or episodes expressed in Sellars's "placing" remark. Assertions must be understood in terms of what they rationally *permit* or *license* or *warrant* and what they *prohibit* or *forbid*. In this way, there are norms or rules that govern the connections between assertions, perception, and non-verbal behavior.

While someone capable of making an assertion can violate these rules from time to time, one can be an "assertor" only if one is generally in conformity with these rules. If one *never* conforms with these rules, none of one's behavior could count as asserting. For instance, a very young child who makes the sounds that we write as 'A bug,' but never in the presence of bugs, and oftentimes in the presence of various non-bugs, and has a limited vocal repertoire besides, won't (yet) count as asserting the presence or existence of bugs. Thus, following rules is an important dimension of asserting. Several issues arise when we try to get more precise about what it is to follow a rule. We shall pursue that in the next chapter.

This type of picture is aptly called 'Normative Functionalism.'[34] It is functionalist because it emphasizes the function of assertions. It is normative because it stresses the place of normative statuses in characterizing those functions. The norms that are relevant are, of course, norms of reasoning or valid inference (not moral or legal norms). The game of giving and asking for reasons is the normatively defined whole within which acts of asserting take their place. In fact, assertion is doubly Normative Functionalist, for it is both *acts* of asserting and believing, as well as the *contents* of such acts, that should be understood in terms of their norm-governed role in the game of giving and asking for reasons.[35]

The commitment to the importance of normative statuses distinguishes Normative Functionalism from other sorts of functionalism in the philosophy of language and mind, which tend to stress causes and effects in the characterization of functions.[36] The emphasis on normative statuses, instead of causes and effects, is another manifestation of the Pittsburgh School's fundamental resistance to apparent instances of the "naturalistic fallacy"—roughly the attempt to analyze normative concepts, properties, or facts in terms of non-normative concepts, properties, or facts. The Pittsburgh School does not deny the importance of the causal relations that asserting bears to episodes of perceiving and acting, but it gives priority to the normative-rational relations.[37]

Now, in accordance with Sellars's Myth of Jones, we can extend this Normative Functionalist picture of assertions to beliefs.[38] Beliefs are like assertions in that they too have contents, contents just like those had by assertions. Beliefs should be understood in terms of their connection to other beliefs, perceptions, and various non-verbal actions. For instance, believing that something is red should lead one to believe that the very same thing is colored; seeing a red tomato should result in believing that there is a red tomato; believing that something is a red tomato, in conjunction with a desire for a red tomato, should lead to an act of reaching for it. These connections between beliefs and other beliefs, beliefs and perceptions, and beliefs and non-verbal action should be understood in normative terms. Like asserting, believing something is the adopting of a normative status.

Beliefs are language-like, but they are not entirely speech-like, for they need not be communicated to anyone, which is plausibly a goal of speech.[39] *But* beliefs do often cause and support acts of speech. For instance, I assert that the city needs a new mayor because I believe that the current mayor is corrupt. The 'because' here reports both a cause of my assertion, as well as part of my rational support for that assertion. Indeed, in Sellars's Myth of Jones, the proposal is that beliefs should be simply defined as states that normally cause assertions. (The 'normally' here is normative and not merely descriptive. The claim is that assertion is what beliefs *should*, in some sense, result in and from.) Thus, the picture of belief that is ultimately preferred by the Pittsburgh School does not treat assertion simply as a model for belief. Assertions and beliefs are partly understood in terms of one another. Assertions are caused and rationally supported by beliefs; likewise, assertions will cause and rationally support beliefs.

This view of beliefs requires a holistic (or non-atomistic) conception of concepts.[40] Sellars puts the idea provocatively:

> [O]ne can have the concept of [e.g.] green only by having a whole battery of concepts. . . . [While] [T]he process of acquiring the concept green may—indeed does—involve a long history of acquiring *piecemeal* habits of response to various objects in various circumstances, there is an important sense in which one has no concept pertaining to the observable properties of physical objects in Space and Time unless one has them all—and, indeed . . . a great deal more besides.[41] (EPM, §19)

Concepts are defined by their place in beliefs, which are in turn understood by analogy to assertions, which are understood in terms of their norm-governed rational relations to other assertions, perception, and non-verbal action. Such a view of concepts is directly at odds with LP, which holds that concepts can be acquired one-by-one, and don't necessarily have a role in reasoning or action.

Let's take stock. Sellars proposes thinking of speech as a model for thought. The big idea here is that thoughts have sententially structured, interpersonally available content. These contents are not defined purely in terms of each individual's experiences, which would threaten to make them unknowable to others, but by their place in a norm-governed, interpersonal "game." Assertions are the model for beliefs. Both contents and acts of assertions should be understood in terms of their place in that "game," which includes not just their rational relation to other assertions, but also to perception and non-verbal action. The same holds for beliefs. Because concepts are the constituents of beliefs—as words are the constituents of sentences—having a concept requires having several other abilities as well. Thus, LP goes wrong in several ways: it threatens to leave beliefs knowable only to the believer herself; it severs the connection between belief, reasoning, and acting; and it overlooks the holistic character of concept-possession.[42]

2.3. Having Beliefs Requires Having Language

Let us now turn to the ontological relation between thought and language. We saw that LP holds that thinking is ontologically prior to using language; you can think, in some robust sense, before you can speak. Philosophers in the Pittsburgh School generally reject that claim.[43] In various forms, they maintain that full-fledged belief depends ontologically on language. I will call that the Ontological Dependence Thesis (ODT).

It is essential to grasp what sort of claim ODT is. In the previous section, we saw that philosophers in the Pittsburgh School think that speech can be used as a model for conceptual thought, belief in particular. That is a claim about the order of understanding: *understanding* belief requires *understanding* verbal behavior, particularly assertion. We are now turning to a related but distinct *ontological* issue. Could a person *have* beliefs prior to and independently of the ability to speak or, more specifically, the ability to assert?

These conceptual and ontological issues are independent. A claim of conceptual priority does not imply a claim of ontological priority, and vice versa. For instance, one could think that language is conceptually prior to thought, but at the same time deny that language is ontologically prior to thought. One important consequence of this independence is that one cannot support a claim of ontological priority simply by appeal to conceptual priority.[44] For instance, the claims in the previous section cannot be straightforwardly used in support of ODT.

What's more, ODT is deeply contentious, for it seems clear that creatures can have beliefs and lack the ability to use a language.[45] Philosophers in the Pittsburgh School grant that there is a sense in which non-linguistic animals have beliefs.[46] However, they tend also to think that they do not have beliefs in the full-fledged sense in which normal adult humans have beliefs. non-linguistic animals have beliefs in a derivative sense; a sense that is parasitic upon the sense in which normal adult humans have beliefs. Of course, that idea is also deeply contentious. So, one of my aims in the following discussion is to draw out some of their reasons for thinking that beliefs—in the sense that normal adult humans have beliefs—depend on language.

Philosophers in the Pittsburgh School say various things in favor of ODT. I will focus on three influential claims made by Sellars, McDowell, and Brandom.

2.3.1. Sellars

Let's look first at Sellars. Beyond his claim about the conceptual priority of language over thought, he makes (and is fairly well-known for making) important claims about the causal and ontological relationships between thought and language.

The causal claim appears clearly in his Myth of Jones. We saw that Jones proposes that inner conceptual episodes (e.g., beliefs) are theoretical posits that are to be understood on the model of overt verbal behavior. Moreover, those episodes are partly defined as ones that result in the overt verbal behavior that is their model. Indeed, according to Sellars, our *evidence* for positing such episodes in an organism is usually the fact that it produces this overt verbal behavior. Thus, someone who is capable of undergoing inner conceptual episodes will normally be someone who produces assertions. That is one way in which Sellars maintains that thought is causally (and not just conceptually) linked to language.

The ontological claim held by Sellars is stronger than the causal claim. Essentially, he claims that the ability to speak a language is necessary for following rules, which is necessary for having beliefs in the full-fledged sense.

In EPM, Sellars introduces a view that he labels "psychological nominalism" (§29).[47] He initially characterizes it thus: "all awareness of sorts, resemblances, facts, etc., in short all awareness of abstract entities is a linguistic affair" (§29). On his way to a more modest formulation, he says:

> [W]hen we picture a child—or a carrier of slabs—learning his first language, we, of course, locate the child in a structured logical space where we are at home. Thus, we conceive of him as a person (or, at least, a potential person) in a world of physical objects, colored, producing sounds, existing in Space and Time. But though it is we who are familiar with this logical space, we run the danger, if we are not

careful, of picturing the language learner as having *ab initio* some degree of awareness—'pre-analytic,' limited and fragmentary though it may be—of this same logical space. We picture his state as though it were rather like our own when placed in a strange forest on a dark night. In other words, unless we are careful, we can easily take for granted that the process of teaching a child to use a language is that of teaching it to discriminate elements within a logical space of particulars, universals, facts, etc., of which it is already undiscriminatingly aware, and to associate these discriminated elements with verbal symbols.[48] (EPM, §30)

The basic idea is clear: Sellars thinks that we should be careful not to assume that (a) pre-linguistic creatures are dimly aware of the same logical relations of which we linguistic creatures are aware and that (b) acquiring a language is simply a means or instrument for tracking and expressing those antecedently grasped relations. With this caution in place, he clarifies his conception of psychological nominalism: "As I am using the term, [it] is the denial that there is awareness of logical space prior to, or independent of, the acquisition of a language" (EPM, §31).[49]

What is this "awareness of logical space"?[50] Why is it necessary for full-fledged belief? Why does having it require language?

This logical space that Sellars is alluding to is the very same "logical space of reasons, the space of justifying and being able to justify what one says" that we saw in Chapter 1.

To see what Sellars thinks it takes to be aware of that logical space, consider two ways in which a thing can be said to be engaged in reasoning. In general, reasoning essentially involves the ability to transition from one thought T1 to another thought T2 that *follows from* T1. For instance, you reason when you infer that Socrates is mortal from the fact that he is human; the thought that Socrates is human supports the thought that he is mortal. The first way in which one can be said to be reasoning is when one simply makes these sorts of transitions—even though one does not explicitly recognize that the one thought is support for the other. This first sort of reasoning does not suffice for "awareness of logical space." Something more is necessary, which marks a second, more fully fledged way in which something can count as reasoning. This something more is an awareness of the rules governing good reasoning. A thing that goes from thinking that Socrates is human to thinking that he is a mortal *need not* be able to think that the first judgment is a reason for believing the second. Such a thing treats the first judgment as a reason for the second *only* to the extent that it is disposed to think the second judgment after thinking the first. Being disposed to make a move that happens to be rational is not necessarily to recognize that transition as rational. Transitioning from one judgment to another might be *in accord* with a rule for good reasoning—e.g., 'If something is a man, then it is mortal'—but such a transition need not occur *from an understanding* of such a rule. Awareness of logical space requires being able to act from an understanding of the rules governing inferences.

The basic distinction between acting in accord with a rule and acting from an understanding of a rule traces to Kant (Kant, 1785/1998). For a simple illustration of the point, suppose that when Sarah leaves her office she invariably descends the stairs at a speed of .78mph. Her descent is uniform, regular. It accords with a rule: 'Descend the stairs at a speed of .78mph.' But she could be utterly ignorant of that rule, in which case she certainly could not count as guiding her behavior in light of it. By contrast, when Sarah drives her car at 35mph in order to stay under the posted speed limit of 40mph, she is acting from an understanding of that rule.

"Awareness of logical space" is the phrase that Sellars uses to talk specifically about that phenomenon—acting from an understanding of a rule—in the realm of reasoning and thought; it is his expression for talking about awareness of *rules of reasoning*. To be aware of logical space is to be able to recognize that something is a reason for something else, that there is a rule governing the connection between two things.

Now, why does Sellars think that awareness of logical space, in that sense, is necessary for having full-fledged beliefs? His basic position is that having full-fledged beliefs requires the ability to reason, which in turn requires the ability to act from an understanding of rules of reasoning.

Sellars says, "To be able to think is to be able to measure one's thoughts by standards of correctness, of relevance, of evidence" (PSIM, p. 6). Having beliefs—believing something—requires responsiveness to reasons for and against that belief. Something that putatively had a belief, but never revised it or searched for support in light of incompatible claims, or recognized anything as incompatible with it, could not really count as having any beliefs. Its putative beliefs would be effectively unaccountable to what they were putatively about. And that would keep them from being beliefs at all, for a mark of belief is that it is both about and accountable to something. So, to have any beliefs is to be able and willing to recognize what counts for and against one's beliefs, the ability to reason.

Now, what does that involve? At bottom, it requires the ability to recognize reasons as reasons. Here we need to be careful about what's involved in recognizing something as a reason. A squirrel that tends to move away from danger, for instance, is clearly rational in some sense. Moving out of danger is, in some sense, a way of recognizing the danger as a reason for moving. But tending to do something that is rational is not yet to recognize that something as rational. (Having a habit that is unhealthy is not yet to recognize that habit or anything else as unhealthy.) By contrast, we humans are capable of taking transitions between judgments to be rational. We have the concept of reason or some surrogate. Not only am I able to think that there is something on the table; I am able also to think that it is rational for me to think that there is something on the table, given that there is a book on the table. In general, we humans are capable of *citing* (what we take to be) rules of reasoning in defense of the inferences we make—for instance, 'If a book is on the table, then something is on the table.'

Making the rules explicit for defense and criticism is, for Sellars, *the* crucial skill. Think about a creature or artifact that has merely a habit of acting in accord with rules of reasoning. Such a thing does not seem to be able to distinguish (explicitly or in practice) between *breaking* a rule and *objecting* to it. Clearly, such a thing can *break* a rule simply by not doing what it requires (or doing what it forbids). But could such a thing object to the rule? Not acting in accord with the rule will not suffice. A dog that defecates in the dining room has not thereby objected to the rule requiring him not to do so. To object to a rule seems to require the ability to attend to the rule as such. A creature would have to be able to make the rule explicit to itself. According to Sellars, a thing that cannot distinguish between *breaking* a rule and *objecting* to it cannot count as genuinely following a rule either. Where there is no possibility of objecting to a rule, there is also no possibility of following it.[51]

So, to repeat, the key idea for Sellars is that having full-fledged beliefs requires the ability to reason, which in turn requires the ability to act from an understanding of rules of reasoning. Indeed, Sellars thinks that our responsiveness to rules or norms marks humans off from other creatures. He writes, "When God created Adam, he whispered in his ear, 'In all contexts of action you will recognize rules, if only the rule to grope for rules to recognize. When you cease to recognize rules, you will walk on four feet'" (LRB, p. 122). Other philosophers in the Pittsburgh School agree that understanding responsiveness to rules is essential for understanding humans.[52]

Now, why does Sellars think following rules requires the ability to use a (natural) language? We won't get the full answer until the next chapter, but we can begin on it here. We've seen that Sellars claims that to *follow* a rule one must be able to have it explicitly available. This does not necessarily mean that one must be occurrently conscious of the rule at the time of following it. It primarily means that one must be able to *formulate* the rule.[53] The ability to speak a (natural) language is just such an ability.[54]

Now, one might agree with Sellars that one must be able to formulate the rules, but disagree with him that doing so requires the ability to speak a natural language. One might instead think that thought itself is or affords the ability to formulate the rule. For instance, one might think that there is a "language of thought" available prior to and independently of any natural language. Sellars rejects that strategy, for it seems to force us back to wondering what "thought itself" is, such that it could enable one to formulate rules. What is it to think? What is it to have discursively articulated thoughts? One aim of the Myth of Jones was to demystify thought, partly by modeling it on speech. But that myth also helps demystify thought by suggesting that it comes with the ability to speak. In the next chapter, we will see that Sellars has other worries about appealing to "thought itself" to explain our ability to follow rules.

2.3.2. McDowell

McDowell adopts two important elements of Sellars's position. First, he maintains that fully fledged human belief requires being situated in the "logical space of reasons."[55] Second, he maintains that humans become so situated because of their initiation into a natural language. McDowell offers a distinctive defense of that second claim.

Consider first how McDowell understands Sellars's claim that full-fledged belief requires awareness of the logical space of reasons. In *Having the World in View,* McDowell glosses Sellars's "logical space of reasons" remark thus:

> There is a special category of characterizations of states or episodes that occur in people's lives, for instance, characterizations of states or episodes as *knowings*; and, we might add, corresponding character-izations of the people in whose lives the states or episodes occur, for instance, characterizations of people as *knowers*. In giving these char-acterizations, we place whatever they characterize in the 'logical space of reasons' ([EPM] §36). (HWV, pp. 4–5)

Like Sellars's original remark, McDowell's gloss clearly concerns know-ing and knowers. However, McDowell believes that the "placing" idea extends to believing (or judging) more generally. He claims that "[judg-ing] is something for which we are in principle responsible;" "[it is] essen-tially a matter of being answerable to criticism in the light of rationally relevant considerations;" "[it is] essentially a matter of responsiveness to reasons" (HWV, p. 6).

This responsiveness to reasons is an ability to "recognize reasons as such" (HWV, p. 128). That is, it requires that one has the concept of rea-son or of justification. Like Sellars, McDowell is drawing on the (Kantian) distinction between merely acting in accord with a rule and acting from an understanding of a rule. McDowell stresses that the "ability to step back and assess whether putative reasons really are reasons . . . is part of the ability to [recognize reasons as such]" (HWV, p. 130).[56]

Now, McDowell's understanding and defense of the claim that aware-ness of the logical space of reasons requires the ability to speak a language differ from Sellars's own. McDowell conceives of language as embodying a tradition. He writes:

> In being initiated into a language, a human being is introduced into something that already embodies putatively rational linkages between concepts, putatively constitutive of the layout of the space of reasons, before she comes on the scene. . . . [T]he language into which a human being is first initiated stands over against her as a prior embodiment of mindedness, of the possibility of an orientation to the world.

> . . . [A] natural language, the sort of language into which human beings are first initiated, serves as a repository of tradition, a store of historically accumulated wisdom about what is a reason for what.[57] (MW, pp. 125–6)

Sellars thinks something similar, as McDowell notices. For instance, Sellars writes, "an essential feature of languages . . . [is that] they enable language users to find their way around in the world, and satisfy their needs" (SRLG, p. 340); they have the distinctive feature of "embodying convictions as to the ways of things" (SRLG, p. 340). McDowell says that for Sellars

> conceptual capacities . . . accrue to us along with a mastery of language, which must embody a familiarity with rational linkages between one concept and another. These linkages include, crucially, materially sound inferential connections, and command of such connections is inseparable from having substantial knowledge of the world. (HWV, 92)

Given that, we can see McDowell as highlighting a theme in Sellars's own work. The important substantive point is that awareness of the logical space of reasons *requires* initiation into language *because* languages themselves embody the very rational connections mastery of which is necessary for that awareness.

Could there be some other way into the space of reasons? Perhaps. McDowell does not argue that there couldn't be. Like Sellars, he holds that we can get a better grip on thought—on being in the space of reasons—by thinking of it as coming with the ability to speak a language, rather than something completely prior to that ability. He holds that, for us humans, learning to speak is connected to learning to reason. That is not the absurd idea that one learns how to speak first, and then learns how to reason, but rather the more plausible idea that one learns how to do both, together.

2.3.3. Brandom

Like McDowell, Brandom accepts Sellars's idea that awareness of the logical space of reasons is necessary for belief. And Brandom accepts McDowell's claim that in learning a language we learn the rational relations between various claims. But Brandom rejects the claim that asserting (believing) and reasoning require the capacity to explicitly formulate the rules that one is following. According to him, that capacity for "explicitation" is made possible by broadly logical vocabulary, paradigmatically conditional sentences, with the form 'If *P*, then *Q*.' One can genuinely assert (believe) and reason without yet having that sort of vocabulary.[58]

Brandom has a different way of supporting ODT. Put very roughly, Brandom claims that to have beliefs one must know how to interpret the claims of others.

Brandom thinks that the term 'belief' is ambiguous. It can be used to talk about both what a person takes herself to believe, as well as whatever is entailed by those beliefs she takes herself as having.[59] For that reason Brandom prefers to use "undertaking a commitment," which he thinks avoids the ambiguity.

According to him, there are two general ways of undertaking a commitment: acknowledging it or having it as a consequence of an acknowledged commitment. Thus, the latter sort of commitment allows for undertaken but *unacknowledged* commitments. Crucially, unacknowledged commitments depend on acknowledged commitments. Without any acknowledged commitments, there could be no consequences of acknowledged commitments for one to be committed to.

The paradigmatic way of acknowledging a commitment is to avow it by asserting it. But one can also acknowledge a commitment by acting as though it is a premise supporting one's conduct. For instance, one could acknowledge a commitment to the claim that it is raining by carrying an open umbrella over one's head in the usual way.

Now, according to Brandom, what is the ontological relationship between undertaking commitments—our new surrogate for belief—and speaking a language?

Brandom endorses a two-stage argument offered by Donald Davidson. I will offer only the barest sketch of it here; Brandom claims that the full argument takes the bulk of *Making It Explicit*, roughly 450 pages of wide-ranging and challenging philosophy.[60]

For the first stage, Brandom quotes a striking remark from Davidson, "someone cannot have a belief unless he understands the possibility of being mistaken, and this requires grasping the contrast between truth and error—true belief and false belief" ("Thought and Talk," p. 170; cited at MIE, p. 151; see also AR, pp. 6–7). In Brandom's preferred terms, the claim is that one cannot undertake a commitment unless one understands the contrast between *merely* undertaking a commitment and *correctly* undertaking a commitment.

In support of that claim, Brandom contends that one cannot undertake a commitment unless one gets that such undertakings might be wrong. For if you do not understand that your undertaking is open to evaluation in this way, you cannot be in a position to support it, or to see it as support for another commitment. And if you cannot grasp that an undertaken commitment needs (or can be adduced as) support, then you have not genuinely undertaken that commitment.

The second stage of the argument addresses what's required for understanding the contrast between commitments merely undertaken and commitments correctly undertaken. Quoting Davidson, Brandom writes, "a grasp of the contrast between correct and incorrect belief, true and false belief, 'can emerge only in the context of interpretation, which alone forces us to the idea of an objective, public truth.' The key claim is that 'the concepts of objective truth and of error necessarily emerge in the context of interpretation'" (MIE, p. 152; citing "Thought and Talk," p. 170).

Let me sketch the basic reasoning in support of this claim. To grasp the possibility of erroneous beliefs, one must recognize that there is something that one's belief is *about*, which one's belief *purports* to get *right*. For instance, I might believe of some book that it is red. That belief is about the book, but it could be wrong, if, say, the book is actually brown. *That* capacity emerges in connection with the capacity to distinguish one's own beliefs and other incompatible beliefs about the same object. For instance, I might believe of some book that it is red, while recognizing that I cannot at the same time believe that it is also brown. *That* capacity, in turn, requires understanding the difference between what one believes oneself and the beliefs one attributes (or might attribute) to others. That is, one must be able to distinguish between different *perspectives* on the *same object* or *state of affairs*. For instance, I must be able to distinguish my belief about some book that it is red, and my attributing to you the belief about that same book that it is brown. And *that* capacity "emerges only in the context of interpretation" of the speech of others.[61]

Specifically, linguistic activity is our way of tracking *who* is referring to *what* and by what *means*. Thus, it enables us track the difference between what a person is referring to (or talking about) on some occasion and the expression used by that person to refer to (or talk about) it.[62]

Consider an example. Suppose that you say to me, 'The manager is in his office.' Suppose also that I believe that John is the manager. It might then seem to me that you believe that John is in his office. Having some reason to doubt that John really is there, I say, 'Why do you think John is in his office?' But you don't actually know that John is the manager, so you reply, 'I didn't say that.'

In this exchange, that John is the manager is a commitment of my own, which I have erroneously attributed to you. Because you believe that the manager is in his office, by my lights you also believe *of* John that he is in his office. But since you do not also believe that the manager is John, you do not believe *that* John is in his office.

Realizing something to this effect, I might say to you, 'Oh! John *is* the manager,' or '"John" is the name of the manager.' In either case, for me to make sense of what you seem to believe (that the manager is in his office but John is not), I need to grasp that (a) the same thing can be referred to or picked out in different ways, and (b) you yourself do not recognize that the manager and John are one and the same person. I need to distinguish between my own commitments and those that I attribute to you.

Just as two people can talk about the very same thing using different expressions, two people can think about the very same thing under different guises (or "modes of presentation" to use an expression from Frege). Brandom's view is that without language, we wouldn't be able to undertake and attribute commitments tracking those kinds of differences in perspective.[63]

To sum up, for Brandom, believing or undertaking commitment requires language because (i) having a belief requires grasp of the possibility of false beliefs, which in turn requires (ii) the capacity to distinguish between one's own beliefs, what they are about, and the (possibly incompatible) beliefs of others, which in turn (iii) can be done only in understanding and assessing what they say. Speaking with others affords the ability to distinguish between perspectives on a common world, which is essential to having any beliefs at all.[64]

In this section, I have sketched three different ways in which philosophers in the Pittsburgh School defend ODT. Sellars claims that full-fledged believing requires following rules of reasoning, which in turn requires being able to formulate those rules in a language. McDowell claims that languages embody the rational relations understanding of which is necessary for having beliefs. Brandom claims that full-fledged belief requires a capacity to distinguish between different perspectives on a common world, which in turn requires language. I have not shown that any of these clams is beyond question. However, anyone who wants to reject ODT must come to grips with these defenses of it. Indeed, even if these defenses do not vindicate ODT, they reveal hidden complexities in the nature of full-fledged belief that are obscured by the Lockean Picture, and other pictures like it.

CONCLUSION

The main aim of this chapter was to get clearer about what philosophers in the Pittsburgh School think about thought, specifically belief. In the broadest terms, they think that acts and contents of beliefs should be understood in terms of their place in reasoning, broadly construed. More specifically, they think of beliefs on the model of overt verbal behavior, paradigmatically, assertion; in turn, they think that both the acts and contents of beliefs should be understood in normative functionalist terms, i.e., in terms of the norm-governed roles of those acts and contents. Further, they tend to think that beliefs, both acts and contents, are ontologically dependent on language. They diverge somewhat on how best to understand and defend that claim. At least to that extent, philosophers in the Pittsburgh School have different pictures of belief.

Nevertheless, for philosophers in the Pittsburgh School, rules or norms play a key role in their preferred pictures of belief. For believing and asserting require the capacity to follow rules of reasoning, and the very meaning of beliefs and assertions are constituted by those rules. So, in the next two chapters, we will look more closely at rule-following and meaning.

3 Following Rules

> When God created Adam, he whispered in his ear, 'In all contexts of action you will recognize rules, if only the rule to grope for rules to recognize. When you cease to recognize rules, you will walk on four feet.'
>
> -Sellars, Language, Rules and Behavior, p. 122

INTRODUCTION

Philosophers in the Pittsburgh School stress the importance of following rules for speaking and thinking. What is it to follow a rule?

In this chapter, I want first to identify some of the problems that philosophers in the Pittsburgh School think attend the issue of rule-following. Since they disagree about how exactly to resolve those problems, my second aim is to look at different resolutions proposed by Sellars, Brandom, and McDowell.

1. VERBALLY CLOTHED RULES

1.1. A Regress

Philosophers in the Pittsburgh School think that human thought depends on the ability to follow rules for the use of words or concepts. In what sense exactly do we follow rules when we use a word (outwardly or inwardly)?[1]

In Chapter 2, I introduced a distinction between acting from an understanding of a rule and merely acting in accord with a rule. Sarah might descend the stairs in accord with a rule, but she could be unaware that her behavior is in accord with any rule, let alone that particular rule; she might even lack the specific concepts needed to conceive of that rule. Acting from an understanding of a rule, by contrast, seems to require the capacity to conceive of the rule, say, by citing it in one's own thoughts or in conversation with others. For the Pittsburgh School, when we use words meaningfully, we act from an understanding of a rule.

What is required for acting from an understanding of a rule?

It is natural to suppose that one must be aware of the rule. What form would such awareness take? It's natural to suppose that the rules need to be verbally (or conceptually) formulated; they must express or say what must (not) or may (not) be done. Otherwise, one would go wrong; one would use the given word incorrectly.

However, if we assume that, then we embark on a regress. The words used to express the rule would require following further rules for their correct application.[2] Following any rule would require following a further rule. For instance, suppose the relevant rule for 'sharp' was expressed in the English sentence 'Apply 'sharp' to rigid things that can cut through steel.' Then, the words in that rule (such as 'steel') would require rules for their correct application.[3] Thus, the thesis that grasp of a word requires the ability to follow rules would be "subject to an obvious and devastating objection" (Sellars, SRLG, §1).

Sellars sketches the regress as follows:

> *Thesis.* Learning to use a language (L) is learning to obey the rules of L.
>
> *But,* a rule which enjoins the doing of an action (A) is a sentence in a language which contains an expression for A.
>
> *Hence,* a rule which enjoins the using of a linguistic expression (E) is a sentence in a language which contains an expression for E—in other words a sentence in a *meta*language.
>
> *Consequently,* learning to obey the rules for L presupposes the ability to use the metalanguage (ML) in which the rules for L are formulated.
>
> *So that* learning to use a language (L) presupposes having learned to use a language (ML). And by the same token, having learned to use ML presupposes having learned to use a *meta*-metalanguage (MML) and so on.
>
> *But* this is an impossible (a vicious) regress.
>
> *Therefore,* the thesis is absurd and must be rejected. (SRLG, §1)

Sellars's regress purports to show that we must reject the thesis that "learning to use a language (L) is learning to obey the rules of L." What are the implications of rejecting that thesis? First, it seems to suggest that one can *learn* to use a language L without necessarily learning to obey L's rules. Second, it seems to suggest that *using* a language need not involve obeying rules at all. That would be an especially striking result. If that's so, it would seem to follow that there's nothing that we must (not) or may (not) do in using a language. One can use words however one likes. 'Sharp,' for instance, could be correctly (or "truly") applied even to non-sharp things.[4] What, then, would 'sharp' mean? Would it mean anything at all? This seems especially problematic for the Pittsburgh School, which holds that rules are essential for language and thought.

1.2. A Regress-Stopper?

Can the regress be stopped?

We might hope for very simple rules, the following of which don't require any further rules, rules which could be followed without guidance from another rule. One might suppose that there are rules that are not verbally (or conceptually) formulated.

Intuitively, these rules would govern our most basic or simplest words (and their corresponding concepts), such as those pertaining to sight, sound, touch, and taste—e.g., 'dark,' 'light,' 'loud,' 'quiet,' 'hard,' 'soft,' 'cold,' 'hot,' 'sweet,' and 'salty.'[5] These words seem to be simple in the sense that we seem to grasp their proper use solely in virtue of having had the relevant experiences. For instance, it is natural to think that your experiences of hardness dictate how to use 'hard' in the future. The feeling itself somehow tells you how to use that word properly.

If this proposal is correct, it would seem that the regress must stop since there are rules that are not "clothed" in words (or concepts); thus, there would appear to be no need for further rules; you simply rely on a verbally naked feeling to guide your application of certain words. While *some* words would require further rules for their proper application, not every rule would require a further rule.

Are there such rules?

1.3. The Problem with a Regress-Stopper

This type of proposal faces a serious problem. Rules themselves can be correctly or incorrectly applied. That fact is what really seems to prompt the need for more rules. Whether the rules are "clothed" in words seems to be beside the point.

Let's look at that problem in greater detail.

In "Some Reflections on Language Games" (pp. 323–4), Sellars considers a version of the proposal I have just sketched. In that version, there is a difference between the verbal formulation of a rule and the rule itself, what it requires or permits. And that seems intuitively plausible: the rule expressed by the English sentence 'Exit here' can be expressed in the Spanish sentence 'Salir aqui;' the rule expressed should not be identified with either linguistic-type. Sellars calls the rule itself a "Demand." (These Demands correspond to the non-conceptual feelings we were recently entertaining.) With this distinction in place, it appears that the regress can be averted, since Demands themselves need not be verbally clothed.[6]

Do Demands stop the regress?

Notice that whatever else Demands are, they are supposed to be *rules*. Of any rule, it can be asked 'What counts as following it?' Following a rule is itself prone to error. For instance, the command 'Turn right!' can be variously interpreted to mean 'Turn right immediately!' or 'Turn right at the upcoming street!' If the first interpretation is intended, turning at the street 200 feet away would be a mistake. Thus, although Demands are verbally naked, they are nonetheless the kind of thing that one can get wrong. Thus, properly complying with a Demand seems to require further Demands. We still have a regress.[7] And the same can be said of our original version of the proposal that appealed to unconceptualized feelings or experiences. Whatever else we are supposed to think of them, such experiences must lay down rules; they must tell you to do something. But as such, one can get them wrong; one can misapply them. Insisting that they are unconceptualized does not seem to help.

Thus, the deeper problem seems to be that one can go wrong in trying to follow a rule. Even rules that are verbally naked threaten us with a regress.[8]

A defender of this proposal might try to deny that following a rule is always something that can be done correctly or incorrectly. Specifically, one might claim that Demands (for instance) are so "clear" that one cannot get them wrong; one cannot misapply them.

Does that revision help?

What should we make of this putative clarity? It cannot be conceptual clarity, since Demands are conceptually bare. It is more like the clarity of a loud bell rung in your ear that makes your body jerk. The ringing does not command you to move; it simply makes you move. You need not have any understanding of how your body will be compelled to move; it just will move in that way. There is nothing that the ringing of the bell calls on you to do and makes *right* for you to do; there is only what your body is physically or causally necessitated to do. Likewise, a Demand that one cannot but comply with seems to obliterate the distinction between what you *will* do and what it is *right* or *correct* for you to do.[9]

Thus, this revised proposal replaces normative requirements with physical or causal compulsion. By pushing the possibility of incorrectness out of the picture, it also pushes the possibility of following a rule out of the picture. Adopting the revised proposal would allow us to halt the regress of rules at the expense of actually following rules. So, Demands don't seem to solve our problem.

1.4. The Given (Again)

Perhaps some of you have suspected that Demands are somehow analogous to the Given. Obviously, the two are alike in being enlisted as regress-stoppers. Furthermore, Demands are supposed to be non-verbal or non-conceptual, like *one* form of the Given. So, they have some similarities. But McDowell goes further, contending that the kind of thing we have been considering is an *instance* of the Given.[10]

McDowell is not obviously right about that. First of all, the two regresses seem to concern different things. Appeals to the Given are part of attempts to provide a foundation for knowledge, a kind of knowledge that could be had without appeal to other knowledge. By contrast, Demands arise in the course of trying to stop a regress of rules for the proper use of words, a kind of rule that could be followed without need of other rules. Also, the Given is supposed to be something that is both epistemically efficacious and epistemically independent. That is, it is supposed to be something that can rationally support beliefs or claims, and which can be had independently of any other knowledge. At the very least, it is not obvious that Demands are supposed to have those features.

So, there are impediments to accepting McDowell's claim that things like Demands are just an instance of the Given. However, one way to see why McDowell thinks that a Demand (or something like it) really is an instance of the Given would be to show that a Demand would need to be epistemically efficacious and independent. Let me sketch such a case.

We already know that a Demand is supposed to be something that (a) tells you when it is correct to use a word, and (b) can be followed without following other rules. To help you see why Demands can be understood as an instance of the Given, I will try to show that (a) corresponds to epistemic efficacy and (b) corresponds to epistemic independence.

Let's start with (a). Because a Demand tells you when it is appropriate to apply a word, it effectively *licenses* certain thoughts. That is, by declaring when it is appropriate to apply a word W, a Demand concerning W *supports* thoughts that contain proper applications of W. For instance, a Demand that "says" 'Apply 'sharp' to rigid things that cut through steel' should support the thought expressed in the claim 'That is sharp,' where 'that' refers to some rigid thing that just cut through a piece of steel. As injunctions on when it is appropriate to apply a word, Demands need to be rational supports for thoughts. So, (a) does indeed seem to correspond to epistemic efficacy; Demands need to be epistemically efficacious.

Now, turn to condition (b). Does it correspond to epistemic independence? Demands are supposed to be non-conceptual; whatever exactly they are, they must not be verbally articulated. The point of that requirement is to avoid the need for a person to follow further rules for the proper application of Demands. Now, if following a Demand requires one to know something else in addition, then we are faced with the re-appearance of words and, hence, more Demands. Thus, it appears that Demands must be epistemically independent. One must grasp them without having any other knowledge.

That's a quick sketch of a case for thinking that Demands (or something like them) are instances of the Given. Let us now suppose that McDowell is right that Demands are instances of the Given. We can see how a Demand could play a part in the dialectic of Chapter 1. The regress of knowledge with which we were concerned there would stop at Demands. They would be a type of non-conceptual Given. Specifically, they would be non-conceptual knowledge that tells one when it is appropriate to apply one's most "basic" words (e.g., those concerning sensation); and that knowledge would be available without need of any further knowledge.

If Demands are an appeal to the Given, then such appeals arise not just in accounting for *knowledge*, but also in accounting for our ability to *think*, i.e., our ability to use words and concepts. That result might not be wholly surprising. For if our ability to use words fundamentally depends on or is a kind of knowledge, and the Given arises in the course of accounting for knowledge, then the Given will arise in our thinking about our ability to use words. Appreciating that possibility is the main value of pursuing McDowell's suggestion that one proposal for what would stop the regress of rules is an appeal to the Given.

2. REGULARISM

2.1. The Intellectualist Assumption

Faced with the regress of rules, we went in search of some way to stop it. We considered a proposal that rejected an assumption that seemed to drive the regress: rules must be verbally articulated. We saw that this proposal doesn't work. Even verbally bare rules are the kind of thing that one can get wrong. All rules seem to require further rules for their proper application. However, by rejecting that proposal, we are left with the regress. Is there some other way to avoid it?

Our discussion of Demands does indeed reveal another claim worth questioning, namely the claim that following a rule R always requires following another rule R′ for R's proper application. Challenging that claim would be a different way of resisting the regress. McDowell puts that idea by saying that we should reject the claim that "grasping a rule is always an interpretation" (WFR, p. 238).[11] Sellars and Brandom concur with McDowell that this is a dubious assumption.[12]

Let me motivate the basic idea. There seem to be plenty of occasions on which we correctly follow rules without need of an "interpretation" of that rule or the need for a further rule. For instance, we just know how to follow a road sign featuring this icon: →. Such an icon points to the right; a sign featuring it indicates that something is to the right; we don't need to interpret it, or consult a further rule. For instance, if we saw a sign that displayed the following

> →
>
> Pittsburgh

we'd just know that it says Pittsburgh is to the right. While it is true that an arrow so oriented *could* mean other things, normally no question arises for us about what it means and (hence) what it requires. Likewise, while it takes some training to know what such a sign means, we are not permanently in a state of needing to appeal to that training when we follow it. Examples like this could be multiplied endlessly.

According to Brandom, the picture of rule-following that seems to be at work in the regress is overly "intellectualist;" it depicts us as needing to "think" or "interpret" any time we manage to follow a rule or abide by a norm (MIE, p. 20). The fact of the matter is that we often manage to follow rules without "thinking about it."

Let us call the offending claim the Intellectualist Assumption (IA):

> IA: Following a rule R always requires following another rule R´ for R's proper application.

Rejecting IA is a first step towards resisting the regress, but it is not the last, for there is a way of rejecting that assumption that lands us with a further problem.

2.2. "Conformity" and Regularism

In "Some Reflections on Language Games," after presenting the regress, Sellars writes:

> [T]here is a simple and straightforward way of preserving the essential claim of the thesis [that learning a language is learning to obey its rules] while freeing it from the refutation. It consists in substituting the phrase 'learning to conform to the rules . . . ' for 'learning to obey the rules . . . ' where 'conforming to a rule enjoining the doing of A in circumstances C' is to be equated simply with 'doing A when the circumstances are C'—regardless of how one comes to do it. (p. 322)

The basic idea here is that there is a way of following a rule according to which one follows a rule so long as one has a disposition or propensity to do what the rule requires in the right circumstances. For instance, a small child can be said to follow the rule (in America) of walking on the right side of a sidewalk, so long as she has a disposition to so walk. Sellars calls that *conformity*, which he contrasts with *obedience*, which requires having the rule in mind and intending to follow it. (Sellars acknowledges that "obedience" and "conformity" are often used interchangeably and that his choice of terms is stipulative (Sellars, SRLG, p. 322).)

Voicing a defense of this appeal to conformity, Sellars writes:

> [T]here are many modes of human activity for which there are rules (let us stretch the word 'game' to cover them all) and yet in which people participate (play) without being able to formulate the rules to which they conform in so doing. Should we not conclude that playing these games is a matter of *doing A when the circumstances are C, doing A´ when the circumstances are C´* etc., and that the ability to formulate and obey the rules, although it may be a necessary condition of playing 'in a critical and self-conscious manner' cannot be essential to playing *tout court*. (SRLG, p. 322)

By distinguishing between conformity and obedience, we avoid the regress. If conforming is a species of following a rule, then one can follow a rule without having it in mind. Conformity requires only that one exhibits regularity in one's performances, a disposition or propensity to do the right thing in the right circumstances. You conform to a rule so long as you do what it says to do, even if you do not do so *because of* what it says, even if you do not have the word or the concepts for expressing or comprehending that rule.[13]

Because regularity is the central idea in this proposal, we will follow Brandom in calling this proposal Regularism.[14] Regularism rejects IA by maintaining that some rule-following consists in conformity.

2.3. Against Regularism

Alas, Regularism cannot be acceptable to philosophers in the Pittsburgh School. You have been primed to recognize why. Conformity with a rule or exhibiting a regularity does not count as *following* a rule. Think of Sarah's descent of the staircase. Regularism seems simply to conflate acting from an understanding of a rule and merely acting in accord with a rule.

Moreover, Regularism faces a related problem.[15] There is no single pattern or regularity that one's verbal performances exhibit; one's performances exhibit a variety of regularities. Indeed, one's past performances are consistent with an *infinite* number of incompatible patterns! If there is no single pattern that one's performances exhibit, then those performances alone leave it indeterminate which rule one is allegedly following. If that's so, then it is also indeterminate what is and is not an error. And if that's true, then one cannot be said to be following a rule at all, for following a rule requires the possibility of error.

Consider an example adapted from Wittgenstein's discussion of the problem (1958, §185). Suppose we walk into a classroom and find Erin writing numbers on a board. We see: 2, 4, 6, 8, and 10. She sets her hand to the board to begin writing the next number. Which number is it going to be? What number *should* she write next, given what she has already written?

It's true that Erin seems to be following the rule that says to add 2 to each predecessor. If that's the rule she's following, she should write '12.' The trouble is that the numbers she has written accord with many other rules that are incompatible with writing '12.' For instance, the numbers written thus far accord with the rule that says to add 2 until 10, then add 4. In that case, Erin should write '14' not '12.' In fact, the numbers she has written also accord with many similar but equally incompatible rules:

> Add 2 until 10, then add 5
> Add 2 until 10, then add 6
> Add 2 until 10, then add 7
> Add 2 until 10, then add 8
> Add 2 until 10, then add 9
> Add 2 until 10, then add 10

It should be clear that this list could go on indefinitely. There are indefinitely many incompatible rules that Erin's past behavior accords or "conforms" with. So, judging *only* from the numbers that have been written (i.e., her past behavior), there is no single rule that she is following. Consequently, there is no settled fact about what she *should* do next. Her past behavior does not suffice to settle which rule, if any, she is allegedly following.

Brandom captures the general problem well: Regularism "must be supplemented with some way of picking out, as somehow *privileged*, some out of all the regularities exhibited" (MIE, p. 28). Brandom calls that the "gerrymandering problem" (MIE, p. 28). Regularism proposes that exhibiting a regularity can count as following a rule, but without some specific regularity, there is nothing that counts as irregularity, hence nothing that counts as *error*.

At this point, a defender of Regularism might appeal to *dispositions* to act, instead of simply one's *past* actions. The hope would be that by expanding the number of cases under consideration (from a finite set to an infinite set) one could settle which rule one is following. Specifically, in our given example, the rule that Erin is following would be given by the answers that she is disposed to give. For instance, if she is disposed to add 2 to each predecessor, then she is following the rule to add 2 to each predecessor. One can exclude other incompatible rules as candidates by saying that she does not have the disposition to produce numbers in accord with those rules. According to this dispositionalist proposal, one follows the rule when one does what one is disposed to do and one violates the rule when one does not do what one is disposed to do.

The main difficulty with this proposal, according to Brandom and Sellars, is that dispositions by themselves do not constitute what one should do; exhibiting a disposition does not necessarily constitute what is right.[16] This proposal forecloses the possibility that a person *tends* to perform an act A in circumstance C while it is nevertheless wrong (or at least not right) to A in C.

Let me summarize the dialectic up to this point. Regularism tries to avoid the regress by rejecting IA. It proposes that merely conforming to a rule or exhibiting a regularity suffices for following a rule. On its face, the proposal seems to conflate merely acting in accord with a rule and acting from an understanding of a rule. Moreover, it faces the gerrymandering problem: one's past behavior exhibits many regularities; it conforms with many (incompatible) rules; the proposal requires some way of specifying which regularity is the *right* one. Appealing to dispositions might seem to help. A main problem here is that dispositions alone don't settle what one should or should not do. There can be a gap between what one is disposed to do and what it is right for one to do. Thus, Regularism rejects IA, but loses sight of genuine rule-following.

3. A RESOLUTION?

We wanted to avoid the regress by rejecting IA. Regularism rejects IA, but at the cost of the possibility of genuinely following rules. We need, then, a way of rejecting IA while avoiding Regularism.

Sellars, Brandom, and McDowell seem to agree that this is the general form a resolution should take. However, they differ over the details.[17] In this section, I will canvass each of their attempts at a resolution.

3.1. Sellars

The kernel of Sellars's resolution is that we need to recognize that there is a false dichotomy between "obeying" a rule and merely "conforming" to a rule (SRLG, p. 325). For him, appeals to obedience lead to the regress (and the need for a regress-stopper); appeals to mere conformity don't make room for genuine rule-following. There is a third option, what Sellars calls "pattern-governed behavior."

What is pattern-governed behavior? Sellars proposes that a person can act in a certain way *because of a rule*, even if she is not aware of that rule, i.e., even if she does not intend to follow it, which would be required for obedience. Consider a rudimentary example. Emily might train her dog to go outside when you say, 'Go outside' and open the door. Emily's dog will plausibly develop the habit of acting in accord with that rule. Moreover, for that to seem plausible we need not suppose that Emily's dog has that rule in mind when he acts in accord with it. Nor must we suppose that he intends to follow the rule. Nevertheless, Emily's dog's conduct on those occasions is not "accidental;" it does not bear an accidental relationship to the rule; it is partly explained by the rule. Emily's dog acts as he does because Emily has the rule in mind and has trained him to act in accord with it. So, the dog's behavior is not merely in conformity with the rule. That is pattern-governed behavior. Now, extend that idea to the conduct of a speaker of a language. Suppose I teach my 15 month old son to say 'Mom' when I point to his mom and say 'Who's that?' My son will (normally) acquire the habit of acting in accord with that rule. As was the case with the dog, we need not suppose that my son initially bears that rule in mind, though he will likely develop the ability to do so. Thus, we are not conceiving of him as "obeying" the rule, in Sellars's sense of that term. Although he does not have awareness of it, the rule is still an essential part of the explanation of his behavior. So, we are not conceiving of him as merely conforming to the rule. When he acts in accord with the rule, it is because I have trained him to act in accord with it. In the case of my son, then, we have neither mere conformity with nor obedience to a rule.

According to Sellars, Emily's dog and my son are governed by "rules of criticism."[18] Such rules say how things ought to (or may) be; they endorse a state of affairs as to be brought about. Such a rule might be expressed thus: 'It ought to be the case that the dog goes outside when I say so and open the door.' Something can be governed by rules of criticism without (yet) being able to "obey" any rules, indeed without having any concepts at all.

Rules of criticism contrast with "rules of action," which say what one ought to (or may) do. Such a rule might be expressed thus: 'I ought to train my dog to go outside when I say so and open the door.' Following rules of action requires that one has the words or concepts for expressing the rule and the capacity to guide one's behavior in light of that rule.

Sellars observes that these two types of rules are connected. First, for there to be rules of action there must be conformity with rules of criticism. If we did not exhibit regularities, we could not guide our own behavior by rules of action. Second, the adoption of rules of criticism by a concept-possessing organism implies rules of action for that organism. For instance, we can think of Emily as espousing a rule of criticism, and reasoning that she should adopt a rule of action: 'The dog ought to go outside when I say so, thus I will train the dog to go outside when I say so.'[19]

Sellars maintains that the rules of language governing a speaker cannot all be rules of action, for that would spark the regress.[20] Furthermore, he maintains that many of our uses of words (outwardly and inwardly) are not properly thought of as *actions*, understood as voluntary or deliberate actions.[21] Rather, when we speak, words often simply flow forth. That seems especially true of thinking (the inner analog of our uses of words); we do not plan or intend what to think and then think it.

With pattern-governed behavior and the distinction between rules of action and criticism, we seem to avert the regress. It is true that some rules of language are rules of action; when we follow them, we "obey" them; we conceive of them and intend to follow them. However, for many of the rules of language, when we abide by them, we are engaged in pattern-governed behavior; we are abiding by rules of criticism, not rules of action. Such conduct does not require conceiving of or intending to follow those rules. The regress gets started because we assume that there are only rules of action and that when we talk about "following the rules of a language" we are talking about following rules of action. Once we see the distinction between the types of rules, we avert the regress.

Is this resolution satisfactory? One might admit that pattern-governed behavior is, as Sellars maintains, explained by the rule that shapes it and yet deny that such behavior is genuine rule-following. Throughout this chapter we have been guided by the vague idea that following a rule requires acting from an understanding of that rule. Sellars claims that in pattern-governed behavior an actor need not intend to follow the rule or even be aware of the rule exhibited in the behavior. Thus, it can seem as if pattern-governed behavior does not require having an understanding of the rule. Pattern-governed behavior can look like merely rule-caused behavior, not rule-following.

In response to this worry, we might try instead to think of pattern-governed behavior as a way of being responsive to a rule that does not yet require being consciously aware of that rule. Such responsiveness to the rule would be a rudimentary form of understanding that rule; hence, pattern-governed behavior would be a rudimentary form of rule-following. We could concede that there are more sophisticated sorts of rule-following, which call for more sophisticated forms of understanding, such as the capacity to cite, defend, or criticize the rule (the capacity to "respond to a reason as such," in McDowell's phrase). That capacity comes after the capacity to engage in pattern-governed behavior.[22] The big idea here would be to distinguish between grades of understanding a rule and, in turn, grades of following a rule.

This alternative is questionable, for it implies that there is some degree of understanding had even by rudimentary artifacts that are designed in accordance with specific rules held in mind by their designers, which is implausible. A microwave is designed to comply with various rules, but it does not understand what it is doing, not even a little bit. Perhaps more importantly we should like to know what is necessary to make the transition from conformity with rules of criticism to explicit awareness of such rules and espousal of rules of action.[23]

3.2. Brandom

Brandom takes up Sellars's general idea that there is a middle way between "conformity" and "obedience" (MIE, p. 26).[24] The kernel of his resolution is that we must distinguish between norms explicit as rules and "norms implicit in practice" (MIE, 20).[25] According to Brandom, rules are explicit statements of norms, e.g., 'Walk on the right side of the sidewalk.' However, he maintains that there can be—indeed, there must be—norms that are not explicitly stated; those would be norms implicit in practice, acts of treating something as appropriate or inappropriate in practice without yet explicitly calling it (or conceptualizing it as) appropriate or inappropriate.

Brandom thinks that the regress results from assuming that all norms are rules and that all norm-following is the following of explicit rules.[26] He calls that assumption 'regulism.'[27] Because regulism generates the regress, it must be rejected. That is why we must acknowledge norms implicit in practice and a corresponding sort of norm-following.[28] For Brandom, the big question is: what is it to abide by norms implicit in practice?[29]

Regularism, according to Brandom, is a failed attempt to answer that question. It proposes that treating an act as appropriate consists in exhibiting a regularity, such as having a disposition to act in that way. In Brandom's words, the task is to "reject intellectualist regulism about norms without falling into nonnormative regularism" (MIE, 32). What, then, is it to treat an act as appropriate (or inappropriate) in practice?

It cannot consist simply in producing the act. Brandom says that "treating a performance as correct cannot be identified with producing it . . . [because that makes] it impossible to treat a performance as incorrect" (MIE, 33). There is a difference between doing A and treating A as appropriate. A man might walk up the down escalator, even though he thinks it is inappropriate to do so; a dog might do the same without any conception of appropriateness. To equate the performance of A with treating A as appropriate would make it impossible to do A and treat it as inappropriate, which is implausible.

Brandom appeals to sanctions to help here.[30] Sanctions are ways of treating things as appropriate or inappropriate. Brandom starts with a simple "retributivist" conception of sanctions, according to which one treats something as inappropriate by punishing it; and one treats something as appropriate by rewarding it. In turn, we can think of punishment and reward in terms of classical behavioral reinforcement, i.e., classical learning theory. Punishing an act is to do something that makes it likely that acts of that sort do not happen in the future, e.g., by "beating with sticks" (MIE, pp. 34, 180); rewarding an act is to do something that makes it likely that acts of that sort do happen in the future. So, Brandom's initial proposal is that you treat something as correct in practice by rewarding it; you treat it as incorrect by punishing it. You treat A-ing in C as correct by rewarding A-ing in C; you treat non-A-ing in C as incorrect by punishing it.

Brandom recognizes that, as it stands, the proposal looks like "a kind of regularity theory" (MIE, p. 35). Specifically, treating something as appropriate or inappropriate is to be understood in terms of sanctioning, which in turn is understood in terms of *dispositions* to reinforce a behavior.[31] According to this proposal, one can count as following a rule simply by having a disposition to reinforce behavior in a certain way. That implies that this proposal faces the problems that face Regularism: gerrymandering and non-normativity.

Brandom's response to this difficulty is intriguing. He claims that one need not understand reward and punishment in non-normative terms, such as dispositions to reinforce. Instead, reward and punishment can be thought of in normative terms. His key move is to stress that sanctioning itself is something that can be done correctly or incorrectly (MIE, pp. 36, 42). For instance, rewarding a piece of behavior is itself something that can be done correctly or incorrectly. I might give a student an 'A' on a logic test, even though he has actually earned a 'C.' And that act of sanctioning can, in turn, be subject to sanctioning. In principle, this could go on forever. Brandom's slogan for this idea is that it is "norms all the way down" (MIE, p. 44). By claiming that sanctioning is "norms all the way down," Brandom appears to avert the worry that he is offering a "kind of regularity theory," since sanctioning is not ultimately analyzed in terms of (or reduced to) regularities.

What picture does that give us of following a norm? According to Brandom, norms need not take the form of explicitly stated rules. At least some norms are implicit in practice. For there to be a norm implicit in one's practice is for one to treat something (a behavior) as appropriate or inappropriate, without yet *saying* or explicitly *thinking* that it is appropriate or inappropriate. One can treat something as appropriate by rewarding it; one can treat something as inappropriate by punishing it. Rewarding and punishing are themselves acts that can be done correctly or incorrectly. So, abiding by a norm implicit in practice—by treating something as appropriate (or inappropriate)—is itself an act subject to normative evaluation; it is itself something for which there are norms implicit in practice.

Is Brandom's resolution satisfactory? In §3 of this chapter, we have been looking for a way of denying IA, the claim that following a rule R requires following another rule R′, while also avoiding Regularism. Brandom seems to avoid Regularism by claiming that it is norms all the way down. He denies IA with the claim that one can abide by a norm implicit in practice by sanctioning. While sanctioning itself is norm-governed conduct, it does not necessarily require following a *rule*, since—according to him—a rule is an explicit codification of a norm. However, he still seems to be saddled with a regress, which was the point of rejecting IA. Abiding by a norm implicit in practice requires abiding by further norms implicit in practice. McDowell insinuates this objection. He writes, "Brandom's invocation of norms implicit in practice prior to their explicitation seems to add a pragmatist variant to [Sellars's idea of Demands]" (HNRPI, fn. 8). Since, as you'll recall, the problem with Demands is that they saddle one with a regress, McDowell is implying that norms implicit in practice do too. That seems to be an unavoidable consequence of Brandom's appeal to the idea that it is "norms all the way down." Thus, it is not clear that Brandom's resolution is wholly satisfactory.

3.3. McDowell

The kernel of McDowell's resolution is that acting from an understanding of a rule need not require an interpretation of that rule. In his words, it is possible "to act immediately on an understanding [of a rule]—to act in a way that is not mediated by an interpretation of what is understood" (HNRPI, p. 103).

McDowell believes that the regress is sparked by the assumption that acting from an understanding of a rule requires an interpretation of it.[32] (That is roughly equivalent to IA.) That assumption leads to the regress, which McDowell maintains is one horn of a dilemma.[33] The other horn of the dilemma is the idea of a "last interpretation," a regress-stopper that is something like the feelings or Demands we considered earlier (WFR, p. 230). McDowell thinks that this dilemma is "intolerable" and that we must reject the assumption about understanding from which it emanates (WFR, p. 230). However, McDowell also thinks that there is a danger in rejecting that assumption. Specifically, he says that "we run the risk of . . . under-mentalizing the behavior" (MIWLP, p. 276). That is, we run the risk of making it seem as if following a rule is just a "mindless" disposition to act in accord with that rule. (That is roughly equivalent to Regularism.) So, according to McDowell, the trick is to (a) reject the claim that acting from an understanding of a rule requires an interpretation of it, while (b) maintaining the idea that following a rule requires acting from an understanding of it.

McDowell believes we must make room for the idea that behavior can be both immediate (or automatic) and imbued with understanding.[34] We can and often do just grasp something immediately. For instance, drivers in America and elsewhere step on the brake when faced with a red stoplight; chefs adjust the angle of their knives as they chop vegetables; pedestrians adjust shoulders and hips as they pass each other. These actions might be immediate or automatic or habitual or rote, but they are nevertheless normally infused with understanding of the norms of the specific activity in which the actor is engaged. Likewise, the words you are reading right now are imbued with meaning. They do not sit there inertly unless and until you seize upon an "interpretation" for them; your grasp of their meaning is not mediated by a supplementary act of interpretation; your understanding of what the words mean is immediate.

Now, if McDowell is right that one can act from an understanding of a rule without an interpretation of that rule—action that is immediate but imbued with understanding—then we avoid the regress of interpretations. However, one might worry that action that is immediate or automatic simply cannot be "from an understanding." Such action can only be action that "conforms" to a rule or is the manifestation of a trained habit. McDowell expresses the worry in a memorable passage:

> [The] problem is to steer a course between Scylla and Charybdis. Scylla is the idea that understanding is always interpretation. . . . We can avoid Scylla by stressing that, say, calling something 'green' can be like crying 'Help!' when one is drowning—simply how one has learned to react to this situation. But then we risk steering onto Charybdis, the picture of a basic level at which there are no norms. (WFR, p. 242)

In response to the possibility of "steering onto Charybdis," McDowell's key move is to emphasize that acquisition of a habit *can be* and often is the development of an understanding of the rules of a practice.[35] McDowell admits that *some* actions that are automatic are indeed "blind," i.e., not done from an understanding. For instance, not just anyone or anything that stops upon seeing a red light does so from an understanding of that rule. Nevertheless, we can be trained to respond to things in a certain way, and that training can constitute the development of an understanding of the relevant rules. For someone who has been initiated into the practice of driving in, for example, America, stepping on the brake immediately upon seeing a red light can be and often is an act imbued with understanding of the rules of driving. To be initiated into the practice is to become directly responsive to what certain things or happenings *call for* or *permit* within that practice, such as a red light's calling for one to stop. To be initiated is to become directly responsive to the rules governing various phenomena within that practice. In Sellars's terms, it is to develop "pattern-governed" behavior.

According to McDowell, it is "tempting" to reason as follows. In following any rule (e.g., a sign that points the way to Pittsburgh), it is possible for one to go wrong; so, to avoid going wrong, one must give the rule the right interpretation.

McDowell wants to reject that whole line of reasoning.[36] First of all, he thinks the inference is dubious. That it is always possible for one to go wrong does not imply that one must always be equipped with an interpretation in order to go right. Second, the assumption that it is always possible to go wrong is false. McDowell thinks that this false assumption is the more insidious aspect of the argument. Once it is granted that there is always a "gap" between a rule and what it means or requires, McDowell contends that there is nothing that will satisfactorily close that gap. (The "unclosability" of the gap is effectively the regress of interpretations or rules.) We must reject that assumption.

Doing so requires thinking that there are forms of understanding a rule that *exclude error*. It is true that sometimes we only properly understand or follow a rule with the aid of an interpretation. But McDowell maintains that this is not always the case; sometimes we understand a rule without need of an interpretation; in these cases, there simply is no risk of error. We can be in a position to have the requirements (or permissions) of a rule directly available to us, without mediation of an interpretation. This idea is comparable to (or maybe just a manifestation of) a "naïve realist" conception of perception according to which we can *just see* that things are thus and so, without need of an inference from how things *seem* to us. (In Chapter 5, we will see that McDowell does in fact have such a conception of perception.)

McDowell's attempt at a resolution differs starkly from both Sellars's and Brandom's attempts. Both Sellars and Brandom think that a resolution must identify a different type of rule-following and a corresponding type of rules or norms. From McDowell's point of view, both Sellars and Brandom seem to endorse the false assumption in the tempting line of thought that we have just considered—that it is always possible to go wrong. It is because they do so that they then seek a distinct sort of rule-following with corresponding rules or norms that can close the gap. As we saw in our discussions of Sellars and Brandom, it is questionable whether they succeed in closing that gap. McDowell, by contrast, thinks we should simply reject that assumption.

McDowell thus offers a clear alternative to Sellars's and Brandom's resolutions. Yet it is not certain that his resolution is superior. For instance, McDowell proposes that some instances of understanding simply exclude error, but if the possibility of error is the hallmark of a normative phenomenon (a phenomenon where rightness and wrongness are an issue), then it appears this sort of understanding is non-normative. By McDowell's own lights, that's an implausible consequence, since understanding a rule seems clearly to be a normative phenomenon. McDowell's resolution must explain how we can avoid that implausible consequence. In any case, adjudicating the dispute between Sellars, Brandom, and McDowell requires assessing the feasibility of rejecting the assumption that it is always possible to go wrong.

McDowell's response to the regress exemplifies a key part of his general philosophical outlook. He thinks that the regress is not a genuine philosophical problem that, in turn, needs to be given a satisfactory answer (e.g., a regress-stopper). Instead, he thinks we must expose the regress as only an illusory problem based on a questionable assumption. As we've seen, Sellars and Brandom also think that we should reject an assumption underlying the regress. However, for McDowell that kind of strategy is the proper strategy for good philosophy more generally.[37]

McDowell thinks that a typical philosophical problem has a certain shape: some important feature of ordinary existence (such as the meaningfulness of our words) is made to look impossible (in this case, because of the regress); the task is then to explain how this thing is nevertheless possible and, indeed, real (our words really are meaningful, despite the regress); typically, however, the explanations don't work (such as the appeal to Demands); they leave the important feature of ordinary existence looking questionable. For McDowell, good philosophy helps expose these putative problems as only apparent problems by showing that they rest on questionable and optional assumptions. Instead of accepting those problems as real, and then seeking an adequate answer to them (which typically fails), the goal is to reject the problem by explaining what faulty assumptions it rests on. Thereby, we restore the important feature of ordinary existence that had been made to seem impossible. This outlook is often called "quietism," for it advises us to remain quiet—to resist developing philosophical theories—once faulty and optional assumptions have been indentified and rejected.

That might make you think that McDowell thinks there are no genuine philosophical problems. But that would be a mistake, for McDowell does think there is real work for philosophy to do. "Quietism," as it applies to McDowell, is not an injunction to stop thinking. The key is to understand that, for him, the illusion of problems is itself a legitimate task for philosophers to address. While this "task" does not have the same shape as "the typical philosophical problem," it nevertheless requires ingenuity, care, and good argument and so may be said to count as a problem.[38]

Does McDowell's "quietism" make him (fundamentally) different from Sellars or Brandom?

Although Sellars and Brandom do not have a "quietist" outlook, they are sympathetic with a key motive underlying it. Specifically, they aspire generally to resist philosophical thinking that posits things like Demands, things that are, ultimately, mysterious—we don't know how they fit into the natural world, how we take account of them, or how they manage to do the work they're enlisted to do.[39]

Nevertheless, despite that shared motive, Sellars and Brandom are comfortable with the sort of philosophical theory-building that McDowell eschews as unnecessary. More specifically, while McDowell is content to undermine questionable and optional assumptions that provoke apparent philosophical problems, Sellars and Brandom think that this is not enough, holding instead that developing alternatives is also an important part of the philosophical endeavor. For instance, with respect to the regress of rules, McDowell is content to subvert the idea that understanding requires interpretation, the assumption that instigates the regress. Doing that requires ingenuity, care, and good argument, but, by McDowell's lights, it need not involve constructing a positive proposal about what it is to understand a rule. By contrast, Sellars and Brandom think that subverting this idea is important, but that in its place, we need a story about how automatic or learned behaviors—exemplified in our use of language—are nevertheless intelligent, norm-responsive behaviors.[40]

CONCLUSION

Let me close by summarizing the dialectic of this chapter. Philosophers in the Pittsburgh School believe that using a language requires the capacity to follow rules for the use of that language. They believe further that a regress is sparked by a faulty assumption about what is required for following a rule (IA): following a rule R always requires following another rule R′ for R's proper application. That assumption should be rejected. But they also recognize a danger in rejecting it: Regularism—the idea that exhibiting a regularity (or merely conforming with a rule) suffices for following a rule. The shared task, then, is to reject IA, while also avoiding Regularism. Sellars, Brandom, and McDowell have different ways of executing that task. One interesting point that separates them is McDowell's claim that there are forms of understanding a rule that exclude error. We will revisit this idea in Chapter 5, on knowledge without the Given. Another interesting point that separates them is McDowell's "quietism." We will return to it at the end of the next chapter.

4 Meaning

" ' . . . ' means—- -" is the core of a unique mode of discourse which
is as distinct from the description and explanation of empirical fact,
as is the language of prescription and justification.

-Sellars, Intentionality and the Mental, p. 527.

INTRODUCTION

In Chapter 2, we saw that philosophers in the Pittsburgh School reject the
conception of meaning in the Lockean Picture, which privileges experience over reasoning in the explanation of the content of beliefs and claims.
It also privileges mind over linguistic practice in understanding meaning.
The Pittsburgh School rejects both ideas. For them, the meaning of a claim
should be understood in terms of its place in linguistic activity, especially in
terms of what it can rationally support and be supported by.

In this chapter, I want to look more closely at those ideas, especially as
they have been developed by Sellars and Brandom. I will begin by looking
at some important parts of Sellars's functional role theory of meaning. I
will then turn to Brandom's "inferentialism," which can be thought of as
an attempt to extend and rework some of Sellars's ideas.[1] I will then sketch
McDowell's main challenge to Brandom's view.

1. SELLARS'S FUNCTIONAL ROLE THEORY OF MEANING

1.1. "Relationalism" about Meaning

What is meaning? We say things such as

(1) 'John' means John.
(2) 'Dog' means dog.
(3) 'Hund' means dog.
(4) 'Der apfel ist grun' means the apple is green.

The expressions mentioned in (1)–(4) didn't have to mean anything. Nor
did they have to mean what they do. What is it for a word to have a meaning? It is natural to think that the meaning of an expression is a relation
between it and some specific part of the world, some kind of "word-world"
relation. On that way of thinking, a word means something at all because
it bears a certain relation to something; and a word means what it means

because it stands in that relation to some particular thing or sort of thing. A natural corollary is that meaning claims, such as (1)–(4), describe or state such relations. For instance, (1) describes the expression-type 'John' as standing in the meaning relation to John, the person.

Saying that the meaning of a word is a word-world relation doesn't get us very far, for we want to know what kind of relation it is. It is natural to think that it is some sort of causal relation. Abstractionism is one version of that kind of view; according to it, a concept (a mental word) means what it does because it was "abstracted" from experiences of objects of a certain type; those experiences are some kind of causal connection between the experiencer and the experienced. But one can think that meaning is a species of causal relation without endorsing Abstractionism.[2] Speaking roughly, we might think that an expression 'E' means E because tokens of 'E' are causally connected to E-type things in a certain way. For instance, we might say 'dog' means dog because tokens of 'dog' are causally connected to dogs in a certain way.

A causal theory seems most plausible when we focus on names as the paradigm of words; names seem like they are just tags for the things that they name.[3] For instance, the meaning of 'John' would just be the individual John, because the first use of 'John' was causally connected in a certain way that particular individual, John.

Any adequate causal theory of meaning must be separated from a "tag" theory of meaning, for the "tag" theory has a few well-known problems. Such a theory treats the meaning of an expression as simply the thing "tagged" by that expression. Consider, for instance, Frege's example.[4] 'The morning star' and 'the evening star' refer to the same object, namely Venus. So, according to the tag theory they have the same meaning. But that is dubious. Consider a pair of sentences in which those expressions occur. 'The morning star is the morning star' seems to be an uninformative or trivial claim; by contrast, 'The morning star is the evening star' is informative; it reports a genuine discovery. Those claims must have different meanings, yet according to any tag theory, they have the same meaning. That kind of difficulty led Frege to posit a further component in the meaning of expressions—their *sense*—which, according to Frege, is a mode of presentation of the object referred to. Two terms can share a reference and yet have different senses: 'the morning star' and 'the evening star' have the same reference but different senses. Frege seems to be right that two terms can "tag" or refer to the same object and yet have different meanings.

The example from Frege poses a problem only for a tag theory, a theory that equates an expression's meaning with its reference.[5] It does not challenge the causal theory per se, for one might separate the two.[6] But a causal theory of meaning faces other difficulties.[7] How should it deal with expressions for things like numbers, such as 'five'? Or with logical expressions, such as 'and' or 'some' or 'not'? (In Chapter 2 we saw that Abstractionism has a similar problem.) It's dubious that there is an appropriate type of object for such an expression to be caused by that could constitute the meaning of those expressions. And what about terms for future events or states of affairs, such as 'my future trip to India'? Or talk of possibilities, such as 'I might go to India'? For some meaningful expressions, it seems there is no appropriate type of thing for such an expression to be caused by and serve as the meaning. Even if we grant that there are things for such expressions to be caused by, it is not clear how their meaning is constituted by those relations. These observations don't show that the theory cannot be made to work; they simply show that it faces difficulties.[8]

However, for Sellars, these observations expose a problem for the root idea that meaning is a relation between words and something else, *whatever that relation is*. If we stick to that idea, we are driven to think that each word is related to something, including words like 'not' and 'five.' Thus, we will be moved to conjecture that there is a "not-thing" and a "five-thing." What are such things? They are not simply physical objects, like chairs; nor are they simply the mental states of some person or set of persons. Whatever they are, how might we *know* them? We don't see them, or feel them; and it's not as if they are like faraway galaxies or incredibly small particles, which we have been able ultimately to detect with sophisticated instruments. Whatever they are, we seem to be in a distinctive relationship with them.[9] Again, those questions by themselves don't prove that the idea that meaning is a relation is wrong, but they do undermine its intuitive appeal.

What would be an alternative?

1.2. Meaning as Functional Classification

Sellars thinks that we should abandon the idea that meaning is a relation, and with it the idea that meaning claims, such as 1–4, simply describe such a relation.[10] For Sellars, the key question in thinking about meaning is this: What are we *doing* when we *say* what the meaning of an expression is?[11]

According to Sellars, such discourse is quasi-normative; it conveys to a speaker how an expression should be used.[12]

In rejecting "relationalism" about meaning, Sellars is *not* rejecting the idea that there are relations between words and the world.[13] There are obviously many such relations. In fact, he believes that expressions would be meaningless if there weren't such relations. What he denies is that such relations on their own (individually or collectively) constitute the meaning of an expression.

We saw in Chapter 2 that Sellars espouses a broadly normative functional role theory of meaning. Such a theory entails that the meaning of any expression is constituted by its *relations* to other expressions and rational activity generally. Thus, Sellars clearly accepts that meaning is relational, in some intuitive sense. Moreover, the meaning of an expression is partly constituted by its place in rational conduct, including speech, thought, perception, and action. Thus, meaning, for Sellars, must involve some word-world relations.[14] For those reasons it is best ultimately to avoid talk of "relational" or "non-relational" conceptions of meaning. I have used that sort of talk because Sellars himself uses it. What matters is that Sellars thinks that meaning claims do not purport merely to *describe* relations between linguistic items and parts of the non-linguistic world.

Sellars articulates a distinctive and insightful alternative conception of meaning claims.[15] Consider again:

(3) 'Hund' means dog.

When we put quotation marks around a word, we seem to create a name for that word. The word itself can then appear as if it is an object about which we can say things. Sellars treats such constructions in a distinctive way. He says that when we put quotes around a word, we create a distributive singular term, exemplified by 'the lion' in 'The lion is tawny.' There 'the lion' does not refer to some single lion but rather to lions as a group. 'Lions are tawny' or 'The lion is tawny' say essentially the same thing. Sellars treats 'Hund' in 3 on that model; it is a way of talking about individual tokens of 'Hund'; that is, it is a way of talking about particular instances of the word 'Hund' as it appears in speech and writing.

Now consider the role of 'dog' in 3. Philosophers normally distinguish between the use and mention of terms. When I say that 'hat' has three letters, I *mention* the word 'hat;' I do not *use* it. By contrast, when I say, 'Your hat is crooked,' I *use* 'hat.' Now, does 3 use or mention the word 'dog'? According to Sellars, it does neither. 3 does not *use* 'dog' because it is not an attempt to say that anything is a dog; it does not predicate doghood or non-doghood of anything. It also does not *mention* 'dog' because if we were to translate 3 into, say, French, we would render 'dog' as 'perro.' Thus, in a meaning claim like 3, we are not simply mentioning the English word 'dog.' So, Sellars thinks we need another way of thinking about the role of 'dog' in "'Hund' means dog."

Sellars proposes that "'Hund' means dog" conveys to an English speaker that 'Hund' plays the role that 'dog' plays in her own language. Thus, 'dog' in "'Hund" means dog' is a way of talking about the *role* of 'dog' in the language of the targeted audience. Sellars says that 'dog' here is an "illustrating sortal" (Sellars, MFC). 'dog' is a sortal term, which means that it functions like 'cat' in 'Tabitha is a cat,' which sorts Tabitha into the cat group. And 'dog' is an *illustrating* sortal because it *displays* to English speakers—speakers of the very language in which "'Hund' means dog' is expressed—which group an item is to be sorted into.[16] When we say "'Hund' means dog" we are effectively conveying that tokens of 'Hund' fall into a certain sort, namely the-role-of-'dog'-in-your-own-language sort. For Sellars, 'means' is really a "specialized form of the copula;" that is, it is a disguised way of saying something of the form 'S *is* a P.' It is in that specific sense that Sellars claims that 'means' is not a relational term (MFC, p. 431).

Sellars introduces dot-quotation to make this analysis clearer. Putting dot-quotes around a word enables us to talk about any word that plays the same role as that word. For instance, ·dog· is a predicate that applies to all words that play (roughly) the same role as 'dog' does in English. So, in a more adequate analysis, 3 should be represented as 3':

(3)   'Hund' means dog.
(3')   'Hund' is a ·dog·.

3' tells a speaker of English that 'Hund' plays the role that 'dog' plays in her own language.

Here we see Sellars's resistance to what he calls "factualism": roughly, the assumption that claims containing terms for philosophically interesting notions (e.g., 'knows,' 'means,' 'causes') are mere descriptions, purporting merely to describe facts, even if very special facts.[17] Sellars thinks such claims often do not merely describe. Instead, they also have a distinctive quasi-normative *function* or *force* in discourse. That revelation, according to Sellars, should prompt us to think differently about the relevant philosophical notions.

We saw that strategy already in Chapter 1, in Sellars's claim that "characterizing an episode as one of knowing is to place it in the logical space of reasons" (EPM, §36). The idea there was that knowledge attributions have a quasi-normative force; they are ways of saying that the knowing subject has done something right or well, functioning as a sort of endorsement of her or her state. Something similar holds for meaning claims. They don't simply state a relation between words and the world. Rather, they tell an audience that an expression should be used like a specific term in her own language.

Sellars extends his analysis of 'means' talk to other important sorts of semantic talk, e.g., ' . . . refers to . . . ' and ' . . . stands for . . . ' He also has a companion conception of ' . . . is true.'[18] However, we have enough for our purposes here by simply focusing on ' . . . means . . . ' What we wanted to see was how one might develop an alternative to "relationalism." In Sellars's case, that starts with getting clearer about what we are doing in talking about meaning. That investigation leads us to the idea of an expression's functional role in a language.

1.3. Material Inferential Roles

For Sellars, meaning claims talk about the functional roles of linguistic expressions. Now, how exactly should we conceive of those roles? What constitutes an expression's role in a language?

In Chapter 2, we learned that the role that matters is the expression's norm-governed role in the public activity of reasoning. And we learned that this includes the expression's rational connections to perception and action, so-called language entries and exits.[19] But there is an additional, distinctive feature of Sellars's view. He does not think that the only sorts of rational connections that matter to the role of an expression E are the *formally* valid inferences that E is involved in.[20] He thinks we must also make a place for *materially good* inferences.

What is the distinction between those two sorts of inference? Why does Sellars think materially good inferences are essential to meaning?

A formally valid inference is valid in virtue of its form. To say that an inference is formally valid is to say that any inference with the same form would also be good. Consider 5:

(5) The book is red and the cup is heavy. So, the book is red.

5 is formally valid, since anything with the form F1 would also be valid.

(F1) *P* and *Q*. So, *P*.

It is common to think that all good inferences must ultimately be understood as formally valid inferences. Call that presumption 'Formalism.'[21] Now consider 6, which appears to be a good inference.

(6)   The book is maroon. So, the book is red.

For Sellars, 6 is a *material* inference; it seems to be good in virtue of the *matter* or *content* of the claims involved in it. As stated, 6 is not formally valid. From the claim that *b* is *M*, one cannot generally conclude that *b* is *R*, for any consistent replacement of 'b,' 'M,' and 'R.' If Formalism is right, we will have to treat 6 as an enthymeme, an argument with an unstated premise. To 6 we could add 'Anything that is maroon is red.' That would yield the form F2:

(F2) *b* is *M*. Every *M* is *R*. So, *b* is *R*.

It is important to see that there are many inferences that are like 6, seemingly good, but formally invalid.

(7) This substance turns litmus paper red. So, this substance is an acid.
(8) It is raining. So, the streets will be wet.
(9) I am releasing this piece of chalk. So, it will fall.
(10) There is lightning. So, there will be thunder.
(11) Pittsburgh is west of Princeton. So, Princeton is east of Pittsburgh.

If Formalism is right, 7–11 must also be treated as enthymemes. We can make them formally valid by adding a suppressed general claim linking the premise and the conclusion.

Sellars rejects Formalism; he thinks that not all good inferences can be converted into formally valid inferences; we must recognize the basic "goodness" of material inferences because such material inferences are an essential part of the role of an expression (IM, §27).[22] Why?

The core issue separating Sellars and Formalism is whether the propriety of the move from the premise to the conclusion in any so-called material inference can be adequately rendered as a premise in the inference proper (e.g., 'Anything that is maroon is red'). Sellars claims that this cannot be done.

He thinks there is a two-step problem for trying to treat material inferences in that way. First, the added premise could not be any mere generalization over actual cases of, say, maroon and red things. It has to cover possible or counterfactual cases as well. The added premise would have to be interpreted that way in order to capture the force of a *rule* of inference. Thus, 'Anything that is maroon is red' would have to be read as a subjunctive conditional: 'If anything *were* maroon, it *would be* red.' More exactly, it should express that for any *x*, '*x* is red' may be inferred from '*x* is maroon.' However—and second—interpreting the added premise in that way effectively re-introduces material rules of inference into the argument![23] A subjunctive conditional would be just a disguised way of expressing a commitment to the propriety of an inference. For instance, when I say, 'If it were to rain, the streets would be wet,' I am not merely purporting to describe how the world is; rather, I am expressing a material rule of inference to the effect that the claim that the streets will be wet *may be inferred from* the claim that it is raining. Thus, while my subjunctive claim seems merely to be *about the world* itself, it is in fact a claim *about proper reasoning.* That is another instance of Sellars's opposition to factualism.

In a material inference, Sellars thinks that the correctness of the move from the premise to the conclusion cannot be adequately rendered as a premise in the inference proper without appealing to material rules of inference. Thus, Formalism cannot be made to work: some material rules of inference must be accepted as genuinely (irreducibly) good.[24]

Given that point, and given that for Sellars the role of an expression includes the good inferences that it can enter into, material inferences are genuine parts of an expression's role in the language. Since Sellars thinks that the meaning of an expression is its norm-governed inferential role in the language, the good material inferences that an expression enters into are an aspect of its meaning.

In this section, we have looked briefly at just a few of Sellars's distinctive ideas about meaning. According to him, meaning is not a mere word-world relation; meaning claims are not mere descriptions of such relations; and the inferential role of an expression includes the good material inferences it enters into. As we will see next, all of these ideas have been picked up by Brandom in his attempt to develop a functional role theory of meaning rooted in linguistic practice.

2. BRANDOM'S INFERENTIALISM

Although Brandom does not adopt Sellars's particular view of meaning claims (or the technical apparatus of dot-quotation), he does agree with Sellars that we should reject conceptions of meaning that treat it as a "word-world" relation.[25] He also agrees with Sellars that to understand meaning we must begin with linguistic practice. Like Sellars, he aims to develop a functional role theory of meaning.[26] His project is ambitious and elaborate. I will aim only to introduce the main aspects of it.[27]

Brandom's big idea is that the meanings of sentences and sub-sentences can be explained in terms of their inferential roles in a norm-governed "game of giving and asking for reasons."

That big idea can be understood as unfolding in two stages. In Stage One, Brandom maintains that meaning should be understood in terms of use; that is, the meanings of words should be explained in terms of what one is *doing* in *using* them. The kind of "use" or activity that matters is asserting, which in turn only makes sense in terms of inferring or reasoning—that is, "the game of giving and asking for reasons."[28] The aim of Stage One is to provide an account of asserting as it figures in an activity of inferring or reasoning. Crucially, that must be done without relying on semantic terms, such as 'means' or 'refers to' or 'is true of,' or even intentional terms, such as 'about,' for the goal at this stage is to show how we can understand practices of inferring or reasoning without appealing to a prior understanding of meaning. In Stage Two, the aim is to explain how sentences and sub-sentences are meaningful in virtue of their place in the activity of inferring or reasoning developed in Stage One.

I will look at each stage in turn.

2.1. Stage One: Normative Pragmatics

In Stage One, Brandom aims to account for the activity of asserting as a move in a norm-governed game. To assert something is simultaneously to undertake a justificatory responsibility to defend what one has asserted, and to issue a re-assertion license of what one has asserted. Players may challenge, rely on, and defer to the assertions of one another. If an assertion is challenged, the player who made it is obliged to defend it with another assertion, to point to some other player who can defend it, or to withdraw it.

In this picture, asserting is fundamentally normative and interpersonal, since asserting is understood in terms of what it *allows* and *requires* players to do in relation to one another. By contrast, one might have thought that asserting was simply a verbal act for the expression of thoughts, caused in the right way by those thoughts. That sort of a story would not have normative and interpersonal dimensions obviously built into it.

The main move in Brandom's game of giving and asking for reasons is *avowing* or *acknowledging* a commitment.[29] Let's suppose that a player does that by placing a chip in front of her. Suppose further that there are many different types of these chips; each type has a distinct color, such as red, green, blue, and so on.

All players keep score on each other and themselves. It helps to think of these scores as kept on scorecards, each player keeping a scorecard for every other player and herself.[30] In the simplest case, when player P avows something, for instance, a red chip, every player should register that on her scorecard for P under a column for commitments. Doing that is to *attribute* that commitment to red to P.

A scorekeeper might take there to be *consequences* of acknowledging such a commitment. For instance, Q might take commitment to red to come with commitment to playing a green chip. In that case, Q must also enter that "committive consequence" on her scorecard for P, also under the commitments column. However, since P herself might not acknowledge that consequence, that committive consequence should be identified as an *unacknowledged* commitment of P.

The distinction between acknowledging and attributing a commitment is, therefore, a crucial aspect of the game. It marks a difference in perspective between players. On the one hand, there's what P takes herself to be committed to; on the other hand, there's what others take P to be committed to.[31] A partial sketch of Q's scorecard for P might look like this:

Player P	
Commitments	
Acknowledged	Unacknowledged
Red	*Green*

By default, when P places the red chip in front of her, every player must also count P as entitled to it. That is, on their scorecards for P, they should enter 'Red' also under a column for entitlements. And just as a scorekeeper might take there to be consequences of one of P's commitments, a scorekeeper might also take there to be consequences of one of P's entitlements. For instance, Q might take it that entitlement to a red chip brings with it entitlement to a blue chip. Such "permissive consequences" also need to be registered on the scorecard, also under the entitlements column. As with commitments, scorekeepers must distinguish between entitlements that are acknowledged and those that are unacknowledged (or merely attributed). So, a scorecard for P would be more complex than what we just saw. It might look like this:

Player P			
Commitments		Entitlements	
Acknowledged	Unacknowledged	Acknowledged	Unacknowledged
Red	*Green*	*Red*	*Blue*

Now, I said that each player is entitled by *default* to any commitment that she acknowledges (or "plays"). However, that default entitlement can be undermined in various ways. In the first place, another player can challenge it. Brandom thus says that entitlement has a "default and challenge structure" (MIE, p. 176).[32] Players have entitlement to their commitments by default, but they can lose it through a challenge.

What does a challenge look like? Player Q can challenge P's entitlement to the red chip by avowing a commitment that Q herself takes to be *incompatible* with commitment to the red chip. Let us suppose she does this by avowing a yellow chip. If other scorekeepers also take yellow to be incompatible with red, they should remove 'Red' from the entitlement box of their scorecards for P. More generally, a scorekeeper treats two commitments as incompatible if she treats commitment to one as precluding entitlement to the other.[33]

A player can respond to a challenge in several ways. First of all, she can simply *disavow* the commitment, entitlement to which has been challenged. (A player might do that by removing the chip from in front of her.) Scorekeepers must then register this removal by deleting that commitment from their scorecard for that player—unless that commitment is also a consequence of some other commitment still held. Entitlement to the commitment should also be removed—unless it is also a (permissive) consequence of another entitlement that remains unchallenged. Here we begin to see how tricky scorekeeping is.

A player can instead respond to a challenge by avowing another commitment that she takes to stand in a permissive consequence relation to the challenged commitment. Suppose P does that by avowing an orange chip. If other scorekeepers take avowal of orange to stand in a permissive consequence relation to red chips, then they will reinstate 'Red' in the entitlement box on their scorecard for P (and also enter 'Orange' in the commitment box for P).

With the idea of incompatibility in place we can identify a further constraint on how scorekeepers should respond to an avowal. We have been assuming that P initially avows red with no pre-existing commitments. But now suppose that at the moment of that avowal, P had already avowed yellow; thus, yellow would be in P's commitment box and, let us suppose, her entitlement box. If other scorekeepers take avowal of red to be *incompatible* with commitment to yellow, then they should enter 'Red' in P's commitment box, but *remove* 'Yellow' from P's entitlement box; they should also not enter 'Red' in P's entitlement box, for her default entitlement to it is undermined by her pre-existing commitment to the yellow chip. That is a crucial practical aspect of taking two commitments to be incompatible. This adds yet another layer of complexity to scorekeeping.

We have seen that when a player avows a commitment, she is granted entitlement to that commitment by default, unless it is incompatible with a pre-existing commitment. Likewise, when one player avows a commitment, scorekeepers should also grant entitlement to it to every other player, unless a player has a commitment that is incompatible with it. Thus, when P avows a red chip, scorekeepers should put 'Red' in the entitlement box of any player who has no commitments incompatible with it. In this way, players *inherit* entitlement from each other. Thus, avowal can also be understood as the issuing of a "re-avowal license." The freedom to issue such licenses comes with a responsibility to respond to challenges to the relevant commitment.[34]

Deference is, then, a third way that a player can respond to a challenge. A player may respond to a challenge by deferring to the player from whom she takes herself to have inherited entitlement to the commitment that has been challenged (say, by pointing to her).

Summing up, we have a game in which players undertake and attribute commitments, while also attributing entitlements. Any particular avowal affects the score of that player and others. Thus, all avowals essentially have a score-changing potential. Exactly how a particular avowal affects the avower's score depends on what else she is committed and entitled to; that, in turn, depends on what she and other players have previously avowed. Moreover, how a particular avowal affects anybody's score depends on *who* is keeping score. Different scorekeepers will not necessarily treat a particular avowal in the same way. *Crucially*, there is no single score for a particular player; there is no "super-scorecard."

Now, this game is supposed to model the pragmatic significance of asserting. According to the model, to assert is to affect one's own "score," as well as that of one's fellow speakers. Less metaphorically, asserting is an undertaking of justificatory responsibility and the issuing of a re-assertion license. Thus, asserting is inextricably connected with justificatory practices. Each assertion affects one's epistemic status in a particular way.[35] Thus, each assertion has a status-changing potential. How one's status changes depends on what else one has asserted and what else one has justification for, which in turn depend on what others have asserted. Moreover, how a particular assertion affects one's epistemic status will vary from perspective to perspective, since not all speakers will treat a particular assertion in the same way.

What's crucial for the next stage of Brandom's account is that the epistemic-status-changing potential of an assertion can be thought of as the inferential potential or inferential role of that assertion.

2.2. Stage Two: Inferential Semantics

In Stage Two, Brandom aims to explain how the avowals in the game of giving and asking for reasons have meaning—or conceptual content—in virtue of their status changing potential in that game. That is, he aims to show how assertions have meaning in virtue of their inferential roles. This stage divides into two parts: (a) an account of the meaning of sentences in terms of their inferential role and (b) an account of sub-sentences in terms of their (indirect) inferential roles.[36] Let's look at each part in turn.

What is the inferential role of a sentence?

Brandom follows Sellars in thinking that the inferential role of a sentence includes its role in good material inferences, not just its role in formally valid inferences.

Validity is often understood in terms of the preservation of truth. For instance, one might say that an inference is valid if and only if the truth of the premises guarantees the truth of the conclusion. However, Brandom cannot use that sort of explanation, since he wants to understand meaning in terms of inference, and inference in terms of the game of giving and asking for reasons. That means he cannot explain validity in terms of semantic relations like reference and truth. Instead, he must think of inference in broadly pragmatic and non-semantic terms.[37] Roughly, he thinks of valid or good inference as the "preservation of status," e.g., the preservation of one's status as entitled to a commitment. For instance, avowing a commitment to X in response to a challenge to Y is a "good" or "valid" move if and only if entitlement to Y preserves entitlement to X.[38] Avowing one thing in response to a challenge to another is good if it preserves one's status as entitled to the thing challenged.

For Brandom, the role of an *act* of assert*ing* is constituted by its appropriate "circumstances and consequences of application."[39] In the first instance, these appropriate circumstances and consequences are other assertings. The appropriate circumstances of an asserting are those circumstances *sufficient* for producing it. The appropriate consequences of application for an asserting are the *necessary* consequences of producing it.

Consider a simplified case. Asserting that John is in Beijing is sufficient for asserting in turn that John is in China. The one act licenses the other. Saying 'John is in Beijing' licenses saying 'John is in China.' A necessary consequence of asserting that John is in China is that John is in Asia. The act of asserting 'John is in China' licenses saying 'John is in Asia.'

Meaning—conceptual content—is "conferred" on the act of saying 'John is in China' by virtue of the other acts it licenses and is licensed by. Thus, the meaning of 'John is in China' is partly constituted by its licensing acts of saying 'John is in Asia' and by its being licensed by acts of saying 'John is in Beijing.' It is only *partly* constituted by its connection to those other acts of asserting because it is related to many other such acts.

Moreover, like Sellars, Brandom thinks the role of an act of asserting includes more than just its connections to other acts of asserting. The circumstances and consequences of application of a claim include language entries and exits, i.e., perception and non-verbal intentional action (MIE, p. 119).[40]

Consider again 'John is in China.' Todd might see John at the Great Wall on live television. Seeing that would be sufficient for him to assert that John is in China. The seeing functions roughly as a premise to the act of asserting. Now, suppose that Todd and David had planned to surprise John by visiting him at his house in Philadelphia. Upon asserting that John is in China, Todd would be right to call David to cancel their plan. The act of calling functions roughly as a conclusion to the premise that John is in China.

In that way, the role of 'John is in China' includes the correctness of these other sorts of non-verbal or non-linguistic moves. Thereby they too partly constitute the meaning of 'John is in China.'

It's natural to balk at this proposed extension of the inferential role of an assertion. While it might be true that it is reasonable for Todd to place that call, the reasonableness of doing so doesn't seem to be part of the meaning of the claim 'John is in China.' A person could understand that claim without recognizing any rational connections between it and acts of canceling plans to visit John. Those connections—this objection continues—are external to the meaning of the claim proper.[41]

It won't do to reply that the reasonableness of the move from 'John is in China' to the call is part of the meaning for some people but not for others. That would imply that what a sentence-type means depends on the speaker (or hearer).[42] While there are certainly many cases of speaker-dependence— exemplified by indexical words, such as 'I,' 'here,' 'now,' 'this,' and 'that'— it seems doubtful that it holds for all sentences.[43] If it did, communication would seem to be precluded; one and the same sentence would mean one thing for one person, and something else, maybe something very different, for another person.

Here is another way of seeing the same problem. One prominent feature of the game of giving and asking for reasons is that an avowal can in fact be treated differently by different scorekeepers; how one and the same avowal actually alters the score of any particular player depends on who is keeping score, and there are many scorekeepers. There is no super-scorecard. Any single avowal does not seem to have just one score-changing potential. That score-changing potential is supposed to model the inferential role of an act of asserting. If an act of asserting does not have one inferential role across all speaker-hearers, then we seem to be precluded from saying that it has one meaning across all speaker-hearers.

Brandom confronts this problem by appealing to inferential norms.[44] The inferential role of a sentence is not determined by *actual* inferences that have been made involving it; nor is it determined by speakers' *dispositions* to make inferences involving it. Rather, it is a matter of the norms governing the inferences involving it. Thus, the inferential role of a sentence is not simply the inferences (or "moves") speakers make with it or tend to make with it, but rather the inferences that it would be *appropriate* for them to make with it. So, speakers count as using one and the same sentence-type because they are subject to the very same inferential norms for their use of tokens of that sentence—not because they actually use the sentence in the same ways, nor because they have habits of using it in the same ways.

For Brandom, players of the game of giving and asking for reasons constantly contest what exactly the norms are, and thus what exactly the meaning of a claim is. That facet of the game was anticipated already in the observation that scorekeeping can vary from one scorekeeper to the next. Scorekeepers might disagree about what the norms are. Contestation of the norms is partly on display when speakers challenge and defend their claims. In such challenging and defending, what's at issue is whether a speaker is entitled (or committed) to a particular claim. And whether a speaker is entitled to a claim is partly a matter of the inferential norms governing that claim.

Such contestation comes to the fore when speakers make the norms explicit in the form of claims—what Brandom calls "explicitation." Conditionals are the paradigm; they allow one to state the propriety of an inference in the form of a claim.[45] For instance, Brandom sees the claim 'If Socrates is human, then he is mortal' as making explicit the propriety of the inference from 'Socrates is human' to 'Socrates is mortal.'[46] Such claims are, of course, moves within the game itself. But they embody the distinctive ability to challenge or defend a putative norm of inference. The same is true of claims about what a claim *means*, and claims that speakers *mean the same thing* by a claim. Such meaning talk brings the inferential norms to the fore.[47]

Brandom extends the idea of explicitation to provide a distinctive conception of logic: "logical expressivism." Roughly put, logical expressivism is the claim that logical vocabulary serves to make inferential proprieties explicit in the form of claims. In fact, Brandom maintains that logical vocabulary just is any vocabulary that serves this "explicitating" function. Thus, in *Making It Explicit*, he ultimately counts verbs of propositional attitude (e.g., 'believes'), intentional vocabulary (e.g., 'about'), and normative vocabulary (e.g., 'should') as logical vocabulary.

Because Brandom conceives of logical vocabulary in that way, he claims that what is distinctive about logic is that it "is the organ of semantic self-consciousness" (MIE, p. xix). He means that we use logical vocabulary to make explicit what our claims mean, what they commit and entitle us to. For Brandom, logical vocabulary is distinguished by what it allows us to do: facilitate rational evaluation.[48] Thus, he rejects a more traditional conception of logic that holds that it is simply for the description of a special class of facts.

Summing up, we have seen that Brandom thinks that the inferential role of a sentence includes the sentences from which it can be correctly inferred and the sentences that can be correctly inferred from it; it also includes those perceptions that rationally support asserting the sentence and the actions that asserting the sentence rationally supports in turn (in conjunction with other commitments or facts). Speakers mean the same thing by a sentence (or word) because they are subject to the same inferential norms governing that sentence (or word). Of course, speakers can and do disagree about the norms governing any particular sentence (or word). "Explicitation"—stating an inferential norm in the form of a claim—makes it possible to directly defend or challenge a (putative) norm of inference. The idea that certain vocabulary has an explicitating function also makes available a distinctive "expressivist" conception of logic, according to which logical vocabulary facilitates inferential evaluation.

Let's now turn briefly to Brandom's conception of the meaning of sub-sentences, that is, names and predicates, like 'John' and 'is a human.' The basic idea here is that just as sentences have an inferential role, so do their parts. Things are not that simple, though, since sub-sentences cannot serve as premises and conclusions of inferences. Thus, one might be skeptical that the idea can be made to work. Brandom's solution is that sub-sentences have an "indirect" inferential role. Roughly, the meaning of a sub-sentence is the contribution it makes to the good inferences involving sentences in which it occurs.

Brandom proposes, in particular, that the meaning of singular terms and predicates should be understood in terms of their role in "substitution inferences." Consider the inferences from 12 to 13 and from 14 to 15.

(12) George Orwell is a human.
(13) The author of *1984* is a human.

(14) George Orwell is a mammal.
(15) George Orwell is an animal.

The inference from 12 to 13 substitutes 'the author of 1984' for 'George Orwell,' while the inference from 14 to 15 substitutes 'animal' for 'mammal.' Both are substitution inferences.

Yet there is a clear and important difference between the two inferences. The first is reversible, whereas the second is not. That is, you may go from 12 to 13, and back, but not so for 14 and 15; you may go from 14 to 15, but you may not go back. In Brandom's terms, the first is symmetric and the second is asymmetric. He uses the notions of symmetric and asymmetric substitution inferences to distinguish two important syntactic categories: singular terms and predicates.[49] Singular terms are those expressions involved only in symmetric substitution inferences. Predicates, by contrast, are those expressions involved in (at least some) asymmetric inferences. So, an expression like 'George Orwell' is a singular term because it is involved only in inferences like the one from 12 to 13.

With those syntactic categories in place, we can consider their meaning or semantics. Brandom's basic idea here is that two expressions have the same meaning if they have the same inferential role. Two expressions have the same meaning if substitution of one for the other into a sentence does not alter the inferential potential of that sentence. For instance, 'George Orwell' and 'the author of *1984*' would have the same meaning if 12 and 13 had the same inferential role. The content of any particular sub-sentential expression consists in which substitution inferences involving that expression count as good. For instance, the content of 'George Orwell' partly consists in the goodness of the inference from 12 to 13. Part of the content of 'George Orwell' is that one is permitted to move from saying that 'George Orwell is human' to saying 'The author of *1984* is human.'[50]

As with whole sentences, the inferential role of a sub-sentence is a matter of the norms governing it. We have seen that Brandom thinks norms are dynamic and contested. They are not settled in advance of the game of giving and asking for reasons, but are instead at issue and worked out in the course of it. Different players can take the norms to be different. According to Brandom, the substitution inferences a particular speaker counts as good are her "simple material substitution-inferential commitments" (SMSICs, for short; MIE, p. 372). These SMSICs embody a perspective on the substitution-inferential norms for the expressions involved.

Like other inferential norms, SMSICs can be made explicit in the form of a claim. For singular terms, that can be done with an expression for numerical identity, such as 'is.' Thus:

(16) George Orwell is (=) the author of *1984*.

For predicates, that can be done with universal propositions, as in:

(17) Anything that is human is mammal.

The capacity to express an SMSIC as the content of a claim (such as 16 or 17) is a capacity to assert—and, in turn, defend or challenge—a putative norm governing the role of the expressions contained in that claim.

That is only the briefest sketch of Brandom's conception of the meaning of sub-sentences. In *Making It Explicit*, he explains further how pronouns, such as 'he,' 'she,' and 'it,' function in his inferentialist framework. They are surprisingly important to his account of our ability to "share" meaning. He also goes on to explain how singular terms and claims can be understood as standing for or "representing" things, even though their meaning is not constituted by what they represent, but by their inferential role. Although these strands of his project are interesting and important, I think enough has been presented to see the core of that project, and to appreciate McDowell's challenge to it.[51]

3. MCDOWELL'S QUIETISM

In this section, I want to sketch one big objection that McDowell makes to Brandom's view of linguistic meaning.[52] In brief, he alleges that Brandom is wrong to think we need to and can provide a "full-blooded" theory of linguistic meaning. Rather, our goal should be to expose those faulty assumptions that make such a theory seem necessary, and which provoke theorizing that nevertheless leaves linguistic meaning looking mysterious. McDowell's view here is a further manifestation of his "quietism," which I introduced in Chapter 3. I will start by sketching McDowell's view of "full-blooded" theories of meaning in general and then turn to his objection to Brandom's view.

3.1. "Full-Blooded" Theories

A "full-blooded" theory of linguistic meaning aims to explain the meaning of the expressions (words and sentences) of a language without appeal to the notion of linguistic meaning.[53] For instance, such a theory would aim to say what 'snow' means by specifying what a person must be able to do in order to count as having 'snow' in her vocabulary. Crucially, in this sort of theory, the explanation of what 'snow' means must not rely on a prior understanding of linguistic meaning. For instance, this sort of theory is not content to say things like

(18) 'Snow is white' means that snow is white.

For a full-blooded theory, the problem with 18 is not that it appears trivial, for such a theory would also be unsatisfied with 19:

(19) 'La neige est blanche' means that snow is white.

Rather, the problem with both 18 and 19 is that in specifying what a sentence means, they rely on talk of meaning. A full-blooded theory aims to avoid such talk. The idea is that we don't really understand meaning until we can articulate it in other terms. Thus, when stating the theory, one must avoid expressions like 'means,' 'expresses,' 'refers to,' 'designates,' 'stands for,' and 'is true of.' So, such a theory is "full-blooded" because it aims to explain linguistic meaning in wholly other terms. In Michael Dummett's words, such a theory aims to explain meaning "as from the outside" (Dummett, 1981, p. 40).[54]

McDowell thinks that a full-blooded theory cannot work; we cannot understand linguistic meaning "from outside" meaning.

For McDowell, a full-blooded theory assumes a "gap" between words and their meanings, which it then fails to bridge. (That is the same sort of gap that we saw previously in Chapter 3.) For McDowell, because such a theory eschews talk of meaning and related notions in order to explain meaning, it is committed to the idea that what makes a particular word (e.g., 'snow') that word and not some other word does not, ultimately, concern the meaning of that word. We must be careful here. The idea is not simply that the scratches or noises that we happen to treat as instances of the word 'snow' need not have had the specific meaning that we attach to them. Rather, the idea is that what makes the *word* 'snow'—what Sellars would represent as ·snow·—that word and not some other word is not, ultimately, a matter of what 'snow' (·snow·) means. Thus, a full-blooded theory is committed to the idea that each word is not, of necessity, tied to its meaning.[55] However, if words aren't connected, of necessity, to their meanings, then it's always an open question why some given use or occurrence of a word really means what it's supposed to mean; indeed, it's always an open question whether such uses or occurrences are meaningful at all. Thus, for McDowell, a full-blooded theory leaves meaning mysterious.

McDowell holds that we can and should avoid the mystery by rejecting the false assumption at the root of the theory. Specifically, we should not assume that the only way to genuinely understand meaning is to explain it in wholly other terms. McDowell writes:

> The wish for . . . [a full-blooded theory] reflects a familiar philosophical attitude to content. The attitude is one in which we wonder at the capacity of language to give expression to thought; we take that capacity to be something we must find mysterious unless we can reconstruct it in conceptually independent terms, and so see how we integrate it into a picture of the world that does not already explicitly make room for it. (McDowell, APM, p. 131)

For McDowell, the alternative is to recognize that our ordinary understanding of the meaning of words is already a genuine form of understanding, not in need of replacement by a form of understanding in wholly other terms. That does not imply that we may not think systematically and productively about meaning or that we may not theorize about meaning. Doing so is philosophically permissible. Such efforts are pursued in contemporary linguistics.[56] However, for McDowell the key is that we should not see such theories as "full-blooded." Rather, we should see them as "modest" in the specific sense that they do not aim to explain meaning in other terms, but instead extend our understanding of meaning "from inside" not "from outside" meaning.[57]

How do these ideas bear on Brandom's project? In brief, McDowell thinks Brandom pursues a "full-blooded" theory, and thus is mistaken.

3.2. Motivating Inferentialism

McDowell wonders: What motivates inferentialism?

In §2 of this chapter, I said simply that Brandom takes up Sellars's project of developing a practice-centered, functional role theory of meaning. That should have made it seem as if Sellars's motive—his rejection of relationalism—is Brandom's too. To a large extent, it is.[58] More exactly, Brandom contrasts his own view with something he calls "representationalism," a class of views that he thinks has traditionally dominated reflection about meaning. Those views share a conception about how to explain meaningful linguistic phenomena. In its plainest form, representationalism starts by specifying what individual words mean (e.g., what they stand for); it then explains how the meanings of whole sentences are built out of the meanings of the words they comprise; it then explains which inferences are valid on the basis of the meanings of sentences; lastly, it explains what sentences can be used to say or do, given what they mean. So, it is committed to a certain order of explanation: you start with sub-sentential semantics, move to sentential semantics, then to inferential relations and pragmatics. Representationalism is often coupled with the view that the mind's representational abilities precede, cause, and explain linguistic meaning and what one is doing in using language, as in the Lockean Picture of Chapter 2.[59] That sort of view is the exact opposite of Brandom's view.

Brandom offers representationalism mainly as a contrast to inferentialism; he does not spend much time criticizing it.[60] However, he clearly thinks it's not the right approach. McDowell agrees, but he denies that inferentialism is the only alternative.[61]

McDowell holds that instead of "inverting" the representationalist order of explanation, we should reject the demand to provide a "linear" explanation of meaning. We could think of representation and inference as "coordinate," treating neither as explanatorily prior to the other.[62] We would not use representation to explain inference, nor would we use inference to explain representation (as Brandom aims ultimately to do in *Making It Explicit*). McDowell observes that Brandom sees that this route is available and opts not to take it.[63] That strikes McDowell as odd. If "the representationalist error is to suppose concepts of representational directedness can be intelligible independently of inferential relations," then inferentialism, by simply inverting the order of explanation, errs in the same way.[64]

Brandom agrees with McDowell that rejecting representationalism does not require one to accept inferentialism. He says instead that "the proof should be in the pudding" (Brandom, Replies, 1997, p. 191). That is, we should accept or reject inferentialism on the basis of whether it adequately explains linguistic meaning.

That opens a huge question: does Brandom's project work?[65]

McDowell is doubtful. The problem at this stage is not simply the order of explanation that Brandom pursues. Rather, it's that Brandom aims to explain linguistic meaning without appeal to the idea of linguistic meaning or related ideas (such as intentionality); instead, as we have seen, he aims to explain it in terms of a norm-governed game of attributing and acknowledging normative statuses.[66] Thus, for McDowell, Brandom aims for a "full-blooded" theory of linguistic meaning.[67] In Brandom's words, McDowell's worry is that "the practices of keeping score on commitments and entitlements and their relations . . . do not suffice to get any intelligible notion of inference, assertion or (therefore) conceptual content in play" (Brandom, Replies, 2005, p. 237). In short, the charge is that the so-called game of giving and asking for reasons is a mere game, devoid of meaning.[68]

Naturally, Brandom is more hopeful than McDowell. In particular, he points to the many aspects of linguistic meaning that he attempts to explain in *Making It Explicit*.[69] The crucial question is whether these attempts are successful. I cannot decide that issue here. You can take McDowell's charge as an invitation to work through the details of *Making It Explicit*.

3.3. Should We Be Quiet?

The big issue dividing Brandom and McDowell is what it takes to adequately understand linguistic meaning.

Brandom thinks we learn about linguistic meaning by trying to explain it in terms of the game of giving and asking for reasons. In a couple of places, Brandom presents his view as a "big, bold conjecture," one that's more readily subject to testing and failure than are weaker conjectures.[70] For him, the virtue of pursuing the bolder conjecture is that if it fails, we can see where and how it fails; likewise, we can see where and how it succeeds.

McDowell worries that the conjecture fails right at the beginning, in the assumption that we don't understand linguistic meaning unless and until we can conceive of it in wholly other terms—in terms of norm-governed practices of attributing and acknowledging normative statuses. Once we make that assumption, we've already given up the idea that our normal understanding of meaning is a genuine form of understanding, not in need of replacement by some other. In this respect, many of the details of the view are irrelevant.

At bottom, McDowell wants to know why we need a "full-blooded" theory of linguistic meaning. Brandom thinks that even if we can't have such a theory, we can learn about linguistic meaning by developing such a theory and subjecting it to criticism.[71]

CONCLUSION

The goal of this chapter was to look more closely at the idea that the meaning of a claim should be understood in terms of its place in linguistic activity, especially in terms of what it can rationally support and be supported by. We have seen a lot along the way. Let me highlight a few things. For Sellars, many views of meaning are problematic because they assume meaning is a "word-world" relation, and that when we talk about meaning, we are simply describing such a relation. Once those ideas are rejected, we are free to see things differently. In particular, one can see the meaning of an expression as its norm-governed role in material inferences. Grasping or understanding an expression is being able to use it in accordance with those norms. Brandom takes up that basic idea, adding a story about the activity of giving and asking for reasons, aiming to explain what it is one must do to count as asserting—making a claim with conceptual content—in the first place. McDowell thinks there are deep questions about the need for such a project.

5 Knowledge without the Given

> [I]n characterizing an episode or a state as that of *knowing* . . . we are placing it in the logical space of reasons, the space of justifying and being able to justify what one says.
>
> -Sellars, Empiricism and the Philosophy of Mind, §36

INTRODUCTION

In this chapter, we return to the problem with which we concluded Chapter 1: how can we resist the regress without appealing to the Given?

I'll begin by refreshing your memory about that problem, and then I'll canvass Sellars's, Brandom's, and McDowell's responses to it.

1. REVIEW: THE GIVEN

In this section, I want to remind you why philosophers most commonly appeal to the Given, and what is wrong with those appeals, according to philosophers in the Pittsburgh School. Mainly, I will be highlighting the big moves of Chapter 1. That should prime you to contemplate knowledge without the Given.

In Chapter 1, we envisioned Mark and Sarah entering their house, walking into the kitchen to put away some groceries, and Sarah recalling that the air conditioning is on. She asks Mark, 'Is the door shut?' Mark looks and sees that the door is shut and says so, thereby passing his knowledge on to Sarah, whom we would normally now count as knowing that the door is shut.

For Sarah to count as knowing that the door is shut, she must not merely believe that it is shut; her belief must also be true and justified. That, anyway, is the standard conception of knowledge. But if her belief must be justified, then she needs to have reasons or evidence for it. And indeed she does: she also believes that Mark said that the door is shut, and that he reliably reports such things. That would support her belief that the door is shut. But what of those beliefs themselves? What supports them? Surely Sarah cannot count as knowing that the door is shut if her supporting evidence isn't itself a case of knowledge. What reason does she have to believe that Mark reliably reports such things? Well, she's spent a lot of time with him and recalls only a few instances where he's been mistaken about this kind of thing. But what entitles her to rely on her memory in that way? If this chain of reasons or justifications doesn't halt somewhere, can Sarah really count as knowing that the door is shut?

Moreover, that difficulty is not unique to Sarah's case. It is a general problem. The difficulty is that knowledge requires justification, which seems to spark a regress of reasons or justifications. If it doesn't stop somewhere, there would seem to be no knowledge at all. The skeptic would be right: we wouldn't know anything.

Foundationalism is the most natural response to the regress: try to stop it; identify a foundation of knowledge. Remember also that the regress is part of a larger problematic, the Agrippan Trilemma. The problem is not simply that there appears to be a regress. Rather, it's that in trying to stop it, one cannot appeal to a brute assumption or something that one has already offered as a reason. Both of those moves would be no more acceptable than the regress itself, for they wouldn't give us knowledge. That constrains what a foundation can be.

The foundation would have to be capable of supporting the rest of one's knowledge, while relying on no further knowledge.

We saw that this non-reliance condition is very demanding. The foundation would have to be more than merely non-inferential knowledge. That sort of knowledge is exemplified in cases of seeing, such as when Mark sees that the door is shut. He gets that knowledge without need of reasoning or inferring. But that sort of knowledge clearly can depend on other knowledge, as Mark's case shows. He could not know that the door is shut without also knowing what a door is and what it is for one to be shut. So, the foundation would have to be independent, not merely non-inferential. That is, it would have to be knowledge that one could have independently of any other knowledge. It would have to be "intrinsically credible," in Williams's words.

The Given just is the idea that there could be a foundation of knowledge in that sense. According to deVries, the Given is something that is both epistemically efficacious and independent. More precisely:

(EI) The Given is *epistemically independent*, that is, whatever positive epistemic status our cognitive encounter with the object has, it does not depend on the epistemic status of any other cognitive state.

(EE) It is *epistemically efficacious*, that is, it can transmit positive epistemic status to other cognitive states of ours. (2005, pp. 98–9)

What might play the role of the Given?

Sellars says that "many different things have been said to be 'Given'" (EPM, §1). Descartes's "I think" can seem initially promising because it seems "indubitable." The trouble is that it doesn't look like it could support the rest of our knowledge, especially our knowledge of things beyond our own minds. It's not that such knowledge is utterly "inefficacious"; rather, it is not adequately "efficacious." Experience or knowledge rooted in experience seems like it would be more able to support that sort of knowledge.

In Chapter 1, we looked briefly at three different conceptions of experience that might show us how it could play the role of the Given. They all shared the idea that there are sorts of experience that are so elementary as not to demand much or anything cognitively of us, furnishing us with elementary bits of knowledge, grounding the rest of what we know. (That's just a way of saying they all share the idea that experience could be the Given.) Yet they all have trouble showing how experience need not require much or any cognition and yet also furnish grounds for the rest of our knowledge. That is, they all have trouble showing how experience jointly satisfies EE and EI.

We followed deVries's suggestion that Sellars's argument against the Given is a dilemma: the Given must be either conceptual or non-conceptual; nothing conceptual can satisfy EI; nothing non-conceptual can satisfy EE; thus, in either case, nothing can fill the role of the Given. When we first worked through that argument we had not discussed concepts or reasoning or meaning in much detail, but we have since done so. It might now be easier to understand how that argument is supposed to work.

Think first about a conceptual version of the Given. Various things could play that role, but the crucial thing is that whatever does so must be conceptual, epistemically efficacious, and epistemically independent.

We have seen that the Pittsburgh School thinks that having concepts requires knowledge. One cannot have any concepts without being able to think in terms of them, especially by forming a judgment or a belief. Judging or believing are, in turn, intentional states or episodes; they have content or meaning. For a state or episode to have any content or meaning at all, it must be embedded in a network of norm-governed rational relations. That is, one who believes must know what one's beliefs support and are supported by; otherwise, one doesn't believe at all.[1]

Thus, the Pittsburgh School's argument against a conceptual version of the Given turns on their ideas about content. For one to believe or make a claim at all, one must already have some knowledge. Thus, nothing could be both conceptual and epistemically independent; the Given cannot be conceptual.

That leads us to a non-conceptual version of the Given. Various things could play that role, but the crucial thing is that whatever does so must be non-conceptual, epistemically efficacious, and epistemically independent.

We have seen that for the Pittsburgh School, for something to be a premise or a conclusion for a person in a piece of reasoning, it must be conceptually structured; it must be sentence-like. Something that is not conceptually structured makes no claim at all, and therefore cannot admit of truth or falsity. It could not rationally support or be supported by anything.

Thus, the Pittsburgh School's argument against a non-conceptual version of the Given turns on its conception of reasoning. For one to wield something as a premise in reasoning, thereby achieving further beliefs or knowledge, it must be conceptually meaningful. Thus, nothing could be both non-conceptual and epistemically efficacious; the Given cannot be non-conceptual.

Thus, the Given can be neither conceptual nor non-conceptual. It appears to be a "myth."

2. KNOWLEDGE WITHOUT THE GIVEN

Alas, the Given was supposed to stop the regress. If it is a myth, we seem to be left with the regress into skepticism. In the rest of this chapter, we want to consider how Sellars, Brandom, and McDowell resist the regress while avoiding the Given.

2.1. Sellars

Sellars writes:

> We might begin by trying something like the following: An overt or covert token of 'This is green' . . . expresses observational knowledge if and only if it is a manifestation of a tendency to produce overt or covert tokens of 'This is green'—given a certain set—if and only if a green object is being looked at in standard conditions. (EPM §35)

The basic suggestion here is that the (overt or covert) occurrence of 'This is green' amounts to observational knowledge if, and only if, it is the exercise of an ability to respond to things that are green (in standard conditions) with 'This is green.' When a person with such a disposition produces 'This is green' she has observational knowledge, and she has observational knowledge only when she responds in that way.

This initial idea is provocative. Indeed, since the publication of EPM, many philosophers have carefully developed theories of knowledge that center on the idea of reliability.[2] Such views are considered forms of "reliabilism." The version of it that Sellars sketches here is a kind of "pure" reliabilism, as it treats reliability as both necessary and sufficient for having knowledge. Pure reliabilism contrasts with more traditional conceptions of knowledge that require that the knowing subject herself be able to provide (or, at least, recognize) reasons for what she knows. Pure reliabilism does not require that; instead, it maintains that being a reliable "detector" of the relevant facts is sufficient, even if the person herself is unable to adduce reasons for what she believes.

Because pure reliabilism allows justification to be "external" to the knowing subject's own consciousness, it has been labeled "externalism" about justification; by contrast, "internalism" is the label for views that espouse the traditional idea that the knowing subject must have some kind of "access" to whatever justifies her. In brief, externalism maintains that one can be justified without being able to justify.

Sellars rejects pure reliabilism because it implies that mere thermometers have observational knowledge, when in fact they do not. More generally, something that is merely reliably disposed to respond with a token of 'This is green' in the presence of green things (and only green things) does not yet have knowledge. So, pure reliabilism sets the bar too low for observational knowledge.

For Sellars, such reliability is nevertheless necessary for observational knowledge. Thus, there is an important externalist element in Sellars's story. The question is what more is necessary for someone to count as having such knowledge.

Sellars says that "to be the expression of knowledge, a report [such as 'This is green'] must not only *have* authority, this authority must *in some sense* be recognized by the person whose report it is" (EPM, §35). That is, not only must the person be a reliable reporter, she must also recognize her own reliability, which in turn requires a capacity to connect reports with what they are reports of, and a capacity to discern their veracity or correctness. Let us call that the Reflexivity Requirement (RR).[3]

Sellars recognizes that RR is a "steep hurdle." Indeed, it can seem too steep. Certainly, a thermometer cannot clear it. More importantly, however, very young children and non-human animals might not be able to clear it, for they don't obviously have knowledge of their own reliability. And yet we often do credit them with knowledge. We say things like, "That squirrel knows where the acorns are" and "Your son knows you're watching him." So, in ruling out thermometers, Sellars also rules out apparently genuine knowers, and his position can seem like an over-reaction.

Why, then, does Sellars espouse RR?

He says that "the authority of the report 'This is green' lies in the fact that the existence of green items appropriately related to the perceiver can be inferred from the occurrence of such reports" (EPM, §35). That is, the report is "authoritative" only because from its occurrence one can infer "the existence of green items appropriately related" to the reporter. What makes a report authoritative for a person is that she can infer certain things from it. Thus, a report is authoritative only for people who can recognize that those things can be inferred from it. A report is not authoritative for someone who does not recognize that such inferences can be drawn from the report. A report is "authoritative" only for someone who recognizes the "authority" of that report—what inferences that report "authorizes" or licenses.

Is this a satisfactory defense against the worry that RR is too "steep"? Well, it does not aim to show that RR is any less steep than it initially seemed. Rather, it helps us understand why we should accept RR despite it being so "steep." Sellars's defense helps us see that knowledge has something to do with authority and especially with the recognition of authority.[4] Putting it roughly, knowers aren't merely pushed around by things; they are also authorized to do things; and they can be so authorized only if they are able to recognize something as authoritative. If that's right, then the question is whether very young children and non-human animals can recognize something as authoritative. If they cannot, we would have a reason not to count them as knowers, at least in the sense that typical adult humans are knowers.

What does it take to recognize something as authoritative? This question brings us back to some of the issues raised in our discussion of rules and rule-following in Chapter 3. Specifically, recognizing something as authoritative cannot consist solely in being moved by it or in being disposed to be moved by it. That would be mere responsiveness. Rather, it would seem to involve being aware of the *rightness* or *wrongness* of being so moved. For one to recognize something as authoritative it seems one must also be able to distinguish merely doing something from the rightness of doing it, and to be able to distinguish not doing something and the wrongness of not doing it. For instance, one would need to distinguish uttering 'This is green' from correctly uttering 'This is green.'

Do very young humans or certain non-human animals make such distinctions? It's not obvious that they do. In degrees, very young children learn to sanction and respond to sanctions. That is surely part of what's necessary for distinguishing doing something and the rightness of doing it. Do they need something more? In Chapter 3, we saw that philosophers in the Pittsburgh School think that it requires an ability to be aware of rules *as such*. The ability to make rule explicit in symbols or language would be one way to do that. Alas, that keeps the hurdle fairly "steep."

On Sellars's view, then, very young children and non-human animals do not enjoy knowledge—at least, not in the same way that typical adult humans do.[5] Rather, one might see them as having something similar to such knowledge: modeled on the knowledge of adult humans, but limited in certain ways.[6] Even if you think that is an implausible consequence, it is important to see that Sellars has given us reasons for doubting that very young children and non-human animals have knowledge in the same sense that typical adult humans do. To soundly reject Sellars's position, one must show what's wrong with his case in favor of RR.

Sellars's proposal faces another difficulty. He writes:

> [I]t might be thought that there is something obviously absurd in the idea that before a token uttered by, say, Jones could be the expression of observational knowledge, Jones would have to know that overt verbal episodes of this kind are reliable indicators of the existence, suitably related to the speaker, of green objects. (EPM, §36)

In other words, Sellars's view seems to be circular. Observational knowledge requires knowledge of one's own reliability as an observer, which in turn seems to require observational knowledge. In fact, Sellars's view seems to be either circular or stuck in a regress. He writes:

> [I]t might be thought there is an obvious regress in the view we are examining. Does it not tell us that observational knowledge at time

t presupposes knowledge of the form X *is a reliable symptom of* Y, which presupposes *prior* observational knowledge, which presupposes *other* knowledge of the form X *is a reliable symptom of* Y, which presupposes still other, and *prior*, observational knowledge, and so on? (EPM, §36)

On Sellars's view, how do you acquire any knowledge at all?

In brief, Sellars responds that one can and must come to have observational knowledge and knowledge of one's reliability all at once (EPM, §37).[7] On that view, one must go from having no knowledge at all to having a whole lot of it. Thus, it can seem as though a huge leap is required, leaving the acquisition of knowledge just as mysterious as it was when we were facing the circle or the regress.

In response, Sellars writes:

> This charge . . . rests on too simple, indeed a radically mistaken, conception of what one is saying of Jones when one says that he knows that-p. . . . The essential point is that in characterizing an episode or state as that of knowing, we are not giving an empirical description of that episode or state; we are placing it in the logical space of reasons, of justifying and being able to justify what one says. (EPM, §36)

For Sellars, to disarm this worry we must recognize that knowers are similar to players of a norm-governed game.

We have seen that for the Pittsburgh School, attributing knowledge and cognitive states to a person has a crucial normative or evaluative dimension. For instance, when we say that Sarah knows that the door is shut, we are appraising her as successful and endorsing her as someone on whom we can rely in further reasoning. Because knowers appraise each other in these ways, and rely on such appraisals in their own performances, knowers are like players in a game. These appraisals and our reliance on them in turn depend on our recognition of authority and rules. That is a further way in which knowing is like playing a game.

Now, how can these similarities between knowing and playing a game help Sellars explain how people become knowers in the first place?

In both cases, as Wittgenstein puts it, and as philosophers in the Pittsburgh School are fond of putting it, "light dawns gradually over the whole" (1969, §141).[8]

Think about the way in which someone comes to count as a player of chess. Gary might start with the ability to physically manipulate all of the pieces on a chess board and the familiar idea that there are two sides, each of which is trying to defeat the other. But he can't yet play chess. No one who tried to play with him would have much fun or get very far, unless she was instructing him at every turn. Gary doesn't know what he's doing. He needs to know that the goal is to checkmate the opponent's king. And he needs to learn that each type of piece must start in a certain position, and that each type of piece can be moved only in certain ways, and that players alternate turns moving their pieces. He must be able to guide his conduct in accordance with those rules. Only when he is able to do that sufficiently well can he play the game. Having that minimal ability does not imply, of course, that he will be good at chess; he might still make lots of mistakes. However, for him to count as a player at all, he cannot make so many mistakes that it is a question whether he even knows the difference between a legal and an illegal move, or a piece that has been captured and a piece that's still in the game. Imagine trying to play a game with such a person.[9] Anyone or thing that lacked that minimal set of skills wouldn't be a bad player, but a non-player. (A tree or a squirrel or an infant would not be a bad player but a non-player.) To be even a bad player—for instance, someone who tries to attack his opponent's king but usually fails—one must have a range of interconnected skills relevant to the game. To count as playing the game at all, Gary must have a minimally adequate understanding of the whole game.

Sellars can be taken as suggesting that becoming a knower is like becoming a player of a game in that respect. To count as a knower—even one that has many false beliefs, and makes many bad inferences—one must at least have some true beliefs and make some good inferences, recognizing that doing so is a guiding aim of being a thinking thing at all.

To understand how this analogy helps Sellars, it is especially important for us to see that becoming a player of a game, such as chess, does not require a mysterious leap. The measure of whether you can play is whether other players can play with you. Likewise, becoming a knower does not require a mysterious leap. The measure of whether you are a knower is whether others can interact with you as a knower. That includes being able rightfully to give and ask you for reasons in service of their own. The point here is not that you wouldn't be a knower if every other knower died or that you wouldn't be a knower if other knowers simply ignored you. Rather, the point is that other knowers would be right to give and ask you for reasons.

We humans start with various dispositions of responding to things in our environment; in time, we develop still more dispositions, some involving words or, anyway, what seem like words; we "label" things, and call for help, and request things; eventually, it stops making sense for others to talk about our dispositions as mere patterns of response; instead, it makes better sense for people to talk of us as thinking, reasoning, and knowing; that sort of talk becomes most obviously appropriate when we start to use the language of reasons; but it likely begins before then, perhaps when we start disagreeing with others, by making claims that are incompatible with what others say. Saying that "light dawns gradually over the whole" is a way of capturing this development. We do not begin knowing everything, nor do we begin knowing just one thing, acquiring more piecemeal. Rather, we start with a bunch of habits that become increasingly sophisticated; they eventually shade into a sort of sophistication that merits the honorific labels "know" and "reason;" once we start to count as knowers, we count as knowing many things, though not especially well, and we gradually come to know these things better—by getting better at reasoning and reporting things more reliably, for instance.[10]

Our guiding question in this chapter is how we can resist the regress without appealing to the Given. Where do we stand with respect to it?

Sellars's conception of observational knowledge has two aspects: (1) such knowledge must be the exercise of a reliable ability to detect the relevant facts; and (2) the knowing subject herself must be aware of her own reliability (RR).

Does that conception of observational knowledge avoid the Given? To avoid the Given one must avoid positing knowledge that is both independent and efficacious. Sellars appears to have achieved that. According to him, one cannot observationally know of some green thing that it is green without knowledge of one's reliability as a reporter of green objects in one's vicinity. Observational knowledge of particular matters of fact depends on knowledge of more general truths about one's own reliability. And, obviously, one couldn't know that one is reliable without knowing that one has correctly reported the presence of green things in the past. Knowledge of general truths depends on knowledge of particular matters of fact. These two sorts of knowledge depend on each other. Observational knowledge, then, is not independent of other knowledge.[11]

But if Sellars does not appeal to the Given, how does he resist the regress?

It is typically held that the main alternative to Foundationalism is Coherentism, which is roughly the view that the totality of our knowledge is justified because it is a maximally coherent whole, not because it rests on a foundation. It differs from Foundationalism because it conceives of the structure of justification differently. Whereas Foundationalism conceives of it as linear, Coherentism conceives of it as non-linear. According to Coherentism, whether a belief or claim is justified depends on the overall coherence of the system of beliefs or claims of which it is a part. That is, justification accrues indirectly to beliefs or claims from the coherence of the system of which they are a part; it is not simply transmitted linearly from one belief or claim to another, as it would be for Foundationalism (Williams, 2001, p. 117). While Foundationalism pictures the structure of justification as a building with upper floors, lower floors, and a foundation, Coherentism pictures it as a web, with a center and a periphery.[12]

Coherentism begins to seem appealing once one sees the trouble Foundationalism faces: the apparent impossibility of the Given. Coherentism gives up trying to find such a foundation of knowledge. It acknowledges that experiences and experiential knowledge are important, but they are not a foundation from which all positive epistemic status is transmitted. Rather, they are one consideration among others in forming a coherent overall view of things.

Coherentism also has some intuitive appeal: experience does not always or automatically get the final say over what we think. It is true that experience often plays that role. But sometimes we rightly reject an experience, rather than allow it to alter what we think. For instance, if I seem to see a black-and-white-striped tomato, I will question whether I do really see such a thing, given that I believe that there are no such things. I might do a double take. If the appearance persists, I might look around for evidence that someone has painted something to look that way, or that someone is tricking me. I will try to make overall sense of how things appear to me, against the backdrop of both past experiences and everything else I already believe. Experience is not the ultimate arbiter here.

Sellars might look like a Coherentist, for he seems to have a non-Foundationalist conception of the structure of justification. For instance, he thinks that observational knowledge requires knowledge of one's own reliability, which in turn relies on observational knowledge. Of course, he will especially look like a Coherentist if that is the only alternative to being a Foundationalist.

But Sellars says that there is some sense in which knowledge does have a foundation, even if Foundationalism (which simply appeals to the Given) is wrong. He writes,

> If I reject the framework of traditional empiricism, it is not because I want to say empirical knowledge has *no* foundation. For to put it that way is to suggest that it is really 'empirical knowledge so-called,' and to put it in a box with rumors and hoaxes. There is clearly *some* point to the picture of human knowledge resting on a level of propositions— [e.g.] observation reports—which do not rest on other propositions in the same way as other propositions rest on them. (EPM, §38)

By defending the idea of a foundation, Sellars seems to be resisting Coherentism here, putting him at odds with both it and typical Foundationalism. And indeed he does reject both. For he next declares:

> *Above all*, the picture [of human knowledge resting on a foundation] is misleading because of its static character. One seems forced to choose between a picture in which an elephant rests on a tortoise (What supports the tortoise?) and the picture of a great Hegelian serpent of knowledge with its tail in its mouth (Where does it begin?) Neither will do. (EPM, §38)

If he rejects both Foundationalism and Coherentism, how does he resist the regress?

Sellars says that "empirical knowledge, like its sophisticated extension, science, is rational, not because it has a *foundation* but because it is a self-correcting enterprise which can put *any* claim in jeopardy though not *all* at once" (EPM, §38). Both Foundationalism and Coherentism mistakenly assume that knowledge is static, which allows it to seem as though every claim or putative piece of knowledge could be supported "all at once." They share that assumption with the regress into skepticism. The proper response to all three is to reject that assumption. Thus, Sellars resists the regress by rejecting an assumption underlying it.[13]

2.2. Brandom

Brandom thinks that Sellars is wrong to espouse RR.[14] His own view replaces that condition with another, and extends Sellars's idea that empirical knowledge is "a self-correcting enterprise which can put any claim in jeopardy, though not all at once."

Brandom thinks that Sellars has a "two-ply account of observation" (TP, 2002).[15] As we saw, Sellars thinks that observational knowledge has two aspects: (1) it must be the exercise of a reliable ability to respond to the relevant facts; and (2) the knowing subject must be aware of her own reliability (RR).[16] Those are supposed to be the two plies of observation.

Brandom thinks Sellars is right that the first ply is necessary: observers must be reliably and differentially responsive to what they observe. An observation need not be the result of a process of reasoning or inferring; it is non-inferential. He thinks Sellars is also right that such reliability is necessary but not sufficient for observational knowledge.

However, Brandom thinks Sellars is wrong about RR; it is too "steep."[17] According to Brandom, RR says that "one is not justified unless one *knows* one is justified. . . . [R]eports should be accorded the status of knowledge only in cases where the knower can cite her own reliability as a reason" (KSASR, p. 905). Brandom claims instead that one can be justified without knowing that one is justified. He writes,

> [T]here is no reason to deny the externalist insight that, once one is capable of achieving standings in the space of reasons—for instance capable of committing oneself to the claim that there is a candle in the room—one can become entitled to such standings without being able to give reasons for them. (KSASR, p. 905)

That is, sometimes people really do know something, even though they cannot offer reasons for it. For instance, Dusty could be good at distinguishing nectarines from peaches, and yet not know what the exact differences are or that he is good at discerning them. Suppose that he points to a nectarine and says, 'That's a nectarine.' It's plausible that his claim expresses knowledge because although he cannot offer us evidence for his claim, it is grounded in his reliability.[18] For instance, as Sellars himself points out, those of us who know that he is reliable would be right to take his word for it.[19]

If we reject RR, we must replace it with something, for reliability alone is not sufficient for observational knowledge. For Brandom, reliability alone is not sufficient because some reliably elicited responses are not even beliefs or applications of concepts, and something that's not even a belief cannot be knowledge (MIE, pp. 213–5).[20] Only reliably elicited *conceptual* responses count as observational knowledge. So, in place of RR, we need to specify what counts as applying a concept.[21]

That connects us with Chapters 1 and 2. There we saw that mere reliable responsiveness is not sufficient for applying a concept, hence for belief. Brandom's preferred case is the sophisticated parrot. It might be disposed to respond reliably and differentially to red things. When and only when in the presence of red things, it produces noises that sound like utterances of 'That's red' (maybe making some mistakes here and there). But the parrot does not thereby believe that the red object in front of it is red, for to have a belief is to take up a position in the "space of reasons." Doing so requires knowing what one's response—one's putative belief or claim—rationally supports and is supported by. The parrot is not capable of that, and so cannot count as believing.[22]

So, for Brandom, observational knowledge has two plies: (1) it must result from the exercise of a reliable ability to respond to the relevant facts and (2′) the observer must know what would rationally support it and what it would be supported by.[23] Notice that 2′ does not say that one must know what does actually—in this particular case—support one's response. 2′ is mainly Brandom's way of saying that the responder must have the relevant concepts and be in the space of reasons. Thus, Brandom leaves open the possibility—expressed in the "externalist insight"—that a person can know something without being able to give reasons for it.

Brandom holds that knowledge is a socially complex status.[24] The standard analysis of knowledge holds that it is justified, true belief. Brandom re-interprets that idea, focusing first on knowledge-attributions. When we attribute knowledge to someone else, we attribute to her commitment to a claim, as well as entitlement to that claim, but we also undertake that very same commitment ourselves. Thus, attributing belief and justification correspond to attributing commitment and entitlement. But to say that a commitment you've attributed to someone else is true is to undertake that commitment oneself. For instance, when we say that Sarah knows that the door is shut, we attribute to her commitment and entitlement to the claim that the door is shut, and we commit to that claim ourselves. Brandom moves from there to a view about *knowledge*. Roughly, he holds that for S to know that P is for it to be appropriate or correct for one to attribute belief in and justification for P to S, while believing P oneself. To say that someone has *observational* knowledge is to remark on both her commitment and her entitlement: it is to say that such knowledge resulted from the exercise of a reliable differential responsive disposition and is thereby warranted. In turn, for S to have observational knowledge that P is for it to be appropriate or correct to attribute to S a reliably formed belief that P, while believing P oneself.

Now, with 2′, Brandom is trying to improve on Sellars's RR. Does he? Brandom wanted mainly to acknowledge the "externalist insight" that one can be justified without being able to justify. He does that by explaining that it is true so long as it is restricted to things capable of applying concepts. But remember that the initial problem with RR was that it seemed too "steep": it keeps very young children and non-human animals from counting as having observational knowledge. Is Brandom better off here than Sellars?

Not obviously. According to Brandom, to have observational knowledge one must satisfy both 1 and 2′, and while very young children and non-human animals satisfy 1, it's doubtful that they satisfy 2′. That is, it's doubtful that they know what their responses rationally support and are supported by. On Brandom's view, the problem is that they don't yet have concepts.

Brandom thinks that is a tolerable implication.[25] He emphasizes that very young children and non-human animals do have something that matters: the reliable differential responsive dispositions necessary for 1 (TP, pp. 538–42).[26] Having those abilities allows them to track facts, even if they don't recognize that they are doing so. He stresses that he does not have a monopoly on the word 'concept' (RP, p. 205), so one could use it to cover reliable differential responsive dispositions, thereby counting very young children and non-human animals as having concepts. Yet the term is not important. What is important for Brandom is that typical adult humans nevertheless have something that very young children and non-human animals lack: an ability to navigate the space of reasons by knowing what their responses rationally support and are supported by.[27]

It should be apparent that Brandom's view of observational knowledge avoids the Given. While observational knowledge certainly supports other knowledge, one cannot have it without having knowledge of other things, such as knowledge of what one's responses support and are supported by. Observational knowledge is not independent knowledge.[28]

But that leaves him with the regress. How does he resist it?

In brief, like Sellars, Brandom rejects an assumption underlying the regress. Recall what Sellars says: "empirical knowledge, like its sophisticated extension, science, is rational, not because it has a *foundation* but because it is a self-correcting enterprise which can put *any* claim in jeopardy though not *all* at once" (EPM, §38). Brandom develops that idea into a view about the structure of the practice of justification, the "default and challenge" structure of entitlement or justification (DC) that we glimpsed in Chapter 4.

In that chapter, we saw that each player of the game of giving and asking for reasons is "entitled" by default to what she asserts, but her default entitlement can be undermined by a challenge. If a speaker meets the challenge, she retains her justification. She can do so by offering a reason in support of her claim, or by deferring to another speaker—which is one facet of the

"social articulation" of the space of reasons. Crucially, challenges themselves can be challenged, and in turn need support. If a player does not meet
the challenge, she loses entitlement to her claim; it ceases to be justified. A
speaker can also lose—or fail to have—entitlement to something she says if
she has already said something that conflicts with it. In that case, although
she would be committed to both claims, she would be entitled to neither.

By espousing DC, Brandom rejects an assumption of the regress. The
key here is that, according to DC, a claim is presumed justified unless it is
put in question by another speaker-knower or it conflicts with something
already admitted as justified. A claim can be justified without having been
reached via a process of reasoning; it can be justified without one yet having offered evidence for it. That contrasts starkly with the conception of
justification that seems to animate the regress: a claim is presumed not to
be justified until evidence has been provided for it.[29] Williams calls that
the Prior Grounding Requirement (2001, p. 24). In practice, that requirement allows speakers to make claims only once they have offered adequate
evidence for it, sparking a regress of claim-making. Brandom rejects the
Prior Grounding Requirement, espouses DC instead, and thereby avoids
the regress.

Where does observational knowledge fit into DC? For Brandom, observation reports are non-inferentially elicited responses to the environment
for which one can have default entitlement. For instance, Mark might look
at the door and say 'The door is shut.' His claim is not the result of an inference, but a non-inferential response to his environment and it is justified
by default. That preserves the "externalist insight:" one can be justified
without being able to justify. All that's required for a response to count as
observational knowledge is that it be a reliably elicited conceptual response
to the relevant fact. Such responses are not the foundation of knowledge,
for they can be challenged like any other belief or claim, sometimes success-
fully. For instance, one might say to Mark, 'But how can you tell without
your glasses?' or 'Can you tell from there?' or 'You're always wrong about
that.' Thus, for Brandom, observations are one important way of taking
up a position in the space of reasons, but they are not the foundation of all
such positions.

One might wonder whether DC is the right conception of justification.
For instance, one might think that it only tells us when a person is "practi-
cally" justified, not when she is truly, "epistemically" justified.[30] Default
justification can look merely like what your peers "let you get away with,"
for it seems to hinge on their ability and willingness to issue challenges.
Or, in the same vein, one might worry that default justification is a license
to think whatever one likes. If that's what it is, it looks like a form of the
Given, something that is both epistemically efficacious and epistemically
independent.

One thing that seems to speak in favor of DC is that it helps us resist the
regress.[31] But that response looks question-begging in this context: the very

issue is whether the conception of justification underwriting the regress is correct. A better response is that DC requires people to be committed to defending their claims.[32] Default entitlement is only defeasible; a player of the game of giving and asking for reasons must respond to appropriate challenges; unless and until she does so respond, her entitlement is undermined. If someone is utterly non-responsive to such challenges, she risks not being in the game at all. Thus, being justified is not simply a matter of what others "let you get away with," nor is it a license to think whatever one likes, for it carries an ongoing commitment to defend what one thinks and says.

Now, that reply keeps DC from appearing like a mere caricature of justification. But we were wondering whether it is the right conception of justification. Brandom holds that it is necessary for counting anyone as making claims and having thoughts at all.[33] That is a claim about meaning: for our claims and thoughts to be meaningful, we must grant that some of them are justified before any evidence has been offered in support of them. Notice that the claim is *not* that without DC, justification is impossible. Thus, it does not beg the question against the skeptic, who holds that justification and knowledge are not possible.

Why think that DC is necessary for speaking and thinking meaningfully?

If everything you putatively said (or thought) had to be justified first, then you could not count as saying (or thinking) anything—let alone count as being justified in saying (or thinking) something. For if we make that assumption about justification, then even your claims (or thoughts) about what words mean (or what concepts apply to) would stand in need of justification. That is, even your attempts to justify that you had said (or thought) one thing rather than another would be in doubt. Indeed, the claim that you had said (or thought) something at all would be in doubt. So, if you must justify every claim (or thought) first, before you make it, then you would never be able to say (or think) anything.[34] It must be possible for you to make claims (or think thoughts) without first defending those claims (or thoughts).

2.3. McDowell

We have seen the gist of Sellars's and Brandom's attempts to resist the regress without appealing to the Given. For McDowell, the key is to have the right conception of experience. He thinks that Sellars comes close to having the right view of it, whereas Brandom has a more problematic view.

McDowell thinks that our goal should be to make sense of the important role of experience in knowledge and thought more generally, while avoiding the Given. In *Mind and World*, the more specific challenge is to do so without sliding into Coherentism. To see that problem, we must keep in mind that Coherentism is a response to the trouble faced by Foundationalism: the Given is a myth. In *Mind and World,* McDowell is mainly concerned with the non-conceptual version of the Given.[35] The problem with it is that nothing non-conceptual can provide one with rational support or reasons. Only something conceptual, such as a thought or a claim, can do that. As McDowell sees things, that problem drives us towards Coherentism. For him, Coherentism holds that "experience is causally relevant to a subject's beliefs and judgments, but it has no bearing on their status as justified or warranted" (MW, p. 14). That is, an experience can cause a belief, but it cannot serve as one's evidence for that belief. For McDowell, Coherentism's conception of experience is captured in a remark from Donald Davidson: "nothing can count as a reason for holding a belief except another belief" (Davidson, 2001, p. 141; cited at MW, p. 14).

McDowell thinks the problem with Coherentism's conception of experience is precisely that it gives experience only a causal role: experience itself never gives you evidence for what you think or say.[36] When faced with the regress of justification, the hope had been that experience could be the foundation of our knowledge by giving us genuine knowledge of the world. Coherentism simply denies that experience affords such rational contact with the world, opting instead for merely causal contact. Experience merely causes, provokes, or instigates thoughts; it doesn't justify them or make them reasonable. Thereby, it seems to leave us without any knowledge at all; it seems to leave us disconnected from the world. Granting experience a causal role is not enough; we need a rational check on what we think. Thus, according to McDowell, Coherentism leaves us "spinning in a void" (MW, p. 11).

McDowell thinks that this problem tends to force philosophers back to the Given, for we realize that we need experience of the world to provide rational constraint on our thinking. Thus, McDowell thinks philosophers can get stuck in an "interminable oscillation" between appealing to the Given and Coherentism (MW, p. 9).

In McDowell's view, this oscillation has a deeper significance. The Given and Coherentism are not simply attempts to show that and how we have knowledge. Rather, they can and should be understood as responses to a worry about content: "how is empirical content so much as possible?" (EI, p. 243). Understood that way, they are attempts to explain "how our intellectual activity can make us answerable to reality at all" (EI, 243). The issue is not just knowledge, but intentionality.[37]

The regress of knowledge takes for granted that we have genuine intentional states or episodes and questions whether any of them amount to knowledge. In that context, the Given and Coherentism are attempts to show that some intentional states or episodes do indeed amount to knowledge. What McDowell is proposing is that the Given and Coherentism can and should be seen as attempts to explain how we have genuinely intentional states or episodes in the first place.

For mental states or episodes to be about or directed at the world they must be answerable to it for whether they are correct or incorrect, true or false. Crucially, such answerability is not a matter of getting a specific type of answer; rather, it is a matter of getting an answer at all. Even false beliefs require the possibility that our mental states or episodes can face the world and answer to it.

As McDowell sees things, an appeal to the Given (the non-conceptual version of it) attempts to explain that and how our mental states or episodes can so face the world and answer to it. Specifically, it attempts to show how thought comes into contact with reality itself in an experience. It conceives of an experience as something that is not itself another thought, and yet also something to which thought can answer. According to McDowell, it fails because it doesn't allow experience to be the right kind of thing: it assumes experience must be non-conceptual. It does so because it also assumes that whatever thought answers to must come from "outside" of thought; it must be something other than another piece of thinking; otherwise, one's thinking would simply answer to one's own thinking, which would not be a genuine check on one's thinking.[38] Yet thought cannot answer to something that is wholly non-conceptual, for such a thing could never be evidence for or against a thought.

Coherentism concedes that experience itself does not really confront thought. It attempts instead to maintain that answerability to the world need be nothing more than causal constraint by the world. It fails because that's not the right sort of constraint. Being causally constrained by the world is not the same as being answerable to it. Everything in the world is causally constrained by other things in the world: people, dolphins, apes, dogs, trees, stars, plankton, DNA. But only some things are answerable to the world. We are certainly provoked by the world into thinking one thing or another, but what we think is also accountable to the world; our thoughts about the world are to be assessed in terms of it. Coherentism leaves us "spinning in a void" not simply because it doesn't allow us knowledge but because it doesn't allow us even to *think*—to be answerable to the world.

McDowell thinks that to escape the interminable oscillation between the Given and Coherentism, we must find a way to think about experience that avoids both.

What the appeal to the Given gets right is that it tries to give experience a justificatory role. It goes wrong in denying that experience itself is conceptual. What Coherentism gets right is that it recognizes that only something conceptual can serve as a premise in further thinking. It too goes wrong in denying that experience is conceptual; it allows experience only to causally constrain our thoughts. With those points in view, McDowell's resolution emerges: appeals to the Given and Coherentism both wrongly embrace the idea that experience itself is not conceptual. We must instead see experience as conceptual.

McDowell proposes we think of experience as similar to thought.[39] Specifically, just as concepts are required for thinking or saying that the door is shut, so too are concepts required for seeing that the door is shut, or for having a visual experience of the door as shut. Thinking of experience that way allows it to rationally support thoughts. However, we must not carry this analogy too far.[40] You often have control over your own thinking, especially when you "make up your mind" and judge that things are one way rather than another. But experience is not active like that; it is passive. Although I often choose where to turn my head or where to sit, I do not similarly choose what I experience once I am so positioned: what I experience is not up to me. In McDowell's words, "In experience one finds oneself saddled with content" (MW, p. 10). So, while concepts are deployed in both thoughts and experiences, McDowell claims that concepts are merely "activated" or "actualized" in experiences; they are not actively used as they would be in judging that things are one way rather than another.

For McDowell, this analogy allows us to treat experience as "openness to the layout of reality," something that is foreclosed by appeals to the Given and Coherentism (MW, p. 26). They both wrongly treat experience of the world as non-conceptual, and thereby leave it unable to rationally constrain our thinking. They do not treat experience as a rational encounter between mind and world.

McDowell recognizes that talk of "openness to the layout of reality" might make it seem as if experience never leads one astray, as if it were infallible (MW, pp. 9, 111–14).[41] Yet experience clearly can lead us astray; it is fallible. For instance, it could look to Mark as though the door is shut when it isn't.

McDowell holds that his conception of experience does not imply that experience is infallible.[42] His view is not that in experience one always takes in how things are; rather, his view is that "in experience one can take in how things are" (MW, p. 25). The crucial aspect of his view is that experience itself is capable of rationally constraining one's thinking.

For McDowell, it is important to see that there is no good inference from the claim that experience can mislead us to the claim that experience never makes facts directly manifest to us. That sort of inference is the heart of the famous argument from illusion. According to it, a misleading experience is subjectively indistinguishable from a veridical experience. For instance, it can appear to Mark that the door is shut, when it isn't. That experience is subjectively indistinguishable from an experience in which the door really is shut. They differ only because in one case things are as they appear as being, and in the other case they aren't. Thus, veridical and misleading experiences are essentially alike: "appearances as such are mere appearances, in the sense that any experience leaves it an open possibility that things are not as they appear" (McDowell, EI, p. 230). McDowell calls that resulting view a "highest common factor" conception of experience (HCF, for short; CDK, p. 386).

The essential feature of HCF is that experiences are never more than mere appearances. That implies that an experience never makes facts directly manifest to a person. For instance, Mark can never simply see that the door is shut. At best, it can appear to him to be shut, and that appearance in conjunction with further knowledge can lend support to the judgment that the door is shut, but the appearance itself is "inconclusive" (EI, p. 230). At best, experiences inconclusively suggest what the facts are; they never show how things really are.

A common objection to HCF is that it makes knowledge of the world impossible. Hume made that sort of worry famous, although he himself did not issue it as an objection. He maintained that we cannot build knowledge of the world on the basis of how things seem to us, our "impressions." HCF effectively restricts us to what we can learn from our impressions. Thus, it makes knowledge of the world impossible. But since it does so—the objection goes—we should reject it. The standard reply to that objection is that it is question-begging. HCF arises in the context of trying to show that we have knowledge of the world. The objection simply assumes that we have it.

Crucially, McDowell does not make that objection to HCF. Rather, he objects that HCF makes intentionality impossible. His core claim is that if experience can never make us directly aware of how things are, then the very idea that experiences (and thoughts more generally) are *of* or *about* the world is mere illusion. For experiences to be about the world, they must be answerable to how things are in that world. Suppose that Mark has an experience of a door as shut. That experience either gets things right or it gets them wrong: maybe the door is not shut, or maybe it's not really a door at all. For it to be an experience of a door as shut, there must be something in terms of which it could be evaluated as mistaken or veridical. That requires it to be possible to experience how things are. So, McDowell maintains that for experiences to be of or about the world, there must be at least some experiences that show how things are, experiences that show more than merely how things might be; experiences that are "conclusive." Alternatively, if we assume that the best an experience can show is how things might be, then it is not clear that any experience could be genuinely answerable to what it is an experience *of* (how things are), and the idea that experiences are *of* or *about* something would cease to make sense.

So, McDowell thinks HCF is unacceptable, and, as I mentioned in passing, he thinks that the reasoning in support of it is flawed: there is no good inference from the claim that experience can mislead us to the claim that experience never makes the world (epistemically) directly manifest to us. Instead of HCF, McDowell prefers a "disjunctive" conception of experience.[43] According to it, experiences can be of two distinct sorts: they can be *either* mere appearances *or* they can make facts directly manifest to a person (as when someone sees how things are). Saying that experience is fallible is simply a way of registering that some experiences are mere appearances. So, when McDowell says that experience can be "openness to the layout of reality" he means *only* that *some* experiences make facts manifest to a person.[44]

Where does all of that put us with respect to our guiding question?

McDowell holds that a crucial implication of his position is that intentionality requires that we have knowledge in some cases.[45] It is relatively obvious that knowledge requires intentionality: no belief could count as true if it was not also about something. McDowell surprises us with the converse claim that no state or episode could be about something if there were not also states or episodes that take in how things really are—knowledge. Thus, McDowell's conception of experience supplies a distinctive response to the skeptic. If knowledge is not possible, then neither is intentionality, but since even the skeptic seems willing to concede that intentionality is possible—she starts with the assumption that we have beliefs—then she must be wrong that knowledge is not possible.

We can now see how McDowell resists the regress of knowledge without appealing to the Given. While he does say things like "The thinkable contents that are ultimate in the order of justification are the contents of experiences" (MW, p. 29), he is not trying to stop the regress of knowledge with experience.[46] Rather, like Sellars and Brandom, he is rejecting an assumption underlying the regress.[47] Specifically, he rejects the claim that there are no mental states or episodes that put one directly in contact with facts. That claim just is a general expression of HCF. As we have seen, on McDowell's way of thinking, that view has the implausible consequence that there are no genuinely intentional states, and that the typical argument for it—the argument from illusion—is invalid. For McDowell, we resist the regress of knowledge without appealing to the Given by rejecting the assumption that no intentional state puts one in direct contact with facts.

The key to McDowell's position is that a person can have experiences in which she directly confronts the facts. He thinks that both Sellars's and Brandom's views of experience have problems.[48] He has a lot to say about both of them, but I will sketch just one of his objections to Brandom, which should reveal an important difference in their views.[49]

For McDowell, one deep problem with Brandom's view is that it doesn't allow a person to directly confront facts in an experience. That's because Brandom's view seems to be a version of HCF.[50] Recall that Brandom thinks knowledge is a socially complex status.[51] When we attribute knowledge to someone else, we attribute to that person a commitment, and entitlement to it, but we also undertake that very same commitment ourselves. To say that someone has *observational* knowledge is simply to remark on both her commitment and her entitlement: it resulted from the exercise of a reliable differential responsive disposition, thereby giving her entitlement. For McDowell, the problematic feature of the view is that justification and truth are fundamentally separate. Attributing to someone entitlement to a claim is one thing; undertaking commitment oneself to that same claim is another. One can always attribute entitlement to a claim, but at the same time refuse to undertake commitment to that claim oneself. Thus, there is no form of attributing an entitlement that excludes falsehood, even in cases of perception. That is characteristic of HCF: all experiences are "inconclusive." Thus, McDowell thinks that Brandom's view does not allow people to directly confront facts in experience.

Recall that, for McDowell, the big problem with HCF is that it makes intentionality impossible. So, if Brandom's view is a version of HCF, it makes intentionality impossible. And that would make knowledge impossible.

CONCLUSION

We've been guided in this chapter by one big question: How can we resist the regress of justification without appealing to the Given? We've looked at answers from Sellars, Brandom, and McDowell. We've seen that they all try to reject an assumption underlying the regress. Sellars and Brandom reject the same assumption. They hold that we cannot treat knowledge as static, but must instead see it as dynamic; in turn, we can refuse the demand to justify all of our knowledge "all at once." While McDowell might agree with that point, for him the key is to reject the assumption that there are no mental states or episodes that put one directly in contact with facts. Along the way, we've seen that they differ on how to think about experience.

From our point of view, it's still an open question who has the best way to think about knowledge without the Given.

6 Intentional Action

A person can almost be defined as a being that has intentions.

-Sellars, Philosophy and the Scientific Image of Man, p. 40

INTRODUCTION

In the preceding chapters, behavior has been a latent theme. In this chapter, I will focus on one sort of behavior, intentional action. I have waited until now to focus on it because understanding what Sellars, Brandom, and McDowell think of it is easier when one knows what they think about content, knowledge, and perception. As we have seen in preceding chapters, they think of one's mind—both its acts and contents—as open to the world and to others. That same idea shapes their thinking about intentional action. For them, intentional actions are a manifestation of one's mind in the world. Sellars, Brandom and McDowell are guided by the idea that intentional action should be seen as analogous to perception. But they disagree about how exactly to implement that analogy.

1. INTENTIONAL ACTION

1.1. What is Intentional Action?

Things happen. Stars shine, planets rotate, bacteria duplicate, rocks roll, terrain erodes, rivers flow, leaves fall, weeds grow, bees fly, dogs bark, phones ring, humans argue.

'Behavior' is an ambiguous word. In one sense of the word, anything that a thing does counts as the behavior of that thing. In that sense of the term, everything behaves in some way or other. Thus, the falling of leaves and the flowing of rivers would count as behaviors. Even rocks behave. But there is also a narrower sense of 'behavior' that is restricted to those happenings that are initiated by the thing itself. That narrower sense of the term tends to restrict behavior to living things. Thus, the growing of a weed would be a paradigm of behavior. In that sense of the word, rocks probably don't behave. That restricted sense of the word relies on the idea of something being initiated by a thing itself, from "within" as it were. Obviously, the growing of a weed depends on factors external to the weed itself, such as sunlight and the availability of moisture and nutrients in its surrounding soil. So, although the growing of a weed is not wholly initiated from within the weed, there does seem to be a sense in which the growing of the weed is *the weed*'s doing, and not something imposed on it from outside. And, of course, there is an even narrower sense of 'behavior' that also appeals to the intuitive idea of "inner" initiation. That still narrower sense of the term restricts behavior to things capable of moving "at will." Thus, the flight of a bee would be a behavior in this sense, but the growing of a weed probably would not be a behavior. In that sense of the term, rocks don't behave, plants don't behave, but animals do. That further restricted sense of the term relies on the idea of movement initiated "at will" or "voluntarily." Like the growing of a weed, the flying of a bee depends on factors external to it, such as atmospheric pressure and wind speed. So, although "at will" or "voluntary" movement cannot be something that is entirely independent of things outside the thing that moves, there does seem to be a sense in which the flying of the bee is something the bee does at will. All of these points about the term 'behavior' apply as well to 'action;' there are broader and narrower senses of that term.

Now, when philosophers profess an interest in *action*, it is generally "at will" or "voluntary" behavior that they have in mind.[1] And, of course, one of the big questions is just exactly how to draw the distinction between a mere event and a genuine bit of voluntary action. That is sometimes called *the* problem of action or the *first* problem of action.[2] Wittgenstein vividly captures one way of thinking about that problem when he writes, "What is left over if I subtract the fact that my arm goes up from the fact that I raise my arm?" (1958, §621).

Philosophers tend to be interested in the voluntary actions of *humans*, which seem to be distinctive. While many animals seem to act voluntarily, humans act intentionally or deliberately. We are able to *conceive of* different actions, deliberate about which is best, select it, and initiate it. Such action seems to be more complex than mere "at will" behavior because of the distinctive awareness, reasoning, knowledge, or control that it involves. Of course, just what exactly counts as intentional action is the big question. That's our topic in this chapter.

1.2. The Hobbesian Picture of Willing

Traditionally, intentional action has been thought to be the operation of "the will," a faculty or aspect of the mind that initiates intentional action. In brief, the idea is that my will is the difference between a mere rising of my arm and my raising my arm.

Let's consider a very rough picture of willing. I will call it the Hobbesian Picture (HP), since you can find a version of it in Thomas Hobbes's *Leviathan*.[3] You can think of it as a complement to the Lockean Picture from Chapter 2.

In HP, the ability to will is one crucial part of the human mind. We humans are responsive to our environment; we can perceive things in it. For instance, Mark can see a red tomato in front of him. We can also reason in light of what we perceive. For instance, Mark can reason that since tomatoes are usually edible, there is something edible in front of him. And, crucially, we can "will" to act on or in our environment. For instance, Mark can elect to reach for the tomato in front of him. What we "will" often results from what we desire most strongly in the given circumstances, depending also on our characters, such as whether we are generous or selfish, patient or impatient, and so on. For instance, Mark might choose to reach for the tomato because he wants to eat it more than he wants not to eat it, and more than he wants to eat something else, and more than he wants to avoid possibly upsetting someone who might also like to eat it. The strongest desire prevails, becoming one's will.

In HP, willing requires thinking, for it requires conceiving of ways things could be but aren't currently. Willing is the distinctive capacity of the mind to make things happen; most immediately, it is your ability to move your body. Willing is what makes a bit of behavior count as an intentional action. Specifically, an action that is initiated by an act of will is an intentional action. Acts not so initiated are unintentional or "non-intentional" actions. Such acts might be initiated by something internal to an agent, but they do not result from what one desires most strongly, which is one's will. Of course, your will is not always effective. Mark might will to eat the tomato, but fail to eat it, if it were to fall from his hand or be snatched by someone else. You also have direct knowledge of your will. Even in cases where your will fails, you know directly what you have willed. Others don't. They infer that you have willed and what you have willed from observing your behavior. If your will fails, they can learn that you have willed and what you have willed from what you tell them, or maybe from other things you do.

In HP, willing is the complement of perceiving. Perception is one's ability to be affected, taking in how things are; willing is one's ability to affect things, changing how they are. Perception can be misleading, and willing can be unsuccessful. And just as I can immediately know how things *look* to me but you cannot, I can also immediately know what I have willed but you cannot.

1.3. Problems with HP

HP can seem appealing, but it has problems. In brief, it makes intentional action seem mysterious. In that respect, it is like LP, which leaves beliefs and communication mysterious.

Let me work through that claim slowly. HP does not fully explain what it is for one's will to be fulfilled or unfulfilled. According to it, an intentional action is initiated by an act of will. Does that mean that any movement resulting from the will counts as an intentional action and a fulfillment of one's will? We know that a willing need not succeed; it could fail. Mark could will to eat the tomato and yet his arm might not move towards it for some reason. Why *should* willing to eat the tomato result in eating the tomato rather than not? Why, for instance, would sitting still after willing to eat the tomato count as a non-fulfillment or failure of the will? It cannot be simply that whatever the will causes counts as a fulfillment of it. For if Mark's willing to eat the tomato causes him, somehow, to reach for the apple instead, that would not count as fulfilling his will.[4] HP leaves it unclear why some things count as fulfillment of one's will and others don't.

HP also has trouble explaining how others can know that you have willed and what you have willed—both acts and contents of willing. This is essentially the same problem LP faced in Chapter 2. For HP, acts of will are fundamentally events that precede and cause a behavior; the content of what you will is what you desire most in the circumstances; any time you will something, you know *that* and *what* you have willed. By contrast, someone else can observe your behavior, and maybe infer those things, but she cannot directly know them. She could ask you whether and what you have willed, but your response is itself one more action, of which the very same questions could be raised: did you intend to say something with those words? If so, what did you intend to say with those words? Like LP's view of beliefs, HP depicts your will as covered by a veil that others can never fully get behind.

And HP faces a third problem: a regress. That an action is willed—initiated by a willing—is supposed to "make" that action intentional. An action that is not so initiated is not intentional. But what of the willing itself? It too is an act, and it too would seem to need to be intentional, that is, something done intentionally. Otherwise, it's hard to understand what about a willing is supposed to make an action intentional. However, if willings themselves are also intentional actions, that would seem to require that they too must result from a willing, for the idea was that something was intentional only if it was initiated by a willing. That sparks a regress of willing.[5]

One might hope to stop this regress by holding that willings are *intrinsically* things done intentionally; they cannot but be intentional or deliberate. Moreover, one might think they are intentional or deliberate all on their own, without need of a separate willing to initiate them. That idea has some intuitive appeal. For instance, talk of willing to will something or of trying to try to do something doesn't seem to make much sense.[6] That suggests that willing is something one can "just do." Of course, your will might not be effective, but that doesn't show that any particular willing needs to be initiated by a prior willing. If HP adopted that strategy, it would then hold that intentional action is partitioned: willings are "intrinsically intentional," while other actions are intentional only if (and only because) they are initiated by a willing.[7]

But then we are left wondering about the important side of that partition: what is it for something to be "intrinsically intentional"? Without an answer to that, this view doesn't really explain intentional action. What we wanted to understand was why some behaviors count as intentional rather than not, and this view tells us merely that there are some "doings" that just are, by their nature, intentionally done. Yet the idea of something intentionally done was the very thing we wanted to understand.

For those reasons, HP looks questionable and with it the very idea of "the will." In response, some philosophers have been tempted towards a behaviorist interpretation of the will.[8] For them, the hope was either that talk of willing could be exchanged for talk of behavioral dispositions or that "the will" could be understood simply in terms of learning history and behavioral dispositions. But surely behaviorism is no better off here than it was in Chapter 2, when we first encountered it. Behaviorism cannot accommodate the idea that one's will might swing free of her learning history. And it is simply not true that willing can be *defined* in terms of a set of behavioral dispositions. To say that someone willed something is not equivalent to say that she is disposed to do certain things in certain circumstances.

The idea of "the will" was supposed to help us understand intentional action. One picture of "the will" seems inadequate. Do we need to abandon the idea of willing altogether and find some other way to think about intentional action? Or can the idea of the will be made to work?

2. INTENTIONAL ACTION IN PITTSBURGH

Sellars, Brandom, and McDowell all think that the idea of the will can be salvaged. In this section, I will canvass Sellars's, Brandom's, and McDowell's attempts to develop a more satisfactory picture of it. We'll see that they are guided by the idea that intentional action is structurally similar to perception, but they disagree about how to implement that idea.

2.1. Sellars[9]

Sellars holds that "language-exits" are similar to "language-entries."[10] Perception is a "language-entry" move: it is a linguistic response to a non-linguistic stimulus. The "linguistic" character of the response is its intentional character; a perception has content or meaning; it is *about* something. Intentional action is similar. It is a non-linguistic response to a linguistic stimulus. Again, the "linguistic" character of the stimulus is its intentional character, its *about-ness*.[11] Rather than talking of acts of will or of willing, Sellars tends to talk of intentions, some of which we act on—these effective intentions are surrogates for willings. Sellars holds that all intentions are thoughts that tend to result in behavior, which itself need not be "linguistic."

Sellars thinks of intentions, like other thoughts, on the model of the overt verbal performances that express them, what he calls "intending-out-loud." Like other thoughts, intentions are meaningful in virtue of their norm-governed inferential relations to other thoughts. Intentions can be premises and conclusions in a piece of reasoning; in this case, it would be *practical* reasoning, reasoning about what to do.

Expressions of intention can and do take many forms, but we must be careful to avoid a couple confusions. For Sellars, an intention is not like a command directed at oneself, such as, 'Chauncey, explain what you mean.'[12] Rather, an "intending-out-loud" would be made in the first-person voice. For instance: 'I intend to explain what I mean' or 'I will explain what I mean.' We must also distinguish between having an intention and ascribing an intention to oneself.[13] When I say things like 'I intend to explain what I mean' or 'It is my intention to explain what I mean,' I could be *expressing* an intention or *describing myself* as having an intention. But having an intention or producing an "intending-out-loud" is not the same as describing oneself as having an intention. An intention is a commitment to a course of action. The difference between having an intention and describing oneself as having it is the difference between committing to a course of action and describing oneself as being so committed. (It is comparable to believing something and describing oneself as having that belief.) The two thoughts or utterances might be expressed in the same form of words, but they have distinct functions or roles.

And we must distinguish between intentions and predictions. When we say things like 'I will explain what I mean,' I could be expressing an intention or predicting what I will do. But intending is not predicting. (Clearly, not all predicting is intending.) To intend is to commit to a course of action, while to predict is to describe how things will be in the future.[14] They too have distinct functions or roles.

For those reasons, Sellars stipulates that intentions are expressed in the form: 'I shall . . . ' For instance, the proper form of my intention to explain what I mean is:

'I shall explain what I mean.'

The 'shall' explicitly marks the expression of an intention.

Sellars holds that we can reason our way to intentions. Perhaps I "reason-out-loud": 'The reader won't understand that expression. I want my reader to understand it. So, I shall explain what I mean.' And part of the meaning or content of that concluding thought—that intention—is what would rationally support it.

Crucially, intentions are distinctive because one facet of their norm-governed role is that, by definition, they rationally ought to lead to the relevant behavior. Thus, one who has not yet learned to follow a putative "intending-out-loud" with the relevant bit of behavior isn't yet capable of having intentions.

For Sellars, learning how to have intentions requires learning to act on "volitions," intentions "whose time has come."[15] Sometimes, an intention is formed well in advance of the relevant action. As time goes by, and "no alternative course of action recommends itself," my intention "grows" into a volition and then action (TA, p. 110).[16] Sellars says, "What differentiates a volition from an act of intending is (a) its *now* character, and (b) the fact that the central place in what is intended is something (putatively) doable here and now" (TA, p. 109). Sellars holds that the form of a volition is 'I shall . . . *now.*' For instance, I might form the intention to eat a tomato in fifteen minutes. I would express my intention in English by intending-out-loud, 'I shall eat a tomato in fifteen minutes.' As time goes by, and nothing undermines my intention, it grows into a volition, which I would express in English by saying, 'I shall eat a tomato *now*,' and which rationally should culminate in my eating a tomato.

Of course, not all intentions are formed in advance of the time of action. I might develop a volition to eat a tomato on the spur of the moment. Likewise, not all intentions formed in advance of the action will "grow" into volitions or actions, even though they are defined as having that tendency. Sometimes, a different course of action recommends itself. I might decide I'd like to eat a peach instead. Or I might simply have another, conflicting intention: I might also have an intention to wait to eat until dinner. And not all volitions culminate in the right sort of action: volitions can be unsuccessful. Many things can keep me from acting in the right way: I might be distracted or clumsy. I might reach for the tomato, but stop when I hear the doorbell; I might try to reach for the tomato, but discover my arm is asleep; I might drop the tomato as I bring it to my mouth. All that is consistent with the idea that intentions *rationally should* "grow" into volitions, which *rationally should* lead to the relevant action. Here we see how intentions should be understood in terms of their normatively defined functional role. That is just another manifestation of Normative Functionalism, which we first saw in Chapter 2.

So, for Sellars, to be capable of intending, one must be capable of producing the relevant behavior once an intention's time has come. A young child might be able to produce the words 'I shall . . . '—or other "intention-talk"—but she hasn't fully grasped their significance until she tends to follow those noises with relevant sorts of behavior. Having intentions, grasping their contents, requires the ability to produce the relevant behavior in response to them.[17]

With this sketch of Sellars's view, we can see that he averts two worries that faced HP. First, on Sellars's view, both acts and contents of intentions are knowable by others. Intending to do something is essentially something that can be expressed out loud for others to hear. And what one intends—the contents of one's intention—is like the content of any other thought (or claim): it is determined by its norm-governed place in interpersonal, rational discourse. Second, on Sellars's view, by definition, volitions rationally ought to lead to the behavior that is the fulfillment of that intention. Someone who is generally incapable of producing such behavior is also incapable of having intentions (or intentions of that sort).[18] Thus, unlike HP, Sellars holds that there is a conceptual connection between volitions and the behavior that counts as their fulfillment.

Sellars holds that intentions are not "actions" but "acts."[19] He wields that distinction to block the worry that the very idea of intentions results in a regress that makes intentional action impossible.[20] But what exactly is the difference between actions and acts?

Sellars says that "An action is the sort of thing one can decide to do," such as eat a tomato (SM, p. 74). That means, for Sellars, it is something that one can do deliberately or on purpose. That does not mean that one always decides to do it. I could eat a tomato without deciding to do so. Acts, by contrast, are not the kind of thing one decides to do or does deliberately or on purpose. For instance, you might feel gratitude for a birthday party that your friends throw for you. But, Sellars says, "feeling gratitude is not something one *does*, save in that broad sense in which anything expressed by a verb in the active tense is a doing" (SM, p. 76).[21] Feelings of gratitude or warmth are *acts* in the sense that they are *activations* of abilities.

Given that distinction, Sellars claims,

> [I]t does not make sense to speak of willing to will to do A anymore than it makes sense to speak of willing to feel sympathy for someone. (In each case, however, there is such a thing as willing to do something which one conceives likely to influence one's mental propensities in the desired direction.) (SM, p. 178)

Volitions are more like something that happens to us than like something that we decide to do or deliberately bring about. They are acts, not actions. Of course, we can decide to influence the dispositions we have, and thus the kind of volitions we have, but that is not the same as willing to will a specific action. So, in holding that volitions are not actions, but only acts, Sellars avoids a regress of intentions.[22]

So, Sellars's view seems to avert the problems facing HP. But his view also invites an objection: can't non-linguistic animals act intentionally? Because Sellars holds not only that thought is modeled on speech, but also that it depends on the ability to speak, animals that cannot speak are precluded from thinking. Thus, they are also precluded from having intentions and acting intentionally.

Part of the issue here is merely verbal, centering on the expressions "act intentionally" and "intentional action." Sometimes those expressions can be used to refer to what I characterized earlier as "voluntary" or "at will" action. Sellars does not deny that animals are capable of that. We have been using the expression "intentional action" to refer to a special class of voluntary actions. Humans are the paradigm of things capable of such action. We are able to conceive of different actions, deliberate about which is best, select it, and do it. Of course, it's not antecedently obvious what exactly separates intentional action from mere at will behavior. Part of the philosophical task is to say how we should draw that line. Sellars draws it in a way that would preclude non-linguistic creatures from genuine intentional action. So, the substantive question is whether Sellars draws the line in the right place. Should intentional action, that special sort of voluntary behavior, depend on a capacity to use a natural language?

Many will say 'No.' For them, such action might involve concepts or reasoning, but that, according to them, does not require language. Sellars would disagree with them on just that point. For him, if it involves concepts and reasoning, then it depends on language. For him, that is the most fruitful way of understanding what it is to have concepts. As we saw in the previous chapter, Sellars holds that sub-linguistic animals are capable of concept possession and reasoning in a derivative sense.[23] That is, such creatures would have something similar to, but not the same as, the human capacity for natural language and thought. In turn, they also would be capable of having intentions and acting intentionally in a derivative sense.

2.2. Brandom

Brandom adopts the core of Sellars's position.[24] As he sees things, just as we should have a two-ply conception of observation, so too should we have a two-ply conception of intentional action.[25]

For Brandom, an observation is an exercise of a reliable disposition to respond differentially to a stimulus. But that does not suffice for observation; that is only the first ply of observation. The response must also be conceptual; that is the second ply of observation. For Brandom, to be conceptual is to be "inferentially articulated," which means the response must stand in inferential relations—relations of rational support—to other things, paradigmatically contents of assertions and beliefs. That means the responder herself must be aware, in some sense, of what the response would rationally support and be supported by. Thus, observation has two plies: it is (1) an exercise of a reliable disposition to respond differentially to a stimulus with (2) a conceptual—inferentially articulated—response.

Intentional action also has two plies. And these two plies are essentially similar to those had by observation. Intentional action involves both reliable differential responsive dispositions and concepts. However, the arrangement of the plies is essentially reversed. Whereas an observation is a reliably and differentially elicited *conceptual response* to the environment, an intentional action is a reliably and differentially elicited response to a *conceptual stimulus*. This reversal of the order of the two plies corresponds to Sellars's conception of language entries and language exits: entries are linguistic responses to non-linguistic stimuli; exits are non-linguistic responses to linguistic stimuli.[26]

Let's walk through Brandom's view of the two plies more slowly. An intentional action is a manifestation of a disposition or tendency. But, as we should expect, that does not suffice for doing something intentionally. Doing something that you tend to do is not necessarily to do it intentionally. For instance, you might tend to fidget when nervous, but when you so fidget you need not do so intentionally. Something more is needed. In line with the classical idea that intentional behavior is the result of willing, Brandom holds that an intentional action must be or result from a conceptually meaningful commitment to so act—or, as he calls it, "an acknowledgement of a practical commitment" (MIE, p. 324).

Intentions, for Brandom, are fundamentally *practical* commitments: they are commitments to *make something true*, and they tend to cause behavior. But intentions are also essentially conceptually meaningful. So, like other conceptually meaningful episodes or states (such as assertions or beliefs), intentions must stand in inferential relations to other conceptually meaningful states or episodes. That means intentions can serve as and stand in need of rational support. Our intentions can and often do result from reasoning, deliberation about what to do. As we saw in Chapter 4, Brandom holds that for one to have any such states or episodes, one must know, in some sense, what those states or episodes rationally support and are supported by; one must be sufficiently competent in the norm-governed, social game of giving and asking for reasons. So, to have any intentions at all one must be competent in the game of giving and asking for reasons. More specifically, to have intentions one must be competent with the relevant sorts of vocabulary, the vocabulary that purports to express commitment to act. In English, that would include the expressions we saw when discussing Sellars's view: 'I will . . . ,' 'I intend to . . . ,' 'I shall . . . ' Like Sellars, Brandom holds that a key aspect of being competent with such vocabulary is knowing what to do or how to behave in response to (earnestly) producing the relevant words. For instance, saying 'I shall eat a tomato' should (defeasibly) lead to my eating a tomato. So, in Brandom's view, as in Sellars's view, an intention fuses the conceptual and the practical. It is a conceptually meaningful commitment to act that should result in (or be responded to with) relevant behavior.

One could raise here the same worry that was raised against Sellars: can't non-linguistic animals and humans act intentionally? Brandom thinks that they cannot, but he also thinks that this is not so implausible. They are certainly capable of voluntary behavior. And they are also capable of having one of the two necessary plies of intentional action: reliable, differential responsive dispositions. But they lack the necessary conceptual capacities to form intentions, for they lack understanding of what would rationally support or follow from such intentions. Without that, activations of their reliable differential responsive dispositions cannot be responses to the content of something. As was the case with Sellars, the substantive question is whether Brandom draws the line between intentional action and mere "at will" behavior in the right place.

Consider one last feature of Brandom's view. Like Sellars, Brandom recognizes that intentions can be formed well in advance of the relevant behavior. For instance, I might intend-out-loud: 'I shall eat a tomato in fifteen minutes.' Sometimes, such intentions are abandoned. Sometimes, they aren't. For Sellars, an intention "whose time has come" is a volition. Brandom prefers to talk of "prior intentions" and "intentions in action," terms introduced by John Searle.[27] Intentions in action are essentially Sellarsian volitions; prior intentions are Sellarsian intentions.

Intentions in action can grow out of prior intentions, but they need not. They can be formed exactly at the time of action. Brandom cites this passage from Searle:

> Suppose I am sitting in a chair reflecting on a philosophical problem, and I suddenly get up and start pacing about the room. My getting up and pacing about are clearly intentional actions, but in order to do them I do not need to form an intention to do them prior to doing them. I don't in any sense have to plan to get up and pace about. Like many of the things one does, I just do these actions; I just act. (Searle, 1983, p. 85)

This leads Brandom to hold that intentional actions either result from or *just are* "acknowledgements of practical commitments," that is, intentions. So, an intentional action can *result from* a prior intention, an intention formed in advance of the behavior and which causes the behavior, but an intentional action itself can also *be* an intention, an intention in action. The idea here is that the action itself is an "acknowledgement of a practical commitment." For Brandom, acknowledging a commitment is doing anything that would make it appropriate to attribute that commitment (MIE, p. 257). In Searle's example, he acknowledges a commitment to get up and pace about *because* in getting up and pacing about, he makes it appropriate for us to attribute that commitment to him, all else being equal.

That marks a difference between Brandom's view and Sellars's view. On Sellars's view, volitions precede, cause, and explain each intentional action. On Brandom's view, that's not always so. An intention can be the action itself. An intentional action isn't always a behavior that results from an intention; rather, sometimes an intentional action is itself a behavior that constitutes an "acknowledgement of a practical commitment," the formation of the intention, an intention in action. We'll see shortly that McDowell questions whether Brandom is really entitled to that view.

2.3. McDowell

McDowell agrees with Sellars and Brandom that we should treat action and experience in parallel.[28] However, he disagrees with them about how to do that. Just as he disagrees with their conceptions of experience, so too he disagrees with their conceptions of action. Let's look first at his view, and then turn to his objection to Sellars and Brandom.

McDowell intends his conception of intentional action to be structurally similar to his conception of experience.[29] Thus, he thinks that "rationality can be *in* bodily activity as opposed to behind it" (SRIA, p. 17).[30] McDowell's big idea is that actions themselves embody conceptual capacities. They are not merely (non-conceptual) bodily movements that result from conceptual happenings (thinking). That idea parallels his view about experience: experiences themselves are conceptual; they are not merely non-conceptual happenings that result in conceptual happenings.

And McDowell's reasoning in favor of his big idea about action also parallels his reasoning in favor of his view of experience. In brief, just as our beliefs must be rationally answerable to our experiences, so too our actions must be rationally answerable to our intentions.

Let's go slower through that parallel. Remember that McDowell holds that the right view of experience must allow us to see how our thinking is "answerable to the world." That is, it must allow us to see how our thinking is genuinely about the world. His primary concern is not to show how experience functions as a regress-stopping foundation of knowledge. Put another way, he is not mainly concerned with how we get a certain kind of answer from the world, but with how we can be answerable to the world at all.

In *Mind and World*, McDowell develops his view of experience in relation to a pair of mistaken views of experience: appeals to the Given and Coherentism. An appeal to the (non-conceptual) Given holds that an experience is something other than another piece of thinking but also something to which a piece of thinking can answer. It is untenable because in holding that experience is not conceptual at all, it keeps experience from being the kind of thing that our thinking can answer to. Coherentism also holds that experiences are not conceptual, but it adds that they need not be. Instead, experiences need only to causally constrain one's thinking. Coherentism is untenable because mere causal constraint is not rational answerability; it doesn't allow our thoughts to genuinely answer to experience; it allows our thoughts to be merely caused by experiences.

For McDowell, the basic resolution is clear: to resist both of those views, we must reject their common assumption; we should hold that experience itself is conceptual.

With intentional action, McDowell thinks that the important question is: How can our actions rationally answer to our intentions?[31] That is, the big issue in thinking about intentional action is how some movements of our bodies can count as the *fulfillment* or *non-fulfillment* of an intention. For instance, when Mark intends to eat a tomato, and in turn reaches for it, grasps it, and brings it to his mouth, he is fulfilling that intention. Those movements are answerable to Mark's intention. They happen to answer it in the affirmative. Other movements would not constitute an "affirmative" answer, such as reaching for the apple, but they would nevertheless be answerable to Mark's intention; they would constitute a negative answer;

they would fail to fulfill his intention. So, McDowell is not especially concerned with how some movements constitute an "affirmative" answer to an intention, but with how they can answer an intention at all, even in the "negative." (HP essentially overlooks that issue.)

Although McDowell himself does not make this point, we should expect there to be views of intentional action that are structurally similar to an appeal to the Given and to Coherentism. A view that is structurally similar to the (non-conceptual) Given would hold that actions are not conceptual, but they are nevertheless rationally answerable to our intentions. A view that is structurally similar to Coherentism would also hold that actions are not conceptual, but maintain nevertheless that it is enough for our actions to be caused by our intentions.[32]

And we should expect McDowell to have an objection to those views that is structurally similar to his objection to the Given and Coherentism. Something like this: both views do not permit actions to be the kind of thing that can genuinely answer to an intention. They both assume that actions themselves are non-conceptual.

As with his view of experience, McDowell's basic resolution should be clear: to resist both of those views, we must reject their common assumption; we should hold that actions themselves are conceptual. That is the key to seeing how our actions can be rationally answerable to our intentions.

McDowell thinks that his view is appealing for two basic reasons. First, it rejects "a familiar picture according to which a person's mind occupies a more or less mysterious inner realm, concealed from the view of others" (McDowell, SRIA, p. 17). Second, it rejects "the tendency to distance a person's body from the mind that is the seat of her rationality" (McDowell, SRIA, p. 17).[33] In McDowell's view, a person's mind—indeed, a person herself—can be directly on display in her actions.

McDowell develops his view by focusing on the idea of an intention in action. His strategy is to make his view plausible by discussing what such a thing would be, what it would be for something conceptual to be "in action."

Like Searle and Brandom, he holds that intentions in action contrast with prior intentions, or intentions for the future. Like Brandom, he holds that prior intentions can become intentions in action.[34] And, of course, intentions in action can arise on the spur of the moment.

For McDowell the key question is: What is the content of an intention in action?

He proposes that the content of an intention in action has the form 'I am doing such-and-such' (McDowell, WCIA, p. 417).

To make his case, he questions Brandom's claim that Sellarsian volitions just are intentions in action. Recall that Sellars holds that volitions have the form 'I shall do such-and-such now.' For McDowell, the 'now' suggests that a volition would be the kind of thing that one would have only immediately before one began acting, or perhaps just as one began acting. Yet

McDowell contends that an intention in action should be in action for the duration of that action (WCIA, p. 416).[35] For instance, Mark's intention in action when eating the tomato should be true of that action for the duration of the eating. Throughout the eating of the tomato, he intends to eat the tomato. So, Brandom appears to be equating Sellarsian volitions with intentions in action. Since McDowell thinks Sellarsian volitions can only mark the beginning of an action, he holds that they can at best mark the *onset* of an intention in action; they cannot *be* intentions in action.

More positively, McDowell holds that the content of an intention in action must be the kind of thing that can be true of what one is doing (WCIA, pp. 428–30). He reasons as follows. Actors can know what they are doing. Following Aquinas and Anscombe, McDowell calls that "practical knowledge." Now, however the actor comes by that knowledge, for it to qualify as *knowledge*, it must be the kind of thing that can be true of what one is doing. For instance, Mark's practical knowledge of what he is doing should just be a first-person counterpart of what someone else would know in observing Mark eat the tomato. The actor and the observer should count as knowing the same objective fact from different perspectives. Someone who observes Mark eating the tomato would know that he is eating the tomato; the observer's knowledge would have the form 'He is doing such-and-such.' The first-person counterpart of that is 'I am doing such-and-such.' That should be the form of one's practical knowledge. Since McDowell also holds that the content of one's intention in action should be identical to the content of one's practical knowledge when one's intention succeeds (WCIA, p. 417), the form of an intention in action must also be 'I am doing such-and-such.'

What about cases in which you intend to be doing such-and-such—you are trying to do it, say—but you are failing at it? In those cases, it would seem that you cannot count as *knowing* something with the form 'I am doing such-and-such,' for in those cases, you are not really doing such-and-such. You cannot know what isn't so. In those cases, what is the content of one's intention?

McDowell holds that in those cases, the content of your intention has precisely the same form that it does when you fulfill your intention. For him, when you fail to fulfill an intention in action, what you say in expressing that intention should be false. For although your intention in action will still be your intention even as you fail to fulfill it, what you say in expressing it—saying what you are doing—should be false on those occasions. On those occasions, you do not know that you are doing such-and-such, for you are not doing such-and-such. At best, you might know that you *intend* to be doing such-and-such.[36]

Summing up, McDowell thinks that intentional actions themselves are conceptual, not simply the result of something conceptual. For him, we can see the appeal of that idea by thinking about intentions in action, intentions being acted out. When all goes well in an intentional action, one has direct knowledge of what one is doing, and what one knows is true of what one is doing at that time. Thus, McDowell holds that the form of an intention in action is 'I am doing such-and-such.' When things don't go well, one's knowledge might be restricted to what one intends to be doing, but is failing to accomplish.

With these basics in place, we can consider McDowell's objection to Sellars's and Brandom's views of intentional action. He alleges that both of them do not let action itself be properly conceptual.

On Sellars's view, as we have seen, intentional actions are "language exits." That means that they are exits from the conceptual; they are non-conceptual responses to conceptual stimuli. But, then, McDowell points out, the action itself is not something conceptual, only a response to something conceptual (PI, p. 121). McDowell thus seems to be right that Sellars doesn't make room for the idea that intentional action itself can be conceptual.[37]

The situation with Brandom is more complex. Recall that Brandom holds that an intentional action can either *be* or *result from* an "acknowledgment of a practical commitment," an intention. Actions that result from prior intentions are actions that merely result from an acknowledgement of a practical commitment. Those sorts of actions would not be conceptual, but only responses to something conceptual. Actions that arise "on the spur of the moment" don't result from such an acknowledgement, but are supposed to be such acknowledgements themselves. Those sorts of actions presumably would be conceptual. Thus, as McDowell himself notes, only part of Brandom's view seems to be subject to McDowell's objection.

McDowell thinks that this asymmetry itself is peculiar. McDowell holds that "If we use the concept of intention in action at all, we must recognize intention in action whenever there is intentional action, whether the action is execution of what used to be a prior intention or not" (PI, p. 126). That is, there are intentions in action even in cases where the action arises from a prior intention. If that's true, then Brandom should hold that even in those cases, the action itself is an acknowledgement of a practical commitment. If Brandom were to modify his view in that way, he would seem to avert McDowell's objection.

But McDowell alleges further that in Brandom's view even cases of "spur of the moment" action aren't really conceptual; they remain only responses to something conceptual. To make his case, McDowell points to Brandom's emphasis on the "two-ply" structure of intentional action. On Brandom's view, an intentional action is an activation of a reliable disposition to respond differentially to something, to a practical, conceptually articulated commitment. Even actions that arise "on the spur of the moment" must have that two-ply structure; the action must be a *response to* something conceptually articulated. It might not be a response to a commitment formed much earlier, but it nevertheless must be a *response to* a commitment; otherwise, it's not an intentional action on Brandom's view. Thus, McDowell thinks that Brandom treats intentional action as behavior that is a response to something conceptual, not something conceptual itself.[38]

Brandom denies the charge (Reply to Rowland Stout, 2010). He grants that even "spur of the moment" actions are responses to practical commitments. But he also holds that those responses themselves are exercises of a rational and conceptual capacity (Reply to Rowland Stout, 2010, p. 329). That's what they must be for them to count as a rational response to the practical commitment (the intention), rather than something that is merely caused by it. The behavior is supposed to rationally answer the intention; it is supposed to be a "making true" of precisely what one has committed to "make true." The behavior cannot serve as a rational and thus conceptually articulated answer unless it is conceptual.

Who is right? This much is clear. McDowell and Brandom agree that actions themselves should be conceptual. Brandom thinks his account allows for that; McDowell doesn't. They disagree as to whether Brandom's two-ply conception of intentional actions allows actions themselves to be conceptual.

2.4. Concepts in Action?

The bigger question is whether McDowell and Brandom are right in their shared view that actions themselves *should* be conceptual. Such a view is highly unorthodox in contemporary philosophy of action.

It can seem implausible for a couple reasons. A more common view is that only *some* intentional actions, namely speech acts, are conceptual. On that view, what distinguishes speech acts from other intentional actions is that they are conceptually structured, whereas non-speech acts are not. Thus, claiming that all intentional actions are conceptual would leave us needing a way to distinguish speech acts from non-speech acts. Moreover, it can seem just *weird* to hold that intentional actions themselves are conceptual. Do they "say" or "mean" something? Are they linguistic? We sometimes say that a gesture is "meaningful" because, for instance, it makes someone feel a certain way. But that is not the same as holding that a non-verbal gesture itself "speaks" or is "linguistic." For that would seem to imply that the gesture itself has something like sentential structure, something with a subject and verb.[39]

Can those challenges be met? Perhaps. There could be other ways of distinguishing speech acts from other intentional actions. For instance, one might think that speech acts tend to be directed at an audience (if only the speaker herself); or one might think that speech acts are explicit in a way that other intentional actions are not, wearing their conceptual structure on their sleeves. And the charge of "weirdness" might be exaggerated. We don't simply think that a gesture can be "meaningful" because it makes someone feel a certain way. We also think that a gesture, like a gentle pat on the back, can express that person's sympathy. That begins to suggest that we think our non-verbal acts themselves can express our thoughts—not in the sense that they simply result from something we think, but in the sense that they embody our thinking itself. Moreover, if thoughts can be expressed by making noise with the mouth and throat, or by configuring the hands, fingers, and arms in certain positions, why can't they be expressed or "embodied" in other ways? Of course, a whole lot more can be said on these issues. What's important to see is that McDowell and Brandom are not obviously wrong.

For McDowell and Brandom, the big idea is to see thought in behavior itself, making it rationally accountable to things we believe and intend, and available for others to engage directly. In that sort of picture, it would be apt to speak not of mind *and* world, but of mind *in* world.[40]

CONCLUSION

In this chapter, our goal was to consider the Pittsburgh School's views of intentional action. We saw that one of the biggest issues in philosophical reflection on action is what makes a bit of behavior count as intentional, as a rational response to a person's deliberations about what to do. Historically, philosophers have faced that challenge by talking of "the will." One way of thinking of the will—the Hobbesian Picture—leaves both the will and intentional action looking mysterious. As with the Lockean Picture of belief, the Hobbesian Picture leaves us wondering how the will does what it does and how it can be accessible to people other than the actor herself. Sellars, Brandom, and McDowell reject that picture, aiming still to preserve the basic idea of the will. They all agree that intentional action should be seen as analogous to perception. In both perception and intentional action, we rationally engage the world. In perception, the world rationally influences us; our thinking answers to the world. In intentional action, we rationally influence the world; the world answers to our thinking. The big idea is to demystify the mind by refusing to see it as something that merely lies behind behavior, available only really to the agent herself. They disagree about what exactly that requires.

Concluding Suggestions

My main aim in this book has been to introduce you to the views of the Pittsburgh School.

In brief, they hold that intentionality cannot be assimilated to being merely affected by things, for genuine thinking requires the ability to reason, which in turn requires responsiveness to norms of reasoning; the very contents of what one thinks and says are constituted by such norms; the holistic character of thinking rules out the existence of anything that can both be known independently of everything else and underwrite the rest of one's knowledge; there is no foundation of knowledge, in that sense; but there needn't be either, for knowledge doesn't suffer from a vicious regress; because intentional action requires the capacity for genuine thinking, it too requires initiation into "the space of reasons;" initiation into that space comes with initiation into natural languages; thus, we learn to think, know, and act intentionally through such initiation.

Now that you have seen the views of the School as a whole, you can look more closely at the details and begin assessing the viability of those views. Here at the end of the book I want to provide some suggestions for doing that. In each chapter, I identify contested issues. Some of those issues are contested mainly between members of the School; other issues are contested between the School and philosophers who don't share the School's commitments. Let me highlight a few issues of both sorts, starting with issues dividing Sellars, Brandom, and McDowell.

In Chapter 1, we saw that they all agree: experience is not the foundation of knowledge; one must avoid treating experience as "the Given"—something that is epistemically independent and efficacious; yet experience can support further claims and thoughts. In Chapter 5 we saw that they disagree about how to work out that last idea, about what experience must be such that it can support claims and thoughts, and yet not be a form of the Given. Must experience itself be conceptual? Is there some other way to avoid both the Given and the regress into skepticism?

That question points to a "parallel" question about action. They all agree that intentional actions must be rationally supportable by one's thinking.

But must intentional actions themselves be conceptual? The big issue here is this: What is the precise place of concepts in human rational activity?

In Chapter 2 we saw that Sellars, Brandom, and McDowell agree that genuine thinking and speaking—genuine use of concepts and words—require responsiveness to norms of reasoning. Yet, as we saw in Chapter 3, they disagree about how to understand that responsiveness. Responding to a rule is not merely being causally compelled to do something. And yet responding to a rule also need not involve—indeed, on pain of a regress, it *cannot* always involve—consulting some explicit interpretation of the rule. Are there "norms implicit in practice" that aren't mere regularities in one's behavior (as Brandom holds)? Can we treat "just seeing" what a rule requires as genuinely intelligent behavior rather than mere causal compulsion (as McDowell holds)?

In Chapter 2 we also saw that Sellars, Brandom, and McDowell agree that the meaning of our words and the contents of our thoughts are constituted by norms of reasoning. Sellars and Brandom think that requires an alternative to traditional "relational" and "representational" theories of linguistic meaning. Sellars takes this to require clarification of the distinctive role of "meaning" talk, as well as a theory of the inferential roles of words in the language. Brandom agrees, and adopts the further task of explaining how meaning can be understood as arising out of a certain sort of norm-governed social practice, a "game of giving and asking for reasons." McDowell doubts whether this more "full-blooded" goal is necessary.

That leads us to a deeper divide that I have not explored in this book. In Chapters 3 and 4, we saw that McDowell has a distinctive view of the task of philosophy, his so-called quietism, a view that Sellars and Brandom do not share. Roughly, McDowell thinks that the main task of good philosophy should be to undermine putative philosophical problems concerning features of everyday human existence, such as whether there really are any norms, or what makes words meaningful, or how we know the world; doing so does not bring with it a burden to advance a positive account of these things. Sellars and Brandom disagree with him. McDowell seems to think that our ordinary conception of ourselves has a privileged place in philosophy; it cannot be dislodged by philosophy. Sellars, however, worries that our ordinary conception of ourselves—what he calls "the manifest image of man"—is threatened by "the scientific image of man," a comprehensive world-view that seems to have no room for whole persons, thoughts, feelings, or norms.[1] For Sellars, the primary task of philosophy is to reconcile these two images.[2] That raises several questions. What is the place of "the manifest image" in philosophy? Could philosophical reflection force us to revise it? More generally, what is the aim of philosophy?

Thus, Sellars, Brandom, and McDowell agree on certain big ideas concerning experience, concepts, norms, and meaning, but they disagree on how to work out those ideas. And despite their agreement on those big ideas, they don't agree entirely on the aims of good philosophy.

Now, disagreement about those big ideas is primarily what distinguishes the Pittsburgh School from other philosophers. Let me highlight a few of the disputes.

The idea that the Given is a myth guides the Pittsburgh School. Many other philosophers deny that the Given is a myth.[3] Part of the issue here is merely verbal, centering on the term "the Given." Many philosophers will concede that, understood one way, the Given is surely a myth, that there is no such thing; understood another way, those same philosophers will hold that there must be a "given." Indeed, even the Pittsburgh School holds that some talk of a "given" is innocuous (e.g., EPM, §1). The more substantive dispute concerns whether certain sorts of appeal are problematic; that is, whether certain sorts of appeal constitute an appeal to the Given in a problematic sense of that term.

One thing that distinguishes the Pittsburgh School from others is the breadth of their conception of the Given. They hold that the Given is anything that is supposed to be both epistemically efficacious and independent. Understood thus, they think it can take many unobvious forms, and is always problematic. Thus, they are inclined to find some views problematic that others don't. In particular, the Pittsburgh School tends to be suspicious of most forms of epistemological foundationalism. Of course, there are sophisticated defenders of that view.[4] Those philosophers must hold either that they are not committed to the Given (in the Pittsburgh sense of the term) or that if they are so committed, the Given is not problematic. Two questions stand out. Can anything be both epistemically efficacious and independent? If not, can foundationalism avoid appealing to something that is both epistemically efficacious and independent?

Norms—especially norms of reasoning—are central to the Pittsburgh School's conception of human rational engagement with the world. Moreover, they hold that norms cannot be understood in non-normative terms. For instance, what *should* or *should not* happen cannot be understood simply in terms of what has happened or will happen or is likely to happen. However, many philosophers think that norms can be understood in non-normative terms. Indeed, some philosophers think that norms must be so understood, if we want to think of ourselves as fully natural (rather than super-natural) creatures. These philosophers hold that there is a tension between the idea of norms and the idea that everything is, in some sense, part of nature, a certain form of "naturalism."[5] As we just noted, norms don't seem to be settled simply by what has happened or will happen or is likely to happen. And yet nature seems to be just that: the sum of facts about what has happened (and what will happen or is likely to happen, given the laws of nature). How can norms "outstrip" nature in that way?

Although I did not focus on that issue in this book, Sellars and McDowell have been responsive to it. Sellars thinks that the right response is to develop a "stereoscopic" vision of humans, one that reconciles "the manifest image" with "the scientific image," one that recognizes the irreducibility of norms, and yet also treats humans as fully natural creatures. McDowell thinks the right response is to reject impoverished conceptions of nature that force us to think that norms are somehow not part of the natural world.[6] Both proposals are intuitively appealing, but the big question is whether the details work.[7]

The relation between thought and language is a third big issue separating the Pittsburgh School from others. As we saw in Chapter 2, the School espouses the widely shared idea that language is a model for at least a certain kind of thinking, discursive thinking. However, the School also espouses a much more contentious thesis: that such thinking depends, in some way, on the ability to speak a language. The rough idea is that one doesn't have concepts unless and until one learns to speak a natural language. That implies that sub-linguistic animals are incapable of discursive or conceptual thought. Many philosophers and cognitive scientists find that deeply implausible. It can seem just obvious that sub-linguistic creatures are capable of such thought. Of course, as we saw, Sellars, Brandom, and McDowell are aware of that implication, and have things to say about it.[8] Adjudicating that dispute requires getting clearer about what one should count as having a concept and why.[9] The challenge here is to acknowledge the apparent intelligence of sub-linguistic animals without assimilating it entirely to the reasoning of normal adult humans.

Looking further into these issues should help you assess how well the views of the Pittsburgh School hang together.

Notes

NOTES TO THE INTRODUCTION

1. How influential are their views? Some indication is given by the honors they have received. All have presented the prestigious Locke Lectures at Oxford. Sellars gave the John Dewey Lectures and the Paul Carus Lectures. McDowell and Brandom have given the Woodbridge Lectures. Both Brandom and McDowell have recently received the Andrew Mellon Foundation's Distinguished Achievement Award, including a grant of $1.5 million. That grant is one of the largest available to humanistic scholars. The Award has been given to three people each year since 2001. Of the thirty recipients, seven have been professors of philosophy, including Brandom and McDowell.
2. For instance: (Castaneda, 1975), (Delaney, Loux, Gutting, & Solomon, 1977), (Pitt, 1978), (Pitt, 1981), (Seibt, 1990), (Smith N., 2002), (Thornton, 2004), (de Gaynesford, 2004), (Knell, 2004), (deVries, 2005), (Wolf & Lance, 2006), (Gaskin, 2006), (Macdonald & Macdonald, 2006), (O'Shea, 2007), (Wanderer, 2008), (Weiss & Wanderer, 2010).
3. (Lance, 2008) is an insightful presentation of Sellars, Brandom, McDowell, and others under the heading "neo-Sellarsian philosophy." (Redding, 2007) treats Sellars, Brandom, and McDowell together, as "analytic neo-Hegelians."
4. "Empiricism and the Philosophy of Mind," Sellars's most famous work, was originally presented as a set of lectures titled "The Myth of the Given."

NOTES TO CHAPTER 1

1. This sort of idea is discussed in Plato's *Theaetetus*. It's not clear whether Plato himself endorses it. It is widely held that the "standard analysis" of knowledge is undermined by (Gettier, 1963). There is an enormous literature on the issue. See, e.g., (Goldman, 1967), (Lehrer & Paxson, 1969), (Dretske, 1971), and (Nozick, 1981).
2. That is one of the topics of dispute in the discussion emanating from (Gettier, 1963).
3. (Klein, 1999) holds that although there is an infinite regress, it is not vicious; so, according to him, there is knowledge despite the infinite regress.
4. For mentions of the regress and the idea of a foundation, see: (EPM, §32), (Sellars, 1989, pp. 7–10), (Brandom, MIE, 1994, p. 177), (Brandom, SG, p. 124), (McDowell, MW, 1994, pp. xiii–xiv), (McDowell, EI, 2009, pp. 243–4). Williams consistently connects the Given with the regress and Foundationalism; see, e.g., (Williams, 1977/1999), (Williams, 1996), and (Williams, 2001).

5. This dialectical situation is commonly known as the Regress Argument for Foundationalism. See, for instance, (Fumerton, 2010).
6. Williams cites (Fogelin, 1994). See also (Sextus Empiricus, 1967).
7. Some philosophers contend that knowledge by testimony or "hearsay" does not involve this sort of reasoning or inferring. See, e.g., (McDowell, Knowledge by Hearsay, 1998).
8. The underlying ideas here are contentious. We will return to them in Chapter 5.
9. In her review of (deVries & Triplett, 2000), Danielle Macbeth disputes their claim that Sellars thinks the Given is always enlisted to play a foundational role (Macbeth, 2002).
10. For a similar characterization, see (deVries & Triplett, 2000, p. xix).
11. And that knowledge depends on what is learned by "the natural light," which Descartes takes as given. Thanks to Willem deVries for the clarification.
12. Cited in (deVries & Triplett, 2000).
13. For some discussion of this sort of view, see (EPM, §26), (Sellars, BLM, §122-8), and (Sellars, FMPP, pp. 11–12).
14. For discussion of this problem, see (EPM, §§2–10). For further discussion from Sellars on the significance of 'as' see (ME, Ch. 4).
15. Sellars presents this kind of challenge in (EPM, §§2–7).
16. See, for instance, (e.g., (Price, 1932))
17. (Sellars, P) and (Williams, 1996) make cases for thinking that such approaches to empirical knowledge are hopeless.
18. This type of argument is developed and scrutinized in (Williams, 1996).
19. Sellars develops this type of objection (EPM, §§10–20).
20. For a different and influential conception of experience that still appeals to something given, see (Lewis, 1929/1956). Lewis talks of the "the given element in experience," which the mind receives from the world to organize.
21. A few scholars have identified a correlation between EPM and the beginning of Hegel's *Phenomenology of Spirit*. On the connection between Sellars and Hegel more generally, see (deVries, 1988), (Pinkard, 2007), (Redding, 2007), (deVries, 2008), (Redding, 2010), and (Redding, 2011).
22. See (deVries & Triplett, 2000) for a similar interpretation.
23. McDowell addresses this in his discussion of the "endogenous" Given (pp. 135-6). There he connects the Given with (Quine, 1956).
24. (Brandom, TP, 2002, p. 525)
25. They trace that idea to Kant. The idea that concepts essentially play a role in judgments is shared by many other contemporary philosophers and cognitive scientists. Fodor is one prominent, contemporary theorist who rejects that conception of concepts, e.g., (Fodor, 2004).
26. See, for instance, (pp. 11–12).
27. Making correct inferences is one way of exhibiting knowledge of inferential norms. One exhibits explicit awareness of the norms by citing them in support of one's reasoning. One might also exhibit such awareness by challenging inferences that do not conform to those norms.
28. The claim here is not that one must be able to make every correct inference to and from that judgment. It is more modest than that. One must be capable of making at least some correct inferences to and from that judgment. Which specific inferential relations matter? Which ones must one know? The quick answer: the inferential relations that constitute the meaning of that particular judgment! But then the question is: which ones are those? For statements of this worry see (Fodor & Lepore, 2001), (Fodor & Lepore, 2007).
29. See (Brandom, 1994, p. 220, ch.4.III passim) and (pp. 48, 109). (Brandom, No Experience Necessary, pp. 10–11) and (Brandom, Conceptual Content and Discursive Practice, pp. 17–8).

30. For a case in favor of parrot intelligence, see (Pepperberg, 1999).
31. McDowell claims that this sort of thing "offers exculpations where we wanted justifications" (1994, p. 8).
32. This stage of the argument corresponds with Sellars's allegation in EPM §3 that some empiricists want foundational knowledge to be both of a fact and of a particular: something both having and lacking conceptual structure.
33. See, for instance, (Heck, 2000) and Heck (2007).
34. Many philosophers do not accept the arguments against the Given. For instance: (Chisholm, 1966), (Fales, 1996), (Sosa, 1997), (Bonevac, 2002), and (Alston, 2002).
35. That there is a difference in kind between attributions of cognitive states (claims like 'S knows that P') and attributions of other states is a career-long theme in Sellars's work. For early instances, see (ENWW) and (Pure Pragmatics and Epistemology, 1947).
36. "Endorse" is the term used by Sellars (EPM, §§16–16bis).
37. This idea is connected with an important and controversial proposal in meta-ethics, known as expressivism. See, for instance, (Ayer, 1936), (Stevenson, 1937), (Hare, 1952), (Gibbard, 1990), (Blackburn, 1993), (Schroeder, 2008). One of the main challenges to this view is presented in (Geach, 1960) and (Geach, 1965).
38. McDowell objects to Sellars's contrasting the "logical space of reasons" with the space of "empirical description" (McDowell, MW, 1994, pp. xiv–xvi). Nevertheless, McDowell does not reject the normative character of epistemic attributions, or the normative character of epistemic states (broadly construed to include states other than knowing). For instance, he says "knowledge is a normative status" (McDowell, MW, 1994, p. 80n12).
39. Such permission or authority typically comes with certain responsibilities. The interaction of authority and responsibility is central to Brandom's philosophy of language (see MIE) and his related conception of reason (see RIP).
40. See also (Sellars, PPPW, p. 230), (Sellars, Abtract Entities, p. 634), and (Sellars, SM, p. 176).
41. For seminal statements of "naturalized" (non-normative) epistemology, see (Quine W., 1969) and (Goldman, 1979).
42. See, for instance, (Sellars, PSIM), (Sellars, SM, ch. 7), (Brandom, MIE, 1994, pp. 124–30), (Brandom, AR, 2000, pp. 69–76), (Kukla, 2000), (Rouse, 2003), (McDowell, Towards a Reading of Hegel on Action in the 'Reason' Chapter of the Phenomenology, 2009), (Brandom, 2009, ch. 2), and (Kukla & Lance, 2009, ch. 7).
43. In a classical conception of democracy, the majority is the arbiter of rightness. But what legitimates majority rule? It cannot be the majority, for that would be circular.
44. Sellars talks of "self-authenticating" episodes in (EPM, §§34, 38).

NOTES TO CHAPTER 2

1. (Wanderer, 2008) and (de Gaynesford, 2004) also use Locke in this way.
2. For instance, (Hobbes, 1651/2009), (Bloom, 2002), and (Prinz, 2002).
3. For a nice statement of the point, see (Haugeland, 1997, p. 5).
4. The expression comes from (Price, 1932).
5. It can be useful to distinguish the "content" of a thought from its "target." I might think that New York is too crowded; you might think New York is a great place to see a good musical. The contents of our thoughts differ, but they share a target: New York. Content and target are not the same thing.

Expressions like "what a thought is about" are ambiguous between content and target. See (Cummins, 1996).

6. The word 'intentionality' derives from medieval discussions of thought. It regained currency because of (Brentano, 1973).

7. In his second meditation, Descartes writes, "But what then am I? A thing that thinks. What is that? A thing that doubts, understands, affirms, denies, is willing, is unwilling, and also imagines and has sensory perceptions" (Descartes, 1996/1641, p. 19).

8. (Anscombe, 1957, §32).

9. There is a further dimension of evaluation. Such states might be based on more or less evidence, better or worse reasons.

10. For a challenge from within the Pittsburgh School, see the discussion of the "declarative fallacy" in (Kukla & Lance, 2009).

11. Of course, philosophers in the Pittsburgh School have explored other sorts of thought. For instance, (Sellars, TA), (Sellars, SM, ch. VII), (Sellars, 1976), (McDowell, Are Moral Requirements Hypothetical Imperatives?, 1998), (McDowell, MW, Lecture V), (Brandom, MIE, pp. 229–71), and (McDowell, BO).

12. For instance, (Fodor, 1998).

13. Sellars calls this idea "concept empiricism" in (ME, p. 195).

14. (Geach, 1957) provides a fuller characterization of abstractionism. McDowell often cites Geach on this topic, e.g., (MW, pp. 7, 20). Brandom discusses abstractionism in Chapter 8 of (RP).

15. This way of thinking is exemplified in the work of Grice (1989) and Searle (1983) and their intellectual heirs.

16. Sellars finds this way of thinking already in Aristotle (Aristotelian Philosophies of Mind, 1949, p. 561)

17. That way of thinking about thought and language is captured nicely in a remark from Augustine (Augustine, Confessions, I.8) memorably quoted in Wittgenstein's *Philosophical Investigations* (p. §1):

When they (my elders) named some object, and accordingly moved towards something, I saw this and I grasped that the thing was called by the sound they uttered when they meant to point it out. Their intention was shown by their bodily movements, as it were the natural language of all peoples; the expression of the face, the play of the eyes, the movement of other parts of the body, and the tone of the voice which expresses our state of mind in seeking, having, rejecting, or avoiding something. Thus, as I heard words repeatedly used in their proper places in various sentences, I gradually learnt to understand what objects they signified; and after I had trained my mouth to form these signs, I used them to express my own desires. (Augustine, Confessions, I.8)

For mentions of Augustine, see (Sellars, EPM, §30), (McDowell, MI, 2008), (McDowell, Sellars's Thomism), and (Brandom, RP, ch.8).

18. For other critical discussion, see, e.g., (Geach, 1957) and (Gauker, 1994)—Gauker was a student of Sellars.

19. See, for instance, (Sellars, ME, pp. 195–228).

20. (Fodor, 1975) is a seminal statement of the idea that there is a "language of thought."

21. In other words, this sort of behaviorism held that mental states or episodes could be *defined* in behavioral terms. This sort of view is expressed in (Ryle, 1949/1984).

22. A version is defended in (Skinner, 1953) and (Skinner, 1957).

23. "Methodological" behaviorism is yet a different view. It holds that the mind ought to be studied by studying behavior; that is the proper method of psychology. See, e.g., (Watson, 1930). Sellars appeals to it in (EPM, §53).

24. See especially (Chomsky, 1959).

25. Sellars mentions this idea from Plato in (Sellars, LTC); McDowell mentions it in (MW, p. 165). They recognize its importance for Thomism, e.g., (Sellars, Being and Being Known) and (McDowell, Sellars's Thomism).

26. (Geach, 1957), (Dummett, 1973/1981), and (Dummett, 1996) also maintain that language is conceptually prior to thought. For a nice summary of some objections, see (Peacocke, 1998). While Sellars thinks that language is conceptually prior to thought (Sellars & Chisholm, 1957), other philosophers in the Pittsburgh School accept a somewhat weaker thesis: they are conceptually coeval. They see Davidson as an ally, e.g., (Davidson, 2001).

27. Thus, Richard Rorty claims that Sellars "may have been the first philosopher to insist that 'mind' is a hypostatization of language" (Rorty, 1997, p. 7).

28. Thus, while this theory shares something with a purely behaviorist conception of the mind, it is not such a conception, for thoughts are not merely dispositions to speak or act.

29. For Brandom, an assertion is the fundamental "move" in the game of giving and asking for reasons, for it is the most basic act that can be offered as or stand in need of a reason. The priority of assertion has recently been questioned by Kukla and Lance (2009, p.11; chs. 2, 6, 7).

30. Brandom attributes to Sellars both the idea of a game of giving and asking for reasons and that very phrase (SG, 123). While the idea might come from Sellars, I have not seen him use the phrase in print.

31. LP errs in making both acts and contents of belief implausibly private, inaccessible to others.

32. You might think the challenge could be avoided by simply denying that there are rational relations between assertion and perception and action. One could maintain instead that there are only causal relations. Perception could cause assertion, but not rationally support it; judgment or assertion could cause non-verbal action, but not rationally support it. That move is a central target of *Mind and World*. It is subject to clear counterexamples. For instance, suppose that Joan goes to the refrigerator. If you were to ask her why she went to the refrigerator, she might respond, 'I wanted some orange juice and thought that there was some in the fridge.' Not only does she offer a cause of her behavior, she also cites a thought with a content that supports her behavior. That is a common sort of reason-giving explanation.

33. Thus, Brandom talks about developing a "normative pragmatics" in *Making It Explicit*. Pragmatics, broadly construed, concerns the use of language. A normative pragmatics, then, focuses on norms of use.

34. For the phrase, see (Rosenberg, 1974), (O'Shea, 2007), (Lance, 2008), and (Brandom, RP, p. 12); for illustrations of it, see also (Sellars, SRLG), (Sellars, Abstract Entities, 1963), (Macbeth, 1994) and (Haugeland, Having Thought, 1998).

35. Generally speaking, one can be a functionalist about mental states, without being a functionalist about the content of those states. See, for instance, (Fodor, 1987).

36. Brandom: "The sense in which we are compelled by the norms that matter for intentionality, norms dictating what we are under various circumstances obliged to believe and to do, is quite different from natural compulsion" (MIE, 31).

37. For discussion of the embodiment of functional roles in this framework, see (Sellars, Abstract Entities, 1963), (Haugeland, Mind Embodied and Embedded, 1998), (Lance, 1998), and (Lance, 2000)

38. (Macbeth, 1994) is an ingenious presentation of these ideas by analogy with the evolution of economies.

39. See, for instance, (Kukla & Lance, 2009, ch. 7). For a partial anticipation of these ideas, see the discussion of "telling" in (Sellars, FD).

40. For one prominent challenge to holism, see (Fodor & Lepore, 1993). See also (Fodor & Lepore, 2001), (Fodor & Lepore, 2007), and (Brandom, Reply to Fodor and Lepore, 2010).

41. Sellars later attached a footnote to that remark, which tempers it somewhat: "The argument can admit of a distinction between a rudimentary concept of 'green' . . . and a richer concept of 'green'. . . . The essential point is that even to have the more rudimentary concept presupposes having a battery of concepts" (deVries & Triplett, 2000, p. 226).

42. To use an expression from Brandom, LP has a "one-sided" conception of the contents of belief (AR, p. 64). Brandom might allege further that LP has only mere "labeling" and not genuine belief in view (RP, p. 199).

43. For a different but sympathetic view, see (Gauker, 1994), which defends the claim that language is both conceptually and ontologically prior to thought.

44. In certain texts, it can be tempting to read Sellars as committing that mistake, e.g. EPM. Gauker, for instance, accuses Sellars of just that (p. 51). The issue arises clearly in the Sellars-Chisholm correspondence (Sellars & Chisholm, 1957). The same worry could be raised about Brandom, e.g., (Brandom, AR, pp. 5–6).

45. For a philosophical overview on animal cognition, see (Andrews, 2011). For an articulation and defense of the idea that the thinking of non-linguistic creatures is not, cannot and need not be "language-like," see (Bermudez, 2003).

46. See, for instance, (Sellars, Behaviorism, Language and Meaning, 1980) (Sellars, Mental Events, 1981), (Brandom, MIE, pp. 155, 142–3, 150–2), (Brandom, RP, pp. 205, 212), (McDowell, MW, pp. 108–26), (McDowell, Conceptual Capacities in Perception), and (McDowell, Avoiding the Myth of the Given, pp. 313–17).

47. The moniker 'psychological nominalism' suggests that the central tenet of the view is that "the psychological"—the mind—is not wholly real but exists in name only, which is not Sellars's intention, and for that reason it is misleading.

48. Wittgenstein makes a similar remark: "Augustine describes the learning of human language as if the child came into a strange country and did not understand the language of the country; that is, as if he already had a language, only not this one. Or again: as if the child could already think, only not yet speak. And 'think' would here mean something like 'talk to itself'" (1958, §32).

49. See also (Sellars, EAE, pp. 444–5). In later work, Sellars develops this thesis in connection with what he calls "verbal behaviorism" (Sellars, MFC).

50. For helpful discussion of the phrase as it is used by Sellars, see (deVries, 2005, pp. 183–91).

51. See, for instance, (SRLG, p. 327).

52. There are many places where this is emphasized. For some representative remarks, see (Sellars, SRLG), (Sellars, LRB), (McDowell, 1979), (McDowell, MW, Ch. 1), (Brandom, 1979), (Brandom, MIE, Ch. 1), (Haugeland, Truth and Rule-following, 1998), (Kukla & Lance, 2009).

53. I have relied on deVries's reconstruction here (2005, pp. 179–91).

54. For Sellars, these ideas suggest that thought has an "essentially social character." He writes, "[T]he essentially social character of conceptual thinking comes clearly to mind when we recognize that there is no thinking apart from common standards of correctness and relevance, which relate what I do think to what anyone ought to think. The contrast between 'I' and 'anyone' is essential to rational thought. . . . Conceptual thinking is not by accident that which is communicated to others, any more than the decision to move a chess piece is by accident that which finds an expression in a move on a board between two people" (PSIM, 16–7).

55. See, e.g., (MW, xi–xii).
56. McDowell intends this conception of recognizing reasons as such to exclude non-human animals, who might be said to count as reasoning in some other sense.
57. McDowell adds, "Initiation into a language is initiation into a going conception of the layout of the space of reasons" (MW, p. 184).
58. See (MIE, pp. xviii–xxi, 383), (AR, ch. 1), and (BSD).
59. See, for instance, (AR, p. 174).
60. (MIE, p. 153). Brandom says that "what he [Davidson] has really given us is not so much an argument as the form of one. Turning it into an actual argument requires . . . the rest of this work" (MIE, pp. 152–3, 599).
61. Summarizing this argumentative arc, Brandom writes, "The notion of objective truth conditions makes explicit what is implicit in our grasp of the possibility of mistaken belief and so of the distinction between what is *merely* held (true) and what is *correctly* held (true). It emerges only in the context of interpretation—that is, discursive scorekeeping—because that is the practical activity in which the commitments acknowledged (held true) by one interlocutor are compared and contrasted with those acknowledged (held true) by another, the scorekeeper who attributes the first set" (MIE, 599).
62. See Chapter 8 of (MIE) and Chapter 5 of (AR).
63. The sort of difference in perspective that is important to Brandom goes beyond merely having different names or descriptions for picking out objects. It crucially includes the different collateral commitments that different believers (or "scorekeepers") have. Thus, our case simplifies drastically.
64. For a similar sort of claim from a developmental psychologist, see (Tomasello, 1999). He writes, "human beings are the only animal species that conceptualizes the world in terms of different potential perspectives on one and the same entity" (Tomasello, 2008, p. 344).

NOTES TO CHAPTER 3

1. To ease exposition, I will focus on rules for the use of words. Similar points can be made for the use of concepts. Throughout this chapter, it is important to bear in mind the main idea of the last chapter: philosophers in the Pittsburgh School think that concepts are not only analogous to terms of a language, but are also developed in the course of acquiring those terms.
2. For an attempt to situate the regress problem within a broader discussion of concepts, see §1.2 of (Margolis & Laurence, 2006).
3. As Brandom explains (MIE, 22), this regress has a connection with the one identified by Lewis Carroll in "What the Tortoise Said to Achilles." Carroll shows that it cannot be the case that all of the rules governing a piece of reasoning must be explicit premises in that piece of reasoning, on pain of an infinite regress. As Brandom puts the point, "One cannot express all the rules that govern inferences in a logical system in the form of propositionally explicit postulates within that system" (MIE, 22).
4. Consider what McDowell has to say: "[G]rasped meanings in particular give a normatively characterizable shape to the space of options in which behavior is undertaken" (MIWLP, 264). And: "The effect of the regress . . . is that we lose our entitlement to the idea that a grasped meaning imposes demands on a person's behavior . . ." (MIWLP, pp. 272–3).
5. In a related context, McDowell talks of "our lowest level conceptualizations" (OSPLA, p. 281) and "concepts that sit as closely as possible to [the ultimate grounds for judgments of experience]" (MW, p. 19).

6. (SRLG, §§7–8). Of Demands Sellars says, "they are entities of which the mind can take account before it is able to give them a verbal clothing" (SRLG, §7).
7. (SRLG, §10).
8. These considerations connect with concerns about the possibility of a so-called private language. For an introduction to the issue, see (Candlish & Wrisley, 2009).
9. Of this sort of proposal, McDowell writes, "The irresistible upshot of this is that we picture following a rule as the operation of a super-rigid yet . . . ethereal machine" (WFR, p. 230). He is commenting on the following remark from Wittgenstein: "What one wants to say is: 'Every sign is capable of interpretation; but the *meaning* mustn't be capable of interpretation. It is the last interpretation" (Blue Book, p. 34).
10. (McDowell, MW, pp. 18–23). DeVries holds that Sellars thinks something similar (2005, pp. 40, 46). In (EPM, §34), Sellars does indeed sketch a view that appeals to something like "Demands" and he explicitly identifies it as an instance of the Given.
11. This language pervades (McDowell, WFR, 1998).
12. E.g., (Brandom, MIE, 20) and (Sellars, SRLG, §12). McDowell calls a version of this idea 'platonism' (MIWLP, 273). For a helpful discussion of such platonism, see (Finkelstein, 2000).
13. Haugeland calls these kinds of rules "exhibited rules," since they are only exhibited by some phenomena; they do not "govern" such phenomena (Haugeland, Truth and Rule-Following, 1998).
14. (Brandom, MIE, p. 26)
15. This problem was made prominent by (Kripke, 1982). Both McDowell and Brandom rely on Kripke's work to develop their own views (WFR, pp. 226–8) (MIE, p. 28). The relevant passages in Wittgenstein's work include (PI, §§138–315). (Boghossian, 1989) is a nice overview of some of the relevant philosophical issues.
16. See (Brandom, MIE, p. 29) and (Sellars, SRLG, p. 323). A separate question is whether the appeal to dispositions avoids the gerrymandering problem. Kripke (1982, pp. 23–4) and Brandom (MIE, p. 28) think that it does not.
17. Some of their differences arise as a result of different interpretations of the problematic up to this point. Brandom takes himself to be developing ideas in Sellars, Wittgenstein, and McDowell. McDowell thinks that Brandom is misreading both Wittgenstein and McDowell's interpretation of Wittgenstein, and possibly Sellars (McDowell, HNRPI).
18. See (Sellars, LTC).
19. (MFC, p. 423).
20. (LTC, p. 98)
21. See (SM, pp. 74–76, 156–7) and (LTC, pp. 95–7). We will return to this idea in Chapter 6. Sellars's distinction between rules of criticism and action, and his insistence that the rules of language are primarily rules of criticism, is relevant to recent discussions of semantic normativity. See (Wikforss, 2001), (Hattiangadi, 2006), (Whiting, 2007), and (Gluer & Wikforss, 2009).
22. (Sellars, LTC, p. 101) and (SRLG, §16).
23. A further worry is that Sellars thinks that for there to be any rules of criticism, there must be some rules of action. Thanks to deVries for stressing this point in correspondence.
24. He also takes himself to be developing McDowell's suggestion that there is a middle way between Scylla (the idea that all understanding requires interpretation) and Charybdis (the idea that conformity with a rule suffices for following a rule).

25. Brandom explains that "Norms explicit as rules presuppose norms implicit in practices because a rule specifying how something is correctly done (how a word ought to be used, how a piano ought to be tuned) must be applied to particular circumstances, and applying a rule in particular circumstances is itself essentially something that can be done correctly or incorrectly. . . . For any particular performance and any rule, there will be ways of applying the rule so as to forbid performance, and ways of applying the rule so as to permit or require it" (MIE, p. 20). Elsewhere, he writes, "there must be some meta . . . metalevel at which one has some understanding of rules that does not consist of offering another interpretation of them . . . but which consists in being able to distinguish correct applications in practice" (MIE, p. 25).

26. McDowell disputes this interpretation of the problem: the regress "does not arise only where what is understood is discursively explicit" (HNRPI, p. 99).

27. Sellars uses the term 'regulism' to describe something different in (LRB).

28. (MIE, p. 20).

29. "What must one be able to *do* in order to count as *taking* or *treating* a performance as correct or incorrect? What is it for such a normative attitude—attributing a normative significance or status to a performance—to be implicit in practice?" (MIE, p. 32).

30. Here he cites (Haugeland, 1982). See also (Haugeland, The Intentionality All-Stars, 1998) and (Haugeland, Truth and Rule-Following, 1998).

31. (Brandom, MIE, p. 35)

32. Which in turn assumes that there is a difference between understanding and interpreting—an assumption one might like to question.

33. (McDowell, WFR, p. 230)

34. This kind of idea is also part of a prominent strand of interpretation of Martin Heidegger's *Being and Time* (Heidegger, 1962), as represented in (Dreyfus, 1991) and (Blattner, 2006). McDowell and Dreyfus debated some of the related issues in (Dreyfus, 2005), (McDowell, What Myth?, 2009), (Dreyfus, 2007), and (McDowell, Reply to Dreyfus, 2009).

35. McDowell writes, "the key to finding the indispensable middle course is the idea of a custom or practice. How can a performance both be nothing but a 'blind' reaction to a situation, not an attempt to act on an interpretation (avoiding Scylla); and be a case of going by a rule (avoiding Charybdis)? The answer is: by belonging to a custom (PI §198), practice (PI §202), or institution (RFM VI–31)" (WFR, p. 342).

36. This type of argument plays an important role at several places in McDowell's thinking, e.g., (CDK), (KI), (WFR), (MIWLP), (KIR), (HNRPI).

37. McDowell speaks of his work as "diagnostic" (MW, p. xi), (KI, p. 890), (MIWLP, p. 278) or as "dissolving" problems (MW, p. 11) or as "exorcizing" problems (APM, p. 131), (MW, pp. xxii, 142n, 176). He takes this idea from (Wittgenstein, 1958), whom he and others interpret as recommending "quietism" in philosophy (McDowell, WQ). For instance, Wittgenstein writes, "The real discovery is the one that makes me capable of stopping doing philosophy when I want to.—the one that gives philosophy peace, so that it is no longer tormented by questions which bring itself in question" (1958, §133). For a nice overview of this aspect of McDowell's view, see (de Gaynesford, 2004, pp. 3–18). For challenges to McDowell's quietism, see (Dummett, 1987), (Friedman, 2002), (Larmore, 2002).

38. For instance, in *Mind and World*, McDowell stresses the need to understand what is appealing about the idea of the Given (MW, pp. xi, xxiii–xxiv, 13–18).

39. For an insightful discussion of how this plays out in Sellars's thinking, see (Kraut, 2010).

40. Brandom questions Wittgenstein's quietism in (MIE, p. 29), (Brandom, Replies, 1997), and (Brandom, Replies, 2005). McDowell questions Brandom's interpretation of Wittgenstein's "quietism" in (McDowell, HNRPI) and (McDowell, WQ).

NOTES TO CHAPTER 4

1. How faithful is Brandom's project to Sellars's project? For some initial discussion, see (Macbeth, 1997), (Macbeth, 2010), and (Millikan, 2005).
2. The lectures published as (Kripke, 1980) defend a causal theory of *reference* for proper names. That view is challenged and augmented in (Evans, 1973). (Lance, 1984) and (Brandom, 1984) criticize the causal theory and suggest an alternative from a "Pittsburgh" point of view. See also (Wolf M., 2006).
3. For that reason, Ryle called this sort of theory the 'Fido'-Fido theory of meaning (1949). Sellars mentions the 'Fido'-Fido theory (EPM, §31). (Quine, 1969, p. 28) calls a similar idea the "museum myth" of meaning, for it treats all words as if they were labels on exhibits. Such a view of meaning is one of the targets in (Wittgenstein, PI, §§1–80).
4. See (Frege, 1892/1997).
5. A further problem for a theory of meaning that assimilates all meaningful expressions to tags or names is that it makes it nearly impossible to understanding the meaning of sentences, for sentences are not simply lists of names. See (Bradley, 1893/2010, pp. 17–19) and (Russell, 1919/1993).
6. Various contemporary approaches to meaning/content build on the initial idea that meaning is constituted by a causal relation between the meaningful item and the thing or things it's *about*. They appeal to notions like law-governed asymmetric dependencies (Fodor, 1990) or indicator functions (Dretske, 1989) or proper function (Millikan, 1984), (Millikan, 1993), and (Millikan, 2005).
7. See (Haugeland, 1985, pp. 26–7) for a brief summary of the initial hurdles facing a causal theory of meaning.
8. One might think that a "divide and conquer" strategy will work: the meaning of *some* terms is constituted by their causal relations to the relevant objects.
9. That sort of issue is part of what drives Sellars's commitment to *nominalism* about so-called abstract entities. For an overview, see (deVries, 2005, ch. 4). For other helpful presentations of this sort of strategy, see also (Kraut, 2010) and (Price H., 2011).
10. (SRLG, §31), (EPM, §§30–31), (ITM), (SM, ch. 3), and (MFC).
11. That type of question is at the heart of a lot of Brandom's work, e.g., (Brandom, 1979), (MIE) and (BSD). More specifically, a common methodological move for him is to transform questions of the form 'What is it for A to be B?' into questions of the form 'What is one *doing* in *saying* that A is B?' or, more generally, 'What is it to treat A as B?' Sometimes that move is referred to as methodological pragmatism.
12. In an early formulation of the idea, he writes, "To say that '"rot" means red' is not to describe "rot" as standing 'in the meaning relation' to an entity red; it is to use a recognized device (the semantical language game) for bringing home to a user of 'red' how Germans use 'rot'" (SRLG, p. 332). In his correspondence with Roderick Chisholm, Sellars writes, " . . . although 'means' is in a *grammatical sense* a 'relation word,' it is no more to be assimilated to words for descriptive *relations* than is 'ought,' and that though it is a 'descriptive' predicate if one means by 'descriptive' that it is not a *logical* term nor constructible out of such, it is not *in any more interesting (or usual) sense* a descriptive term" (Sellars & Chisholm, 1957, pp. 523–4). And: " '" . . ." means—- -' is the core

of a unique mode of discourse which is as distinct from the *description* and *explanation* of empirical fact, as is the language of *prescription* and *justification*" (ITM, p. 527). (Lance & Hawthorne, 1997) extend and defend this idea. They claim that meaning claims are normative.

13. Brandom makes a similar point (MIE, p. 325); (McDowell, BIR, p. 159fn.1) sketches a criticism of that claim.

14. This aspect of language is addressed by Sellars in his discussion of the "picturing" dimension of language. See, for instance, (TC) and (SM, ch. V).

15. Sellars summarizes the basic ideas in (BLM, §§138–89).

16. In technical jargon, it is a *metalinguistic* illustrating sortal, not an object-language sortal. Our particular example is a sortal in English in which we are expressing a claim about another language, German.

17. (Sellars, ENWW, p. 29). This idea is similar to what J. L. Austin calls the "descriptive fallacy" (Austin, 1962). A similar idea is expressed in (Wittgenstein, PI, §23).

18. See (Sellars, Abstract Entities, 1963), (SM), (NO), and (TTP).

19. There is some debate on Sellars's position here. (Brandom, AR, p. 28), (deVries, 2005, pp. 30, 38–9), (O'Shea, 2007, pp. 60–1, 78), and (Rosenberg, 2008, p. 20) think that Sellars thinks that an expression's role in all three sorts of move is constitutive of its meaning. Macbeth denies that in (Macbeth, 1997) and (Macbeth, 2010). She claims that Sellars thinks that an expression's role in entries and exits is not constitutive of meaning; only their role in a limited class of language-language moves is constitutive of their meaning.

20. In IM, Sellars contrasts "material" rules of inference with "logical" rules of inference, which are now commonly called "formal" rules of inference.

21. That is Brandom's name for it (MIE, p. 98).

22. Sellars writes: "Everyone would admit that the notion of a language which enables one to state matters of fact, but doesn't permit argument, explanation, in short reasoning, in accordance with the principles of formal logic, is a chimera. It is essential to the understanding of scientific reasoning to realize that the notion of a language which enables one to state empirical matters of fact, but contains no material moves is equally chimerical. The classical 'fiction' of an inductive leap which takes its point of departure from an observation base undefiled by any notion as to how things hang together is not a fiction but an absurdity. The problem is not 'is it reasonable to include material moves in our language?' but rather 'Which material moves is it reasonable to include?'" (SRLG, p. 355)

23. Sellars writes, "The language of modalities is . . . a 'transposed' language of norms" (IM, §39). He says that subjunctive conditionals are "object-language expressions of material rules of inference" (IM, §28).

24. (Brandom, MIE, pp. 100–1) points out that (Carroll, 1895) makes a similar point: not all rules of inference on which an argument relies can be rendered as explicit parts of that argument proper, on pain of an infinite regress.

25. This rejection is best seen in his deflationary, expressivist approach to semantic vocabulary. See, e.g., (REA), (PPT), and (MIE, ch. 5).

26. Brandom writes, "[the view] is a kind of conceptual-role semantics that is distinguished first by the nature of the functional system with respect to which such roles are individuated and attributed: what is appealed to is role in the implicitly normative linguistic social practices" (MIE, p. xvi).

27. Currently, the best systematic exposition of the essentials of Brandom's inferentialism is (Wanderer, 2008).

28. Brandom writes, "The explanatory strategy pursued here is to begin with an account of social practices, identify the particular structure they must exhibit in order to qualify as specifically *linguistic* practice, and then consider what different sorts of semantic contents those practices can confer on states,

performances, and expressions caught up in them in suitable ways" (MIE, p. xiii).

29. Appealing to avowing and acknowledging here runs the risk of smuggling in semantic or intentional notions, which are unavailable.

30. Bear in mind that, strictly speaking, Brandom is not allowed to appeal to such things, given his aspiration to account for semantics in terms of pragmatics; we cannot assume that players have the ability to write scorecards, since that would require language; scorecards are just a way of talking about a non-linguistic ability players have. Scorecards are simply a useful heuristic.

31. It underpins the distinction between acknowledged and unacknowledged—or merely attributed—commitments. We saw this difference in perspective in Chapter 2, in the brief discussion of Brandom's view about the ontological relationship between thought and language.

32. Here Brandom builds in a substantive conception of the structure of practices of justification, to which we will return in Chapter 5.

33. Notice that incompatibility is not defined in semantic terms. A common definition of incompatible propositions is that they cannot both be true; they are mutually exclusive. Here incompatibility is defined in terms of statuses that one cannot simultaneously have. A and B are incompatible if commitment to A precludes entitlement to B (or vice versa).

34. Brandom develops his views on the freedom and responsibility characteristic of speaking a language in (RP, chs. 1–3).

35. That is one way in which Brandom develops Sellars's placing remark: "characterizing an episode as one of knowing is to place it in the logical space of reasons, of justifying and being able to justify what one says."

36. One initial and important difference between Sellars's functional role theory and Brandom's is that Sellars's focuses on sub-sentential terms (e.g., 'rain' or 'copper'), whereas Brandom focuses on sentences. In (MEV), Sellars emphasizes that sentences are basic. Thanks to Willem deVries for this clarification.

37. For a discussion of how to think about entailment in pragmatic and normative terms, see (Lance, 1995).

38. What, then, is Brandom's conception of truth? He adopts a deflationary theory of truth called an "anaphoric" theory of truth, which builds on the prosentential theory developed in (Grover, Camp, & Belnap, 1975). Deflationary theories reject the idea that truth is a substantive property of propositions, sentences, or utterances (MIE, ch. 5). He has a similar approach to reference, first expounded in (Brandom, REA). See also (Lance, 1997) and (Brandom, Expressive vs. Explanatory Deflationism about Truth, 2002).

39. The phrase is due to (Dummett, 1973/1981). Brandom treats this as another way of talking about Sellarsian entries, exits, and intralinguistic moves.

40. Calling these relations "non-inferential" initially might seem right, but it is ultimately confusing, since they are supposed to be genuinely part of a claim's inferential relations.

41. Sellars himself maintains that the intra-linguistic moves that are constitutive of the meaning of an expression are only those inferences that are underwritten by physical necessity, i.e., by physical laws. See, for instance, (Sellars, CDCM).

42. This is a question about what the sentence-type means. It is not a question about speaker-meaning, nor is it a question about "what is conveyed" or "implicated" by the use of a sentence on a given occasion. There is an enormous literature on these issues, rooted mainly in (Grice, 1989).

43. But for a defense and sketch of such a "radical contextualism" see (Travis, 2006) and (Travis, 2008). Thanks to Nat Hansen for the phrase.

44. Another important part of his answer is his account of how anaphora (pronouns, such as 'he' and 'it' and 'that') enable different speakers to talk about

the same things. Anaphoric "chains" help ensure that different speakers' claims share meaning. For a good overview, see (Wanderer, 2008, ch. 7).

45. Here Brandom picks up Sellars's idea about the special role of subjunctive conditionals that we saw in §1 of this chapter.

46. The corresponding universal claim—'Any human is mortal'—would express the propriety of inferring from the claim that a given thing is human to the claim that it must also be mortal.

47. For more on this way of thinking about meaning-talk, see (Lance & Hawthorne, 1997).

48. Brandom compares different conceptions of rationality in (TMD, pp. 1–20).

49. Brandom writes, "Substitution inferences materially involving singular terms are de jure symmetric, while all predicates are materially involved in some asymmetric substitution inferences" (AR, p. 135). And: "singular terms are grouped into equivalence classes by the good substitution inferences in which they are materially involved, while predicates are grouped into reflexive, transitive, asymmetric structures or families" (AR, p. 135).

50. At least, one is permitted to do that in simple cases like 12 and 13. Things are more complicated in sentences like 'Ted believes that George Orwell is human' and 'Necessarily, the author of *1984* is an author,' so-called opaque contexts. See Chapter 5 of MIE.

51. Challenges to Brandom's inferentialism abound, but I will focus on just one from McDowell. See (Weiss & Wanderer, 2010), the book symposia on *Making It Explicit* in *Philosophy and Phenomenological Research* (1997), and in *Pragmatics and Cognition* (2005). See also the critical discussions in (Graham, 1999), (Habermas, 2000), (Rouse, 2003), (McCullagh, 2003), (McCullagh, 2005), (Loeffler, 2005), and (Kukla & Lance, 2009).

52. He makes a similar objection to Sellars's view, but I won't sketch the details here. See (McDowell, Intentionality as a Relation, 2008) and (McDowell, Sellars's Thomism, 2009).

53. McDowell takes the expression "full-blooded" from (Dummett, 1993). McDowell's objections to "full-blooded" theories are initially made in response to Dummett's discussion of Davidson's view, e.g., (Davidson, 1984), see (McDowell, IDM) and (McDowell, APM). McDowell does not use the expression in his critiques of Sellars and Brandom.

54. Cited in (McDowell, IDM, p. 90).

55. McDowell writes, in a full-blooded theory, "particular episodes of language use must be recognizable for what they essentially are without benefit of understanding the language" (McDowell, IDM, p. 99).

56. See, for instance, (Chierchia & McConnell-Ginet, 2000/1990) and (Heim & Kratzer, 1998).

57. For the origin of "modesty," see (McDowell, APM, p. 108n.3)

58. Brandom carries further the rejection of "word-world" conceptions of meaning in his expressive approach to semantic terms. See especially (REA), (PPT), and (MIE, ch. 5).

59. For a helpful discussion of the assumptions and consequences of representationalism, see (MacFarlane, 2010).

60. Representationalism is the main target of (Rorty, 1979). Rorty was Brandom's dissertation advisor and long-time interlocutor.

61. He wonders in passing whether it is anything more than a "straw man" (McDowell, MI, p. 292), (McDowell, BIR, p. 159).

62. McDowell says that even for Brandom assertion and inference come together as a package. Brandom agrees (Brandom, Replies, 2005, p. 235). But McDowell thinks that once we have assertion, we already have at least one form of

representation. So, even for Brandom inference and representation are coordinate concepts, on McDowell's interpretation.

63. (McDowell, BIR, p. 159) and (Brandom, MIE, p. 669, n. 90)
64. (Kremer, 2010) develops this challenge further.
65. (McDowell, MI, p. 305) and (Brandom, Replies, 2005, pp. 236–41).
66. (MIE, pp. xiii–xiv).
67. See (McDowell, MI, p. 290). McDowell does not use "full-blooded" when formulating this objection to Brandom. However, I think it is useful to see McDowell as making the same sort of criticism of Brandom that he makes of Dummett in (IDM) and (APM).
68. In the terms of McDowell's *Mind and World*, Brandom's "game of giving and asking for reasons" is simply a "self-contained game" (MW, p. 5).
69. See especially (Brandom, Replies, 2005).
70. (Brandom, Replies, 1997, p. 189) and (Brandom, Replies, 2005, p. 238). He is alluding to the work of Karl Popper, e.g., (Popper, 2002/1935).
71. Brandom develops this idea in the "Afterword" to *Between Saying and Doing*.

NOTES TO CHAPTER 5

1. For further discussion of Sellars's conception of the way in which observational knowledge depends on knowledge of general truths, see (deVries & Triplett, 2000, pp. 67–9, 95–9) and (Williams, 2010).
2. See especially (Goldman, 1976).
3. deVries calls it the Epistemic Reflexivity Requirement (2005, p. 123).
4. See especially (Kukla, 2000).
5. See (Sellars, The Structure of Knowledge, 1975) and (Sellars, Mental Events, 1981) for careful qualifications.
6. For helpful discussion, see (deVries, 1996). For criticism of Sellars on this point, see (Sosa, 1997), (Alston, 2002), and (Sosa, 2003).
7. For a nice gloss on this remark, see (deVries & Triplett, 2000, p. 89).
8. For instance: (McDowell, CDK, p. 333), (McDowell, Knowledge by Hearsay, 1998, p. 414), (McDowell, EI, p. 157), (Brandom, SG, p. 162), (Brandom, TP, p. 541).
9. Likewise, it would be hard to count him as a player at all if he never corrected or protested against flagrantly illegal moves, his own or anyone else's. See (Haugeland, Truth and Rule-Following, 1998).
10. 'Honorific' is used in this way in (Williams, 2001, p. 11).
11. This essentially completes Sellars's critique of an *empiricist* version of the Given. One might still hold out hope for a *rationalist* version of the Given, one which appeals to a priori intuition.
12. That sort of image has been made famous by Quine, e.g., (Quine, 1956).
13. (Williams, 2010) argues that what I have said here is only part of the story. See especially (Sellars, MGEC).
14. McDowell does too, e.g., (KI, p. 890n.24) and (KIR, p. 101)
15. McDowell thoroughly critiques Brandom's reading of Sellars in (McDowell, BO, 2010), the predecessor of which is (McDowell, Why Sellars's Essay is Called 'Empiricism and the Philosophy of Mind,' 2009). Brandom replies in (Weiss & Wanderer, 2010). I will leave aside the question of whether Brandom gets Sellars right.
16. As McDowell stresses in (BO), Sellars also thinks there is a further "experiential" dimension to observation.
17. See, for instance, (Brandom, SG), (Brandom, KSASR).

18. See, for instance, the discussion of grounding, evidence, and epistemic responsibility in (Williams, 2001, chs. 1–2).
19. Brandom calls this the "reliability inference" (MIE, pp. 217–21), (SG, p. 158), (AR, ch. 3).
20. See also (PRC, pp. 250–1), (AR, ch. 3), and (TP, p. 526).
21. Brandom claims that RR is part of Sellars's attempt to do that (KSASR, p. 905), (TP, p. 527).
22. Thus, Brandom rejects pure reliabilism or pure externalism not because it has the wrong view of justification, but because it has the wrong view of concept-application or belief-formation. That preempts the objection that Brandom simply begs the question against pure reliabilism by assuming that reliability is not sufficient for justification.
23. Thus, 2′ appears to be a generalization of Sellars's 2. With 2, Sellars claims that one must know about one's own reliability. By contrast, with 2′, Brandom claims that one must know what would support and follow from one's response, which is not limited to knowledge of one's own reliability.
24. See (Asserting), (MIE, ch. 4), (KSASR), and (AR, ch. 4).
25. See (Brandom, KSASR, pp. 899–900 fn.3).
26. He also thinks that the distinctness of the two plies can help explain the acquisition of concepts. One gets the first ply first, then the second ply. First one develops relevant RDRDs. One doesn't yet know what such responses rationally support or are supported by. Then, eventually, one masters enough of that, to count as knowing and applying concepts. The measure of whether one has mastered enough is the community of knowers and thinkers: "whether or not one's utterance has the significance of endorsing a claim, and so of applying a concept, is a question of how it is treated by the other members of the linguistic community" (541).
27. McDowell contends that there is a sense in which young children and non-human animals really do have knowledge, reason, and concepts. See, for instance, (McDowell, KIR), (McDowell, Conceptual Capacities in Perception, 2009), (McDowell, Towards a Reading of Hegel on Action in the 'Reason' Chapter of the Phenomenology, 2009).
28. Brandom admits that McDowell might see him as a Coherentist (Brandom, No Experience Necessary, Unpublished).
29. See (MIE, pp. 176–8).
30. See, for instance, (Williams, 1977/1999, p. 188).
31. See (MIE, p. 177).
32. See (Williams, 1977/1999, pp. 189–90).
33. Brandom acknowledges Donald Davidson as an important predecessor, e.g., (Davidson, Inquiries into Truth and Interpretation, 2001). Davidson holds that to treat someone as speaking or thinking at all requires treating her as having beliefs and making claims that are, largely, true by your own lights.
34. Unless, of course, there were "self-justifying" claims or thoughts, but that looks like the Given.
35. He does discuss something he calls the "endogenous Given" in *Mind and World* (pp. 135–6).
36. Brandom objects to McDowell's conception of Coherentism (PRC, pp. 253, 257–8). Williams also questions this part of McDowell's view, emphasizing that there is a reliabilist component to knowledge. See, for instance, (Williams, 1977/1999, pp. 192–8).
37. See (McDowell, MW, pp. xii–xiv), (McDowell, EI, pp. 243–4), and (McDowell, HWV, pp. 3–4, 6–8).
38. For McDowell, this view goes wrong in conflating acts and contents. He writes, "What we need is constraint from outside thinking and judging, our

exercises of spontaneity. The constraint does not need to be from outside thinkable contents" (MW, 28).

39. McDowell rightly finds that idea in Sellars, e.g., (EPM, §§16–16bis). He emphasizes that it is essential to Kant's project, e.g., (McDowell, HWV, pp. 3–43), (McDowell, AMG).

40. He also rightly finds that idea in Sellars, e.g., (EPM, §§16–16bis).

41. Furthermore, it implies that the "layout of reality" itself is conceptually structured.

42. For some discussion of this type of view, see (Travis, 2005).

43. For some critical discussion of disjunctivism, see (Burge, 2005), (McDowell, Tyler Burge on Disjunctivism, 2010), and (Burge, 2011).

44. He has a similar conception of knowledge in general. See especially (McDowell, KI) and (McDowell, KIR).

45. See (McDowell, EI, p. 252). See also (McDowell, The Disjunctive Conception of Experience as Material for a Transcendental Argument). For a similar claim, see (Haugeland, Authentic Intentionality, 2002).

46. Williams alleges that McDowell is here treating experience as a foundation of knowledge, and is consequently at risk of simply appealing to the Given (Williams, Exorcisim and Enchantment, 1996), (1977/1999, pp. 192–8).

47. See (MW, pp. xxiii–iv); see also (McDowell, HWV, pp. 4–6) and (McDowell, EI, pp. 253–4).

48. McDowell focuses on Sellars's view of the sensory character of experience, which includes the look, feel, smell, sound, or taste of an experience. Sellars discusses experience in many places, see especially (Sellars, EPM), (Sellars, PSIM), (Sellars, FMPP), and (Sellars, Sensa or Sensings, 1982). (deVries, 2005, ch. 8) is a helpful summary. McDowell discusses Sellars's views on experience in several places; see especially (McDowell, MW, pp. xii–xiv, 140–6) and (McDowell, HWV). His views have changed over time; see especially (HWV, pp. 13n.15, 19). For critical discussion of McDowell's interpretation, see (deVries, 2006) and (Williams, 2006).

49. See also (McDowell, BO), which is the successor to (McDowell, Why Sellars's Essay is Called 'Empiricism and the Philosophy of Mind,' 2009).

50. See, e.g., (McDowell, KIR).

51. See (Brandom, A), (Brandom, MIE, ch. 4), (Brandom, KSASR), and (AR, ch. 4).

NOTES TO CHAPTER 6

1. Aristotle captures the phenomenon well when he describes a typical case of action: "a staff moves a stone, and is moved by a hand, which is moved by a man" (Physics, 256a). Actions, in the relevant sense, are initiated by whole organisms or persons.

2. See, for instance, (Frankfurt, 1978), (Dretske, 1989), (Bishop, 1989), and (Enc, 2003)

3. See *Leviathan*, Chapter 6, "Of the Interior Beginnings of Voluntary Motions; Commonly Called the Passions; and the Speeches by Which They Are Expressed."

4. This leads to worries about so-called "causal deviance" or "wayward causal chains." Suppose Mark wills to eat the tomato, but grunts loudly instead, which frightens Sarah, who bumps his arm towards the tomato. His willing makes his arm move towards the tomato, but surely his will has not been fulfilled *in the right way*. See, especially, (Ducasse, 1925), (Ryle, 1949/1984), (Chisholm, 1964), and (Davidson, Freedom to Act, 1980).

5. See (Ryle, 1949/1984).

6. Brandom points this out (MIE, pp. 294–5) and (AR, p. 94).

7. Don't confuse the idea of a happening that is "intrinsically intentional" with the idea of "intrinsic intentionality," the idea that some things are intrinsically "about" something (Searle, 1983).

8. For instance, (Ryle, 1949/1984).

9. In addition to his views on the nature of intentions that I will discuss here, Sellars also developed detailed views of the logic of intentions and practical reasoning, as well as views about freedom and determinism, which I will not discuss here. For critical discussion of those views see especially his exchanges with Hector-Neri Castaneda and Bruce Aune.

10. See (Sellars, TA, p. 108).

11. See, e.g., (Sellars, FD, p. 150).

12. (Sellars, TA, pp. 106–7).

13. For instance, (Sellars, TA, pp. 128–9) and (Sellars, SM, p. 185).

14. That remains true even if it is granted that committing to a course of action involves a belief about the way the future will be, a prediction.

15. The phrase is due to (Solomon, 1977).

16. "Grows" appears elsewhere. Sellars writes, "Intentions . . . *grow* . . . into doings" (Sellars, FD, p. 155).

17. See (TA, 108–9) and (FD, 158).

18. See (Sellars, FD, pp. 157–8).

19. See, for instance, (Sellars, PSIM, p. 11), (Sellars, FD, pp. 151–3, 156–7), (Sellars, SM, pp. 74–76, 156–7, 178).

20. See (FD, pp. 156–7)

21. For helpful discussions of responsibility for involuntary behavior, see (Adams, 1985), (Smith A., 2005), (Sher, 2006), and (Smith A., 2008).

22. One question lingers. How should we make sense of the idea that our *actions*—things we do deliberately—are rooted in *acts*—things that are non-voluntary?

23. For a nice summary of Sellars's position, see (deVries, 1996).

24. (Brandom, MIE, p. 233), (Brandom, AR, p. 79), and (Brandom, Reply to Rowland Stout, 2010, p. 329)

25. (Brandom, MIE, pp. 233–8), (Brandom, AR, p. 83), and (Brandom, Reply to Rowland Stout, 2010, pp. 327–8)

26. See (SRLG, p. 329).

27. See (Brandom, MIE, pp. 256–9), (Brandom, AR, pp. 94–5), and (Searle, 1983, pp. 84–5).

28. McDowell first sketched his ideas about action in Lecture V of (MW). Subsequently, he developed those ideas in the Hägerström Lectures at the University of Uppsala in 2005. Revised versions of some of these lectures have now been published. Material from Lectures II and III appears in (McDowell, SRIA, 2011); material from Lecture IV appears in (McDowell, PI, 2011); material from Lecture V appears in (McDowell, WCIA, 2010). Thanks to John McDowell for clarifying these connections for me.

29. McDowell writes, "The parallel is this: intentional bodily actions are activations of our active nature in which conceptual capacities are inextricably implicated" (MW, p. 90).

30. In other words, "physical activity can be rationality in action, as opposed to a mere result of exercises of rationality" (SRIA, p. 17). And yet another formulation: "our intentional interventions in the world are themselves cases of our conceptual capacities in operation" (WCIA, p. 431).

31. The idea that our actions are or must be responsive to reasons is central to debates about responsibility for action. See, especially, (Fischer & Ravizza, 1999) and (Korsgaard, 1996).

32. In holding that (non-verbal) intentional actions are conceptual McDowell's proposal is relatively unique in contemporary philosophizing about action.
33. Elsewhere McDowell writes that his proposal "can serve as a corrective against the philosophical tendency to locate thought—the operations of intelligence—in a more or less mysterious inner realm, concealed from people other than the thinker herself" (PI, p. 118).
34. He questions Searle, who holds that prior intentions only give rise to intentions in action (SRIA, pp. 2–11).
35. McDowell writes, "[An intention in action] persists . . . through the time it takes to do whatever it is" (SRIA, p. 5).
36. McDowell suggests that this calls for a disjunctivist conception of practical knowledge (WCIA, p. 431).
37. If McDowell is correct about Sellars, then Sellars would appear to be guilty of a mistake analogous to endorsing the Given. In this case, the mistake would be to think that intentional action is both rationally supportable and yet non-conceptual. Thinking that intentional action is rationally supportable corresponds to EE; thinking that it is non-conceptual corresponds to EI. However, it is not obvious that McDowell is correct.
38. (Stout, 2010) makes a similar objection to Brandom.
39. That line of thought can be pressed further. Is the meaning of a non-verbal act composed out of the meaning of its parts—is it "compositional"? Can non-verbal acts be linked with "connectives" into other "larger" non-verbal acts, with new meanings?
40. Apart from their work on Hegel's philosophy itself, that is one of the reasons why McDowell and Brandom are often seen as neo-Hegelians. See (Redding, 2007), (Redding, 2010), and (Redding, 2011).

NOTES TO CONCLUDING SUGGESTIONS

1. See (Sellers, PSIM).
2. Sellars's views here are a topic of dispute. For helpful initial discussions, see (O'Shea, 2007, chs. 1, 7) and (deVries, 2005, ch. 10). For critical discussion of the dispute here between McDowell and Sellars, see (Williams, 2006) and (Williams, 2010).
3. For instance: (Chisholm, 1966), (Fales, 1996), (Sosa, 1997), (Bonevac, 2002), and (Alston, 2002).
4. For an overview, see (Fumerton, 2010).
5. The term 'naturalism' can denote many, incompatible things. I'm using it here in only one limited and vague way.
6. See especially MW.
7. There are many deep and difficult issues here concerning science, causation, laws of nature, and modality. See (Sellars, 1948), (Sellars, CDCM), (Lange, 2000), (Rouse, 2003), (Brandom, BSD), (Brandom, Pragmatism, Inferentialism, and Modality in Sellars's Arguments against Empiricism, 2010), and (Brandom, Modal Expressivism and Modal Realism, Unpublished).
8. For a good start, see (deVries, 1995) and (Garfield, Peterson, & Perry, 2001).
9. This will partly involve getting clearer about the many different uses of the word 'concept.' See (Brandom, HAPFCS).

Works Cited

Adams, R. (1985). Involuntary Sins. *The Philosophical Review, 94*(1), 3–31.

Alston, W. (2002). Sellars and the Myth of the Given. *Philosophy and Phenomenological Research, 65*, 69–86.

Anscombe, G. (1957). *Intention.* London: Basil Blackwell.

Austin, J. (1962). *How to Do Things with Words.* (J. Urmson & M. Sbisa, Eds.) Cambridge, MA: Harvard University Press.

Ayer, A. (1936). *Language, Truth and Logic.* London: Dover.

Bishop, J. (1989). *Natural Agency.* New York: Cambridge University Press.

Blackburn, S. (1993). *Essays in Quasi-Realism.* New York: Oxford University Press.

Blattner, W. (2006). *Heidegger's Being and Time.* New York: Continuum.

Bloom, P. (2002). *How Children Learn the Meaning of Words.* Cambridge, MA: MIT Press.

Boghossian, P. (1989). The Rule-Following Considerations. *Mind, 98*(392), 507–549.

Bonevac, D. (2002). Sellars vs. the Given. *Philosophy and Phenomenological Research, 64*(1), 1–30.

Bradley, F. (1893/1969). *Appearance and Reality* (2nd ed.). New York: Oxford University Press.

Brandom, R. (1979). Freedom and Constraint by Norms. *American Philosophical Quarterly, 16*(3), 187–196.

Brandom, R. (1983). Asserting. *Nous, 17*(4), 637–650.

Brandom, R. (1984). Reference Explained Away. *The Journal of Philosophy, 81*(9), 469–492.

Brandom, R. (1987). Pragmatism, Phenomenalism and Truth-Talk. *Midwest Studies in Philosophy, 12*, 75–93.

Brandom, R. (1994). *Making It Explicit.* Cambridge, MA: Harvard University Press.

Brandom, R. (1995). Knowledge and the Social Articulation of the Space of Reasons. *Philosophy and Phenomenological Research, 55*(4), 895–908.

Brandom, R. (1995). Perception and Rational Constraint. *Philosophy and Phenomenological Research.*

Brandom, R. (1996). Perception and Rational Constraint. *Philosophical Issues, 7*, 241–259.

Brandom, R. (1997). Replies. *Philosophy and Phenomenological Research, 57*(1), 189–204.

Brandom, R. (1997). Study Guide. In W. Sellars (Ed.), *Empiricism and the Philosophy of Mind* (pp. 119–181). Cambridge, MA: Harvard University Press.

Brandom, R. (2000). *Articulating Reasons.* Cambridge, MA: Harvard University Press.

Brandom, R. (2002). Expressive vs. Explanatory Deflationism about Truth. In R. Schantz (Ed.), *What is Truth?* (pp. 103–119). New York: de Gruyter.

Brandom, R. (2002). *Tales of the Mighty Dead*. Cambridge, MA: Harvard University Press.

Brandom, R. (2002). The Centrality of Sellars's Two-Ply Account of Observation. In R. Brandom, *Tales of the Mighty Dead* (523–552). Cambridge, MA: Harvard University Press.

Brandom, R. (2005). Replies. *Pragmatics and Cognition, 13*(1), 227–249.

Brandom, R. (2007). Conceptual Content and Discursive Practice. Unpublished.

Brandom, R. (2008). *Between Saying and Doing: Towards an Analytic Pragmatism*. Cambridge, MA: Harvard University Press.

Brandom, R. (2009). How Analytic Philosophy Has Failed Cognitive Science. In R. Brandom, *Reason in Philosophy* (pp. 197–224). Cambridge, MA: Harvard University Press.

Brandom, R. (2009). *Reason in Philosophy*. Cambridge, MA: Harvard University Press.

Brandom, R. (2010). Pragmatism, Inferentialism, and Modality in Sellars's Arguments against Empiricism. In W. deVries (Ed.), *Empiricism, Perceptual Knowledge, Normativity, and Realism* (pp. 33–62). New York: Oxford University Press.

Brandom, R. (2010). Reply to Fodor and Lepore. In B. Weiss & J. Wanderer (Eds.) (pp.332–337). New York: Routledge.

Brandom, R. (2010). Reply to Rowland Stout. In B. Weiss & J. Wanderer (Eds.) (pp. 327–331). New York: Routledge.

Brandom, R. (Unpublished). Modal Expressivism and Modal Realism.

Brandom, R. (Unpublished). No Experience Necessary.

Brentano, F. (1973). *Psychology from an Empirical Standpoint*. (A. Rancurello, D. Terrell, & L. McAlister, Trans.) London: Routledge.

Burge, T. (2005). Disjunctivism and Perceptual Psychology. *Philosophical Topics, 33*(1), 1–78.

Burge, T. (2010). *Origins of Objectivity*. New York: Oxford University Press.

Burge, T. (2011). Disjunctivism Again. *Philosophical Explorations, 14*(1), 43–80.

Candlish, S., & Wrisley, G. (2009, September 29). *Private Language*. Retrieved January 12, 2011, from Stanford Encyclopedia of Philosophy: http://plato.stanford.edu/entries/private-language/

Carroll, L. (1895). What the Tortoise Said to Achilles. *Mind, 4*(14), 278–280.

Castaneda, H.-N. (Ed.). (1975). *Action, Knowledge, and Reality*. Indianapolis: Bobbs-Merrill.

Chierchia, G., & McConnell-Ginet, S. (2000/1990). *Meaning and Grammar* (2nd ed.). Cambridge, MA: MIT Press.

Chisholm, R. (1964). The Descriptive Element in the Concept of Action. *Journal of Philosophy, 61*, 613–625.

Chisholm, R. (1966). *Theory of Knowledge*. Englewood Cliffs, NJ: Prentice Hall.

Chomsky, N. (1959). Review of Skinner's Verbal Behavior. *Language, 35*, 26–58.

Cummins, R. (1996). *Representations, Targets, and Attitudes*. Cambridge, MA: MIT Press.

Davidson, D. (1973/1980). Freedom to Act. In D. Davidson, *Essays on Actions and Events* (pp.63–81). New York: Oxford University Press.

Davidson, D. (1978/1980). Intending. In D. Davidson, *Essays on Actions and Events* (pp. 83–102). New York: Oxford University Press.

Davidson, D. (1967/1984). Truth and Meaning. In D. Davidson, *Inquiries into Truth and Interpretation* (pp.17–42). New York: Oxford University Press.

Davidson, D. (1984/2001). A Coherence Theory of Truth and Knowledge. In D. Davidson, *Subjective, Intersubjective, Objective* (pp. 137–153). New York: Oxford University Press.

Davidson, D. (1984/2001). *Inquiries into Truth and Interpretation*. New York: Oxford University Press.

de Gaynesford, M. (2004). *John McDowell*. New York: Polity.

Delaney, C., Loux, M., Gutting, G., & Solomon, D. (Eds.). (1977). *The Synoptic Vision*. Notre Dame, IN: University of Notre Dame Press.

Descartes, R. (1996/1641). *Meditations on First Philosophy*. (J. Cottingham, Ed., & J. Cottingham, Trans.) New York: Cambridge University Press.

deVries, W. (1988). *Hegel's Theory of Mental Activity*. Ithaca: Cornell University Press.

deVries, W. (1995). *Sellars, Animals and Thought*. Retrieved July 20, 2011, from Problems from Wilfrid Sellars: http://www.ditext.com/devries/sellanim.html

deVries, W. (2005). *Wilfrid Sellars*. New York: McGill-Queen's University Press.

deVries, W. (2006). McDowell, Sellars, and Sense Impressions. *European Journal of Philosophy, 14*(2), 182–201.

deVries, W. (2008). Sense-Certainty and the 'This-Such.' In D. Moyar & M. Quante (Eds.), *Hegel's Phenomenology of Spirit: A Critical Guide* (pp. 63–75). New York: Cambridge University Press.

deVries, W., & Triplett, T. (2000). *Knowledge, Mind and the Given*. New York: Hackett.

Dretske, F. (1971). Conclusive Reasons. *Australiasian Journal of Philosophy, 49*, 1–22.

Dretske, F. (1989). *Explaining Behavior*. Cambridge, MA: MIT Press.

Dreyfus, H. (1991). *Being-in-the-World*. Cambridge, MA: MIT Press.

Dreyfus, H. (2005). Overcoming the Myth of the Mental. *Proceedings and Addresses of the American Philosophical Association, 79*(2), 47–65.

Dreyfus, H. (2007). The Return of the Myth of the Mental. *Inquiry, 50*, 352–265.

Ducasse, C. (1925). Explanation, Mechanism, and Teleology. *Journal of Philosophy, 22*(6), 150–155.

Dummett, M. (1973/1981). *Frege: Philosophy of Language*. London: Duckworth.

Dummett, M. (1981). Frege and Wittgenstein. In I. Block (Ed.), *Perspectives on the Philosophy of Wittgenstein* (pp. 31–42). Oxford: Blackwell.

Dummett, M. (1987). Reply to John McDowell. In B. Taylor (Ed.), *Michael Dummett: Contributions to Philosophy*. Dordrecht: Martinus Nijhoff.

Dummett, M. (1993). What is a Theory of Meaning? I. In M. Dummett, *Seas of Language* (pp. 1–33). New York: Oxford University Press.

Dummett, M. (1996). *Seas of Language*. New York: Oxford University Press.

Enc, B. (2003). *How We Act*. New York: Oxford University Press.

Evans, G. (1973). The Causal Theory of Names. *Proceedings of the Aristotelian Society, 47*, 187–225.

Evans, G. (1982). *Varieties of Reference*. (J. McDowell, Ed.) New York: Oxford University Press.

Fales, E. (1996). *A Defense of the Given*. Lanham, MD: Rowman & Littlefield.

Finkelstein, D. (2000). Wittgenstein on Rules and Platonism. In R. Reed & A. Crary (Eds.), *The New Wittgenstein* (pp. 53–73). New York: Routledge.

Finkelstein, D. (2003). *Expression and the Inner*. Cambridge, MA: Harvard University Press.

Fischer, J. M., & Ravizza, M. (1999). *Responsibility and Control*. New York: Cambridge University Press.

Fodor, J. (1987). *Psychosemantics*. Cambridge, MA: MIT Press.

Fodor, J. (1990). *A Theory of Content and Other Essays*. Cambridge, MA: MIT Press.

Fodor, J. (1998). *Concepts: Where Cognitive Science Went Wrong*. New York: Oxford University Press.

Fodor, J. (2004). Having Concepts. *Mind & Language, 19*(1), 29–47.

Fodor, J., & Lepore, E. (1993). *Holism: A Shopper's Guide*. Cambridge, MA: MIT Press.

Fodor, J., & Lepore, E. (2001). Brandom's Burdens. *Philosophy and Phenomenological Research, 63*(2), 465–481.

Fodor, J., & Lepore, E. (2007). Brandom Beleaguered. *Philosophy and Phenomenological Research, 74*(3), 677–691.

Fogelin, R. (1994). *Pyrrhonian Reflections on Knowledge and Justification*. New York: Oxford University Press.

Frankfurt, H. (1978). The Problem of Action. *American Philosophical Quarterly, 15*(2), 157–162.

Frege, G. (1892/1997). On Sense and Reference. In M. Beaney (Ed.), *The Frege Reader* (pp. 15–171). London: Blackwell.

Friedman, M. (2002). Exorcising the Philosophical Tradition. In N. Smith (Ed.), *Reading McDowell* (pp. 25–57). New York: Routledge.

Fumerton, R. (2010). *Foundationalist Theories of Epistemic Justification*. Retrieved February 1, 2012 from Stanford Encyclopedia of Philosophy: http://plato.stanford.edu/entries/justep-foundational/

Garfield, J., et al. (2001). Social Cognition, Language Acquisition and the Development of the Theory of Mind. *Mind & Language, 16* (5), 494–541.

Gaskin, R. (2006). *Experience and the World's Own Language: A Critique of John McDowell's Empiricism*. New York: Oxford University Press.

Gauker, C. (1994). *Thinking Out Loud*. Princeton, NJ: Princeton University Press.

Geach, P. (1957). *Mental Acts*. London: Routledge and Kegan Paul.

Geach, P. (1960). Ascriptivism. *Philosophical Review, 69*, 221–225.

Geach, P. (1965). Assertion. *Philosophical Review, 74*, 449–465.

Gettier, E. (1963). Is Justified True Belief Knowledge? *Analysis, 23*, 121–123.

Gibbard, A. (1990). *Wise Choices, Apt Feelings*. Cambridge, MA: Harvard University Press.

Ginet, C. (1990). *On Action*. New York: Cambridge University Press.

Gluer, K., & Wikforss, A. (2009). Against Content Normativity. *Mind, 118*, 31–70.

Goldman, A. (1967). A Causal Theory of Knowing. *Journal of Philosophy, 64*, 355–372.

Goldman, A. (1970). *A Theory of Human Action*. New York: Princeton University Press.

Goldman, A. (1976). Discrimination and Perceptual Knowledge. *Journal of Philosophy, 73*, 771–791.

Goldman, A. (1979). What is Justified Belief? In G. Pappas (Ed.), *Justification and Knowledge* (pp. 1–23). Amsterdam: D. Reidel.

Graham, P. (1999). Brandom on Singular Terms. *Philosophical Studies, 93*, 247–264.

Grice, H. (1989). *Studies in the Way of Words*. Cambridge, MA: Harvard University Press.

Grover, D., Camp, J., & Belnap, N. (1975). A Prosentential Theory of Truth. *Philosophical Studies, 27*(2), 73–125.

Habermas, J. (2000). From Kant to Hegel. *European Journal of Philosophy, 8*(3), 322–355.

Hall, G. S. (1878). The Muscular Perception of Space. *Mind, 3*(12), 433–450.

Hare, R. (1952). *The Language of Morals*. Oxford: Clarendon.

Hattiangadi, A. (2006). Is Meaning Normative? *Mind & Language, 21*(2), 220–240.

Haugeland, J. (1982). Heidegger on Being a Person. *Nous, 16*(1), 15–26.

Haugeland, J. (1985). *Artificial Intelligence: The Very Idea*. Cambridge, MA: MIT Press.

Haugeland, J. (1997). What is Mind Design? In J. Haugeland, *Mind Design II* (pp. 1–28). Cambridge, MA: MIT Press.

Haugeland, J. (1998). *Having Thought* . Cambridge, MA: Harvard University Press.

Haugeland, J. (1998). Mind Embodied and Embedded. In J. Haugeland, *Having Thought* (pp. 207–237). Cambridge, MA: Harvard University Press.

Haugeland, J. (1998). The Intentionality All-Stars. In J. Haugeland, *Having Thought* (pp. 127–170). Cambridge, MA: Harvard University Press.

Haugeland, J. (1998). Truth and Rule-Following. In J. Haugeland, *Having Thought* (pp. 305–361). Cambridge, MA: Harvard University Press.

Haugeland, J. (2002). Authentic Intentionality. In M. Scheutz (Ed.), *Computationalism: New Directions* (pp. 159–174). Cambridge, MA: MIT Press.

Heck, R. (2000). Non-Conceptual Content and the Space of Reasons. *The Philosophical Review,109*(4), 483–523.

Heck, R. (2007). Are There Different Kinds of Content? In B. McLaughlin & J. Cohen (Eds.), *Contemporary Debates in Philosophy of Mind* (pp. 117–138). Blackwell.

Heidegger, M. (1962). *Being and Time*. (M. A. Robinson, Trans.) New York: Harper.

Heim, I., & Kratzer, A. (1998). *Semantics in Generative Grammar*. Oxford: Blackwell.

Hobbes, T. (1651/2009). *Leviathan*. New York: Oxford University Press.

Hume, D. (1748/2011). *An Enquiry Concerning Human Understanding*. New York: Hackett.

Kant, I. (1785/1998). *Groundwork for the Metaphysics of Morals*. (M. Gregor, Trans.) New York: Cambridge University Press.

King, J. (2001). *Structured Propositions*. Retrieved February 1, 2012 from Stanford Encyclopedia of Philosophy: http://plato.stanford.edu/entries/propositions-structured/

Klein, P. (1999). Human Knowledge and the Infinite Regress of Reasons. *Philosophical Perspectives, 13*, 297–325.

Knell, S. (2004). *Propositionaler Gehalt Diskursive Kontofuhrung Sprachabhangigkeit*. Berlin: Walter de Gruyter.

Korsgaard, C. (1996). *Creating the Kingdom of Ends*. Cambridge, MA: Harvard University Press.

Kraut. R.(2010). Universals, Metaphysical Explanations and Pragmatism. *The Journal of Philosophy, 107*(11), 590–609.

Kremer, M. (2010). Representation or Inference. In J. Wanderer, B. Weiss, J. Wanderer, & B. Weiss (Eds.), *Reading Brandom* (pp. 227–246). New York: Routledge.

Kripke, S. (1980). *Naming and Necessity*. Cambridge, MA: Harvard University Press.

Kripke, S. (1982). *Wittgenstein on Rules and Private Language*. Cambridge, MA: Harvard University Press.

Kukla, R. (2000). Myth, Memory, and Misrecognition in Sellars' 'Empiricism and the Philosophy of Mind.' *Philosophical Studies, 101*, 161–211.

Kukla, R., & Lance, M. (2009). *Yo! and Lo! The Pragmatic Topography of the Space of Reasons*. Cambridge, MA: Harvard University Press.

Lance, M. (1984). Reference without Causation. *Philosophical Studies, 45*(3), 335–351.

Lance, M. (1995). Two Concepts of Entailment. *Journal of Philosophical Research 20*, 112–137.

Lance, M. (1997). The Significance of Anaphoric Theories of Truth and Reference. *Philosophical Issues, 8*, 181–198.

Lance, M. (1998). Reflections on the Sport of Language. *Philosophical Perspectives, 12*, 219–240.

Lance, M. (2000). The Word Made Flesh. *Acta Analytica, 15*(25), 117–135.

Lance, M. (2008). Placing in a Space of Norms. In C. Misak (Ed.), *The Oxford Handbook of American Philosophy* (pp. 403–429). New York: Oxford University Press.

Lance, M., & Hawthorne, J. (1997). *The Grammar of Meaning*. New York: Cambridge University Press.

Lange, M. (2000). *Natural Laws in Scientific Practice*. New York: Oxford University Press.

Larmore, C. (2002). Attending to Reasons. In N. Smith (Ed.), *Reading McDowell* (pp. 193–209). New York: Routledge.

Lehrer, K., & Paxson, T. (1969). Knowledge: Undefeated Justified True Belief. *Journal of Philosophy, 66*, 225–237.

Lewis, C. (1929/1956). *Mind and the World Order*. Mineola, NY: Dover.

Loeffler, R. (2005). Normative Phenomenalism. *European Journal of Philosophy, 13*(1), 32–69.

Macbeth, D. (1994). The Coin of the Intentional Realm. *The Journal for the Theory of Social Behavior, 24*, 143–66.

Macbeth, D. (1997). Brandom on Inference and the Expressive Role of Logic. *Philosophical Issues, 8*, 169–179.

Macbeth, D. (2002). Review of Knowledge, Mind and the Given. *The Philosophical Review, 111*(2), 281–284.

Macbeth, D. (2010). Inference, Meaning and Truth in Brandom, Sellars and Frege. In J. Wanderer & B. Weiss (Eds.), *Reading Brandom* (pp. 197–212). New York: Routledge.

Macdonald, C., & Macdonald, G. (Eds.). (2006). *McDowell and His Critics*. New York: Blackwell.

MacFarlane, J. (2010). Pragmatism and Inferentialism. In B. Weiss & J. Wanderer (Eds.), *Reading Brandom* (pp. 81–95). Cambridge, MA: Harvard University Press.

Margolis, E., & Laurence, S. (2006, February 22). *Concepts*. Retrieved January 12, 2011, from Stanford Encyclopedia of Philosophy: http://plato.stanford.edu/entries/concepts/

McCullagh, M. (2003). Do Inferential Roles Compose? *Dialectica 57*(4), 430–437.

McCullagh, M. (2005). Inferentialism and Singular Reference. *Canadian Journal of Philosophy, 35*(2), 183–220.

McDowell, J. (1979). Reason and Virtue. *The Monist, 62*, 331–350.

McDowell, J. (1994). *Mind and World*. Cambridge, MA: Harvard University Press.

McDowell, J. (1995). Knowledge and the Internal. *Philosophy and Phenomenological Research, 55*(4), 877–893.

McDowell, J. (1997). Brandom on Inference and Representation. *Philosophy and Phenomenological Research, 57*(1), 157–162.

McDowell, J. (1998). Another Plea for Modesty. In J. McDowell, *Meaning, Knowledge and Reality* (pp. 108–131). Cambridge, MA: Harvard University Press.

McDowell, J. (1998). Are Moral Requirements Hypothetical Imperatives? In J. McDowell, *Mind, Value and Reality* (pp. 77–94). Cambridge, MA: Harvard University Press.

McDowell, J. (1998). Criteria, Defeasibility and Knowledge. In J. McDowell, *Meaning, Knowledge and Reality* (pp. 369–94). Cambridge, MA: Harvard University Press.

McDowell, J. (1998). Knowledge by Hearsay. In J. McDowell, *Meaning, Knowledge and Reality* (pp. 414–443). Cambridge, MA: Harvard University Press.

McDowell, J. (1998). Meaning and Intentionality in the Wittgenstein's Later Philosophy. In J. McDowell, *Mind, Value and Reality* (pp. 263–278). Cambridge, MA: Havard University Press.

McDowell, J. (1998). *Mind, Value and Reality*. Cambridge, MA: Harvard University Press.

McDowell, J. (1998). One Strand in the Private Language Argument. In J. McDowell, *Mind, Value and Reality* (pp. 279–296). Cambridge, MA: Harvard University Press.

McDowell, J. (1998). Wittgenstein on Following a Rule. In J. McDowell, *Mind, Value and Reality* (pp. 221–262). Cambridge, MA: Harvard University Press.

McDowell, J. (2002). Knowledge and the Internal Revisited. *Philosophy and Phenomenological Research, 64*(1), 97–105.

McDowell, J. (2005). Sellars and the Space of Reasons. Unpublished.

McDowell, J. (2008). Intentionality as a Relation. In J. McDowell, *Having the World in View* (pp. 44–65). Cambridge, MA: Harvard University Press.

McDowell, J. (2008). Motivating Inferentialism. In J. McDowell, *The Engaged Intellect* (pp. 288–307). Cambridge, MA: Harvard University Press.

McDowell, J. (2009). Avoiding the Myth of the Given. In J. McDowell, *Having the World in View* (pp. 239–272). Cambridge, MA: Harvard University Press.

McDowell, J. (2009). Conceptual Capacities in Perception. In J. McDowell, *Having the World in View* (pp. 127–144). Cambridge, MA: Harvard University Press.

McDowell, J. (2009). *Having the World in View*. Cambridge, MA: Harvard University Press.

McDowell, J. (2009). How Not to Read Philosophical Investigations. In J. McDowell, *The Engaged Intellect* (pp. 96–111). Cambridge, MA: Harvard University Press.

McDowell, J. (2009). Sellars's Thomism. In J. McDowell, *Having the World in View* (pp. 239–255). Cambridge, MA: Harvard University Press.

McDowell, J. (2009). *The Engaged Intellect*. Cambridge, MA: Harvard University Press.

McDowell, J. (2009). The Disjunctive Conception of Experience as Material for a Transcendental Argument. In J. McDowell, *The Engaged Intellect* (pp 225–240). Cambridge, MA: Harvard University Press.

McDowell, J. (2009). Towards a Reading of Hegel on Action in the 'Reason' Chapter of the Phenomenology (pp. 166–184). In J. McDowell, *Having the World in View*. Cambridge, MA: Harvard University Press.

McDowell, J. (2009). What Myth? In J. McDowell, *The Engaged Intellect* (pp. 308–323). Cambridge, MA: Harvard University Press.

McDowell, J. (2009). Why Sellars's Essay is Called 'Empiricism and the Philosophy of Mind.' In J. McDowell, *The Engaged Intellect*. Cambridge, MA: Harvard University Press.

McDowell, J. (2009). Wittgensteinian 'Quietism.' *Common Knowledge, 15*(3), 365–372.

McDowell, J. (2010). Brandom on Observation. In B. Weiss & J. Wanderer (Eds.), *Reading Brandom* (pp. 129–144). New York: Routledge.

McDowell, J. (2010). Tyler Burge on Disjunctivism. *Philosophical Explorations, 13*(3), 243–255.

McDowell, J. (2010). What is the Content of an Intention in Action? *Ratio, 23*(4), 415–432.

McDowell, J. (2011). Pragmatism and Intention-in-Action. In R. Calcaterra (Ed.), *New Perspectives on Pragmatism and Analytic Philosophy* (pp. 118–129). New York: Rodopi.

McDowell, J. (2011). *Some Remarks on Intention in Action*. Retrieved January 2, 2012, from Amherst Lecture in Philosophy: http://www.amherstlecture.org/mcdowell2011/index.html

Millikan, R. (1984). *Language, Thought and Other Biological Categories*. Cambridge, MA: MIT Press.

Millikan, R. (1990). Truth-Rules, Hoverflies and the Kripke-Wittgenstein Paradox. *Philosophical Review, 99*(3), 323–353.

Millikan, R. (1993). *White Queen Psychology*. Cambridge, MA: MIT Press.

Millikan, R. (2005). *Language: A Biological Model*. New York: Oxford University Press.

Millikan, R. (2005). The Father, the Son and the Daughter. *Pragmatics and Cognition, 15*(1), 59–71.

Moore, G. (1903/2008). *Principia Ethica*. New York: Cambridge University Press.

Nozick, R. (1981). *Philosophical Explanations*. New York: Oxford University Press.

O'Shea, J. (2007). *Wilfrid Sellars*. New York: Polity.

Peacocke, C. (1998). Concepts without Language. In R. Heck (Ed.), *Language, Thought and Logic* (pp. 1–33). New York: Oxford University Press.

Pepperberg, I. (1999). *The Alex Studies: Cognitive and Communicative Abilities of Grey Parrots*. Cambridge, MA: Harvard University Press.

Pinkard, T. (2007). Sellars the Post-Kantian? In M. Wolf & M. Lance (Eds.), *The Self-Correcting Enterprise* (pp. 21–52). Amsterdam: Rodopi.

Pitt, J. (Ed.). (1978). *The Philosophy of Wilfrid Sellars*. Dordrecht: D. Reidel Publishing Co.

Pitt, J. (1981). *Pictures, Images, and Conceptual Change: An Analysis of Wilfrid Sellars' Philosophy of Science*. Dordrecht: D. Reidel Publishing Co.

Popper, K. (2002/1935). *The Logic of Scientific Discovery*. New York : Routledge.

Price, H. (1932). *Perception*. London: Methuen.

Price, H. (2011). Naturalism without Representationalism. In H. Price, *Naturalism without Mirrors* (pp. 184–199). New York: Oxford University Press.

Prinz, J. (2002). *Furnishing the Mind*. MIT Press: Cambridge, MA.

Quine, W. (1956). Two Dogmas of Empiricism. In W. Quine, *From a Logical Point of View* (pp. 20–46). Cambridge, MA: Harvard University Press.

Quine, W. (1969). Epistemology Naturalized. In W. Quine, *Ontological Relativity and Other Essays* (pp.69–90). New York: Columbia University Press.

Quine, W. (1977). *Ontological Relativity and Other Essays*. New York: Columbia University Press.

Redding, P. (2007). *Analytic Philosophy and the Return of Hegelian Thought*. New York: Cambridge University Press.

Redding, P. (2010). The Possibility of German Idealism after Analytic Philosophy: McDowell, Brandom and Beyond. In J. Chase, E. Mares, J. Williams, & J. Reynolds (Eds.), *Post-Analytic and Meta-Continental Thinking*. New York: Continuum.

Redding, P. (2011). The Analytic Neo-Hegelianism of John McDowell & Robert Brandom. In S. Houlgate & M. Baur (Eds.), *The Blackwell Companion to Hegel* (pp. 576–593). New York: Blackwell.

Rorty, R. (1979). *Philosophy and the Mirror of Nature*. Princeton: Princeton University Press.

Rorty, R. (1997). Introduction. In W. Sellars, *Empiricism and the Philosophy of Mind* (pp. 1–15). Cambridge, MA: Harvard University Press.

Rosenberg, J. (1974). *Linguistic Representation*. Dordrecht: Kluwer.

Rosenberg, J. (2008). *Fusing the Images*. London: Oxford University Press.

Rouse, J. (2003). *How Scientific Practices Matter*. Chicago: University of Chicago Press.

Russell, B. (1919). *Introduction to Mathematical Philosophy*. London: Allen and Unwin.

Russell, B. (1997/1912). *Problems of Philosophy*. New York: Oxford University Press.

Ryle, G. (1949). Discussion of Rudolf Carnap: 'Meaning and Necessity.' *Philosophy, 24*, 69–76.

Ryle, G. (1949/1984). *The Concept of Mind*. Chicago: University of Chicago Press.

Schroeder, M. (2008). *Being For*. New York: Oxford University Press.

Searle, J. (1983). *Intentionality*. New York: Cambridge University Press.

Seibt, J. (1990). *Properties as Processes: A Synoptic Study of Wilfrid Sellars' Nominalism*. Atascadero, CA: Ridgeview Publishing Co.

Sellars, W. (1947). Pure Pragmatics and Epistemology. *Philosophy of Science, 14*(3), 181–202.

Sellars, W. (1947/2005). Epistemology and the New Way of Words. In W. Sellars, *Pure Pragmatics and Possible Worlds* (pp. 645–660). Atascadero, CA: Ridgeview Publishing Company.

Sellars, W. (1948). Concepts as Involving Laws and Inconceivable without Them. *Philosophy of Science, 15*(4), 287–315.

Sellars, W. (1949). Aristotelian Philosophies of Mind. In R. Sellars, V. McGill, & M. Farber (Eds.), *Philosophy for The Future: The Quest of Modern Materialism* (pp. 544–570). New York: Macmillan.

Sellars, W. (1949/2005). Language, Rules and Behavior. In W. Sellars, *Pure Pragmatics and Possible Worlds* (pp. 117–134). Atascadero, CA: Ridgeview Publishing Company.

Sellars, W. (1953/2005). A Semantical Solution to the Mind-Body Problem. In W. Sellars, *Pure Pragmatics and Possible Worlds* (pp. 180–214). Atascadero: Ridgeview Publishing Co.

Sellars, W. (1953/2005). Inference and Meaning. In W. Sellars, *Pure Pragmatics and Possible Worlds* (pp. 215–237). Atascadero, CA: Ridgeview Publishing Co.

Sellars, W. (1954/1963). Some Reflections on Language Games. In W. Sellars, *Science, Perception and Reality* (pp. 321–358). Atascadero: Ridgview Publishing Co

Sellars, W. (1956). Empiricism and the Philosophy of Mind. In H. Feigl & M. Scriven (Eds.), *Minnesota Studies in the Philosophy of Science* (Vol. I, pp. 253–329). Minneapolis, MN: University of Minnesota Press.

Sellars, W. (1958). Counterfactuals, Dispositions, and the Causal Modalities. In H. Feigl, M. Scriven, & G. Maxwell (Eds.), *Minnesota Studies in the Philosophy of Science* (Vol. II, pp. 225–308). Minneapolis, MN: University of Minnesota Press.

Sellars, W. (1963). Abstract Entities. *Review of Metaphysics 16*(4), 627–671.

Sellars, W. (1963). Empiricism and Abstract Entities. In P. A. Schilpp (Ed.), *The Philosophy of Rudolf Carnap* (pp. 431–468). La Salle, IL: Open Court.

Sellars, W. (1963). Fatalism and Determinism. In K. Lehrer (Ed.), *Freedom and Determinism* (pp. 141–174). New York: Random House.

Sellars, W. (1963). Imperatives, Intentions and the Logic of 'Ought.' In H. Castañeda & G. Nakhnikian (Eds.), *Morality and the Language of Conduct* (pp. 159–214). Detroit, MI: Wayne State University Press.

Sellars, W. (1963). Phenomenalism. In W. Sellars, *Science, Perception and Reality* (pp. 60–105). Atascadero: Ridgview Publishing Co.

Sellars, W. (1963). Philosophy and the Scientific Image of Man. In W. Sellars, *Science, Perception and Reality*. Atascadero, CA: Ridgeview Publishing Company.

Sellars, W. (1963). Thought and Action. In K. Lehrer (Ed.), *Freedom and Determinism* (pp. 105–139). New York: Random House.

Sellars, W. (1963). Truth and 'Correspondence'. In W. Sellars, *Science, Perception and Reality*. Atascadero, CA: Ridgeview Publishing Company.

Sellars, W. (1967). *Science and Metaphysics*. Atascadero, CA: Ridgeview Publishing Co.

Sellars, W. (1969). Language as Thought and as Communication. *Philosophy and Phenomenological Research, 29*(4), 506–527.

Sellars, W. (1973). Actions and Events. *Nous, 7*, 179–202.

Sellars, W. (1974). Meaning as Functional Classification. *Synthese, 27*, 417–437.

Sellars, W. (1975). The Structure of Knowledge. In H. Castañeda (Ed.), *Action, Knowledge and Reality: Studies in Honor of Wilfrid Sellars* (pp. 295–347). Indianapolis: Bobbs-Merrill.

Sellars, W. (1976). Volitions Re-Affirmed. In M. Brand & D. Walton (Eds.), *Action Theory* (pp. 47–66). Dordrecht: Reidel.

Sellars, W. (1980). Behaviorism, Language and Meaning. *Pacific Philosophical Quarterly, 61*, 3–30.

Sellars, W. (1980). *Naturalism and Ontology*. Atascadero, CA: Ridgeview Publishing Company.

Sellars, W. (1980/2005). Language, Rules and Behavior. In W. Sellars, *Pure Pragmatics and Possible Worlds* (pp. 117–134). Atascadero, CA: Ridgeview Publishing Company.

Sellars, W. (1980/2005). *Pure Pragmatics and Possible Worlds* (2nd ed.). (J. Sicha, Ed.) Atascadero, CA: Ridgeview Publishing Co.

Sellars, W. (1981). Foundations for a Metaphysics of Pure Process. *The Monist, 64*, 3–90.

Sellars, W. (1981). Mental Events. *Philosophical Studies, 39*, 325–45.

Sellars, W. (1982). Sensa or Sensings. *Philosophical Studies, 41*, 83–111.

Sellars, W. (1983). Towards a Theory of Predication. In J. Bogen & J. McGuire (Eds.), *How Things Are* (pp. 281–318). Dordrecht: Reidel.

Sellars, W. (1989). *Metaphysics of Epistemology*. (P. Amaral, Ed.) Atascadero, CA: Ridgeview Publishing Co.

Sellars, W. (1991). *Science, Perception and Reality*. Atascadero, CA: Ridgeview Publishing Co.

Sellars, W., & Chisholm, R. (1957). Intentionality and the Mental. *Minnesota Studies in the Philosophy of Science, 2*, 521–539.

Sextus Empiricus. (1967). *Outlines of Pyrrhonism*. (R. Bury, Trans.) Cambridge, MA: Harvard University Press.

Sher, G. (2006). Out of Control. *Ethics, 116*, 285–301.

Skinner, B. (1953). *Science and Human Behavior*. New York: Macmillan.

Skinner, B. (1957). *Verbal Behavior*. New York: Copley Publishing Group.

Smith, A. (2005). Responsibility for Attitudes. *Ethics, 115*, 236–271.

Smith, A. (2008). Control, Responsibility, and Moral Assessment. *Philosophical Studies, 138*, 367–392.

Smith, N. (Ed.). (2002). *Reading McDowell*. New York: Routledge.

Solomon, D. (1977). Ethical Theory. In S. Delaney, M. Loux, G. Gutting, & D. Solomon (Eds.), *Synoptic Vision: Essays on the Philosophy of Wilfrid Sellars* (pp. 149–188). South Bend, IN: University of Notre Dame.

Sosa, E. (1997). The Mythology of the Given. *History of Philosophy Quarterly, 14*, 275–286.

Sosa, E. (2003). Are There Two Grades of Knowledge? *Proceedings of the Aristotelian Society, Supplementary Volumes, 77*, 91–130.

Stevenson, C. (1937). The Emotive Meaning of Ethical Terms. *Mind, 46*(181), 14–31.

Stout, R. (2010). Being Subject to the Rule to Do What the Rules Tell You to Do. In B. Weiss & J. Wanderer (Eds.), *Reading Brandom* (pp. 145–156). New York: Routledge.

Thomasson, A. (2009). *Categories*. Retrieved January 15, 2010, from Stanford Encyclopedia of Philosophy: http://plato.stanford.edu/entries/categories/

Thornton, T. (2004). *John McDowell*. Montreal: McGill-Queen's University Press.

Travis, C. (2001). *Unshadowed Thought*. Cambridge, MA: Harvard University Press.

Travis, C. (2005). A Sense of Occasion. *Philosophical Quarterly, 55*(219), 286–314.

Wanderer, J. (2008). *Robert Brandom*. Montreal: McGill-Queen's University Press.

Watson, J. (1930). *Behaviorism*. New York: Norton.

Weiss, B., & Wanderer, J. (Eds.). (2010). *Reading Brandom*. New York: Routledge.

Whiting, D. (2007). The Normativity of Meaning Defended. *Analysis, 67*(2), 133–140.

Wikforss, A. (2001). Semantic Normativity. *Philosophical Studies, 102*, 203–226.

Williams, M. (1977/1999). *Groundless Belief* (2nd ed.). Princeton: Princeton University Press.

Williams, M. (1996). Exorcism and Enchantment. *The Philosophical Quarterly, 46*(182), 99–109.

Williams, M. (1996). *Unnatural Doubts*. Princeton: Princeton University Press.

Williams, M. (1999). Skepticism. In J. Greco & E. Sosa (Eds.), *The Blackwell Guide to Epistemology* (pp. 35–69). New York: Blackwell.

Williams, M. (2001). *Problems of Knowledge*. New York: Oxford University Press.

Williams, M. (2004). The Agrippan Argument and Two Forms of Skepticism. In W. Sinnott-Armstrong (Ed.), *Pyrrhonian Skepticism* (pp. 121–145). New York: Oxford University Press.

Williams, M. (2006). Science and Sensibility. *European Journal of Philosophy, 14*(2), 302–325.

Williams, M. (2010). The Tortoise and the Serpent. In W. deVries (Ed.), *Empiricism, Perceptual Knowledge, Normativity, and Realism* (pp.147–186). New York: Oxford University Press.

Wittgenstein, L. (1958). *Philosophical Investigations* (3rd ed.). (G. Anscombe, Trans.) New York: Blackwell.

Wolf, M. (2006). Rigid Designation and Anaphoric Theories of Reference. *Philosophical Studies, 130*, 351–375.

Wolf, M. P., & Lance, M. (Eds.). (2006). *The Self-Correcting Enterprise*. New York: Rodopi.

Index